Tomb Treasures of the
Late Middle Kingdom

Tomb Treasures of the Late Middle Kingdom

The Archaeology of Female Burials

WOLFRAM GRAJETZKI

PENN

University of Pennsylvania Press

Philadelphia

Published by
University of Pennsylvania Press
Philadelphia, Pennsylvania 19104-4112
www.upenn.edu/pennpress

Printed in the United States of America on acid-free paper
10 9 8 7 6 5 4 3 2 1

Library of Congress Cataloging-in-Publication Data

Grajetzki, Wolfram.
  Tomb treasures of the late Middle Kingdom : the archaeology of female burials /
Wolfram Grajetzki. — 1st ed.
      p. cm.
  Includes bibliographical references and index.
  ISBN 978-0-8122-4567-7 (hardcover : alk. paper)
  1. Tombs—Egypt. 2. Burial—Egypt. 3. Women—Egypt—History—To
500. 4. Egyptians—Funeral customs and rites. 5. Excavations (Archaeology)—
Egypt. 6. Egypt—Civilization—To 332 B.C. 7. Egypt—Antiquities. I. Title.
DT62.T6G73 2014
932'.013—dc23
                                                                  2013024963

For

Danielle Darrieux

Catherine Deneuve

Isabelle Huppert

Emmanuelle Béart

Fanny Ardant

Virginie Ledoyen

Ludivine Sagnier

Firmine Richard

Contents

Introduction

The late Middle Kingdom in ancient Egypt, c. 1850 to 1700 BCE, is exceptionally rich in undisturbed burials of women. These tombs are often lavishly equipped with jewelry of the highest quality. Much of this jewelry has been regularly depicted in books on ancient Egypt. The burials are not often discussed as a whole, however; the other object types found in them are frequently barely mentioned. In this book my aim is to fill this gap. In the first part I provide a description and synthesis of the latest research on several of the most important late Middle Kingdom burials belonging to women. In the second part I give an overall view of late Middle Kingdom burial customs, again with the main focus on burials of women. An advantage of studying female burials is that in them certain trends in burial customs are particularly visible, such as concentration on the social identity of the tomb owner and "Osirification" (discussed in Chapter 4) in the "court type burials." The technology of jewelry production, already covered by several other expert studies, is not the subject of the book.[1]

Studies of ancient Egyptian burial customs often concentrate on inscribed objects of the funerary industry. These include coffins, canopic jars, *shabti* figures, funerary papyri, and amulets. Especially from the Ramesside Period onward, these are certainly the most important items placed in the burial chambers, next to or on the deceased. Looking at the whole of Egyptian history and across all social classes, however, the picture is different. A wide range of uninscribed objects was placed in the tomb, including many items that had already been used in daily life, such as pottery vessels, cosmetic items, tools, and jewelry. Taken together, these latter types of burial goods constitute by far the highest proportion of items placed in burials, while purpose-made funerary objects were restricted to certain periods and to higher social levels. Few of the objects that appear in general books on Egyptian funerary customs, such as coffins, canopic jars, and mummy masks, were found in the tombs discussed in this book. Mummification was not yet fully developed in the Middle Kingdom, and all the women described in this book were found as skeletons.

Particularly in more popular works, it is often stated that ancient Egyptian women had special rights compared to women from other ancient cultures.[2] This impression may date back to the late nineteenth century, when most Egyptologists had undergone a broad classical education. They compared Egyptian women with those of classical antiquity and of European societies in their own time, where women indeed had few rights. In contrast, on many monuments Egyptian women appear next to their husbands and almost equal in size, while texts reveal that in court cases women and men had identical rights. Despite this, however, there is no doubt that ancient Egypt in the late Middle Kingdom, the period covered by this book, was a fully patriarchal society. Among the three hundred rulers during some three thousand years of ancient Egyptian history up to about 300 BCE, there were only a few female rulers with the full royal titulary[3] (Neferusobek, Hatshepsut, Neferneferuaton, and Tawesret). There are several cases where a king's mother ruled for her son in his infancy. This too has been taken as evidence that women had special power in ancient Egypt. Such instances of maternal coregency prove almost the opposite, however: a mother ruling for her son is typical of a patriarchal society, where the mother often plays an important part in family life.[4] In religion too the dominant role of men is visible. Indeed, in the burial equipment of the Middle Kingdom and later, women were identified with the male underworld god Osiris. It was only in the Ptolemaic Period that they were identified with a female deity.[5]

What remains true is that women in ancient Egypt had the same legal rights in court cases as men. There were some women with a certain amount of economic power, and women were fully present in the public sphere, not hidden away in the house as in classical Athens, for example. The Egyptian evidence can be compared with that for women in Mesopotamia, where there were also a few female rulers and where there was even a female poet at the end of the third millennium BCE (something ancient Egypt cannot offer, as no named poets are known for certain there).

THE LATE MIDDLE KINGDOM

After the First Intermediate Period, when Egypt was divided into two political units, the country was reunited around 2000 BCE under the Eleventh Dynasty king Mentuhotep II. This marks the beginning of the period Egyptologists call the Middle Kingdom. Until the end of the Eleventh Dynasty the royal cemeteries of the ruling family and its court were at Thebes, in the south of the country. Here the king built a huge mortuary temple with the tombs of the courtiers around it, including those of the royal women[6] and the highest officials. Mentuhotep II reorganized the administration of the country, launched a building project renovating many temples in Upper Egypt, and began military campaigns against Egypt's neighbors.

At the beginning of the ensuing Twelfth Dynasty, around 1975 BCE, a new residence was founded: Itjtawy ("seizer of the two lands"), in the north of the country, about sixty kilometers south of modern Cairo at the border of Upper and Lower Egypt, in a region the Egyptians considered to be the middle point of their country. Near this capital, at a place today called Lisht, were built the pyramids of the first two kings of the new dynasty, Amenemhat I and Senusret I. Around these pyramids a huge cemetery developed where the national ruling class of the early Twelfth Dynasty was buried. Amenemhat II, the third king of the dynasty, chose Dahshur as the new site for his pyramid, but Lisht remained an important cemetery till the end of the Middle Kingdom in the late Thirteenth Dynasty.

The Eleventh Dynasty and the first part of the Twelfth Dynasty constitute the most decentralized period of ancient Egyptian history. Certainly, in all periods people of wealth lived not only in the royal residence but also in important towns, and there were temples and tombs all over the country. In the first half of the Middle Kingdom, however, there were many wealthy and powerful local governors in different parts of Egypt who were able to quarry huge rock-cut tombs decorated with paintings and reliefs. The burial chambers of these monumental tombs have most often been found looted, but the few remains in them show that these regional governors were buried with a rich array of objects, most of them from the local workshops of a funerary industry.[7] In this period, tombs were often equipped with wooden models showing carpenters, potters, ships, servants, and the production of food. Coffins were decorated on the inside with long religious texts known as Coffin Texts.

In about the middle of the Twelfth Dynasty, after the reign of Senusret II, major changes in the political landscape of ancient Egypt are visible. These mark the beginning of the late Middle Kingdom. First of all, the large provincial tombs of governors disappeared, and there were no longer cemeteries for the local ruling classes who worked for them. People were still buried in the provinces, and there are still some quite rich tombs of people not belonging to the local government. The early Middle Kingdom governor tombs are a most important source for coffins with religious texts. As a result of the disappearance of local governor court cemeteries, decorated coffins are much rarer in the late Middle Kingdom and seem to be restricted to just a few cemeteries, most of them in one way or another connected to the royal court. The wooden models so typical of the early Middle Kingdom also disappeared in the middle of the Twelfth Dynasty. Evidently this reflects a shift in religious beliefs. The wooden models seem to indicate that a major concern of the deceased was to secure the eternal food supply and the supply of material goods. With the disappearance of these wooden models, other aspects clearly became more important for the eternal afterlife.

In the late Middle Kingdom, local governors are still attested, for example on seals and temple statues, but it seems that they had diminished resources. The wealth of the country was now concentrated at a few places connected with royal activities. One was the region between Memphis and the Fayum. It was here that the royal pyramids were built, and most likely the royal residence, and here also were the burials of the highest court officials. In the Fayum several temples were erected, the most famous being a complex next to the pyramid of Amenemhat III at Hawara, known in later periods as the "labyrinth." Another focal point was Abydos. This was the center of the cult of the underworld god Osiris. Here, king Senusret III built a huge tomb where he may have been buried, although he also had a pyramid in the north at Dahshur. Statues and stelae of officials were placed in the temple of Osiris. In the cemeteries next to the town, officials erected small chapels equipped with stelae and statues. These officials wanted to be, at least symbolically, close to the offerings made to Osiris. The third center of the late Middle Kingdom was Thebes. Here there was a royal palace, where it seems the kings spent a considerable amount of time. Officials followed the king, and there is good evidence for a flourishing late Middle Kingdom cemetery in Thebes. Although most tombs were found heavily looted, the available evidence indicates many richly equipped burials.

Preserved from the late Twelfth Dynasty are a large number of undisturbed burials of royal women, buried close to the pyramids of the kings. These burials were especially well equipped with jewelry of the finest quality. They also included a set of royal insignia identifying the deceased with Osiris. The late Middle Kingdom was without question the classical period of Egyptian gold work. The pectorals and other items found are of the highest aesthetic and technical quality. Such workmanship reaches a high point under Senusret II and his successor Senusret III, while under Amenemhat III a decline is already detectable. Although some of these burials were close to the pyramid of Amenemhat II and to those of Senusret II at Dahshur and Lahun, it seems that all these women were buried after Senusret II and therefore belong to the late Middle Kingdom.

After the Twelfth Dynasty with its long reigns, the Thirteenth Dynasty, by contrast, had many short-reigning kings. In terms of culture, there is no visible break. Few royal pyramids of this period have been excavated, which might be one reason there are so few comparable royal "jewelry tombs." From the Thirteenth Dynasty, however, at least one burial of a royal woman is known, showing the same pattern of burial goods as for the royal and high-status women of the Twelfth Dynasty.

In addition to these burials of royal and high-status women, excavators have found and recorded several other burials of women from all around the country, which are also richly equipped with jewelry, though often with few other burial items. For comparison, these tombs are also discussed in this book. In terms of jewelry there are some similarities to the tombs of the princesses in the royal cemeteries. The rest of the tomb equipment, however, is often very different and even quite limited. Without the presence of jewelry many of the tombs would in fact appear rather poor. Nevertheless, the burials of these women, who did not belong to the royal court, attest to a wider spread of wealth in the late Middle Kingdom.[8]

BURIAL GOODS: AN OVERVIEW

In many cultures around the world people were buried with objects. These range from single items to the richly equipped tombs of the Egyp-

tian New Kingdom or the similarly richly equipped burials in many periods of Chinese history. Burial goods are not found in all cultures. This
is especially true for the modern (Western) world, where burial goods are
not common at all, although the Christian and the Islamic faiths teach
belief in an afterlife. Nevertheless, some kind of burial arrangement is
found even in Christianity and in the Islamic world. In a medieval Islamic
cemetery in southern Egypt personal adornments were still sporadically
present, and the deceased were sometimes found wrapped in a decorated
sheet of linen.[9] In Europe people are placed in a coffin or urn and wrapped
in a shroud or some other type of garment; even priests are buried in their
official garments.[10] It is said that the actor Bela Lugosi, who gained fame
playing Dracula, was buried in his iconic Dracula cape.[11] Today, flowers
are typical grave goods often presented by family members and friends of
the deceased and placed on the coffin.[12]

Grave goods generally had the function of providing the deceased with
some kind of support for the afterlife, but in some cultures or contexts
they had almost the opposite purpose, being put there to prevent the dead
from coming back.[13] To complicate matters, objects in graves are sometimes not grave goods at all. It is reported that the few objects sometimes
placed in graves of the Nankanse people in Ghana belong to living people
working at the funeral whose souls are thought to get trapped in the grave.
To avoid death, an item belonging to each of these people is placed in the
burial.[14]

In general terms there are two types of burial goods. There are the objects of a funerary industry, and there are the objects taken from daily life.
A subgroup of the objects of a funerary industry are those used in rituals
performed in funerary rites and afterward placed in the tomb chamber.
It is evident that there are overlaps between these groups. Coffins are
most likely always specially prepared for a tomb, though in ancient Egypt
deceased children were often placed in boxes or vessels,[15] objects perhaps
already used in daily life.[16]

The following discussion tries to collect some of the most common
reasons for placing burial goods in graves. There are certainly overlaps
between the categories mentioned. A servant figure placed in the burial of
an official might have had the function of providing physical help so that
the deceased was not forced to work in the afterlife. Such a figure, however, might also confirm the social status of the deceased, emphasizing
that he or she was an owner of servants and an estate.

Containers for the Body

Containers for the body of the deceased are the most common burial goods, found in most cultures around the world. In Egyptian burials these are boxes, pottery vessels, coffins,[17] and in a wider sense mummy masks and perhaps also the burial chamber in general. In Egypt there developed for high-status burials the custom of a nest of coffins, one inside another, something also often found in China,[18] where burial customs were elaborate and perhaps comparable to those of Egypt. In Egypt there also developed the custom of placing masks over the face of the deceased, something again attested in Han Dynasty China, although the Chinese "masks" are actually protective shields placed over the head.[19] Indeed, masks for the deceased are quite widely known all over the world. Metal burial masks are attested in South America.[20] Gold masks appear in Parthian Mesopotamia, but they are also known from the Black Sea and Sidon.[21] Other containers for bodily remains are urns, common in cultures where the body of the deceased was burned, and ossuaries, boxes into which only the bones of the deceased were placed.

Equipment for the Journey into the Afterlife

Burial equipment for the journey into the afterlife implies a belief in another world to or though which the deceased travels. As most cultures have a belief in an underworld,[22] equipping the deceased with objects important for a journey is common in many cultures.[23] It is well attested in the Hellenistic world, where the deceased was buried with an obol for Charon, the ferryman to the underworld. Similar ideas are known from China, where the deceased were dressed comfortably for the journey. Furthermore, they received rice to feed dangerous dogs that were believed to attack the travelers on their way, and staffs for beating them off.[24] Certain Mesopotamian cuneiform texts clearly state that burial goods were provisions for the deceased's journey. These included footwear, a belt, water, and some food.[25]

In most cultures mainly known from archaeology, however, written sources are absent, and the reasons objects were placed in tombs remain guesswork. Equipping the deceased for the journey into the next world is often given as an explanation for burial goods, although hard evidence is lacking. For burials in Bahrain, vessels placed in the burial were explained in this way.[26] Lamps found in tombs are sometimes explained as providing light for the journey into the dark underworld, which in many cultures was indeed situated underground, although that is only one possible explanation for lamps in burials.[27]

The same explanations have been proposed for some late Middle Kingdom burials. It has been observed that many of the burial goods in tombs of this period might be objects of daily life that would especially be needed for a journey. These include gaming boards for leisure, food supplies, and writing equipment, including papyri.[28]

Participating in Special Events in the Underworld

Pottery vessels in burials belong to the most common burial goods from all cultures and often seem to indicate a need to supply food. This might be either food required for the journey or a general symbolic food supply for all eternity. Tableware found in graves in Bahrain has been explained as important for the deceased so that he or she could join the afterlife banquet.[29] Underworld banquets are part of the underworld beliefs of the Greeks and Etruscans. The same explanation is given for tableware found in an early Iron Age cemetery on Crete: "Offerings seem to express a respect for the good things of life—banqueting."[30]

The Tomb as a House for the Afterlife

During the First and Second Dynasties[31] the whole tomb was seen as the "house of the afterlife." We find furniture and a vast quantity of pottery storage vessels for the eternal food supply. This concept appears again in tombs of the Eighteenth Dynasty. It appears also in other cultures, for example in the case of certain Etruscan tombs whose architecture seems to copy contemporary houses very closely.[32] In many cultures it is common for urns or ossuaries to have the shape of a house, most likely also reflecting the idea of the tomb as a house for the afterlife. Examples include ossuaries of the Ghassulian culture in Palestine dating from the fourth millennium BCE.[33]

Helping Hands

In many cultures a sacrifice for the burial of an important member of society is attested.[34] There are various possible reasons for this custom. One might be practical. Persons of high status wanted to have their servants in the afterlife so that they would not have to work. In Egypt this is found as early as the First Dynasty, when people of slightly lower status were buried around their masters. Burial goods indicate that they were often craftsmen.[35] Whether they were actually sacrificed is still under discussion. It appears, however, that the subsidiary tombs around the tomb of the First Dynasty king Semerkhet were integrated with the king's tomb as one unit, which seems to indicate the servants were buried at the same time as the king and were most likely killed for the royal burial.[36] The same idea can be found in several other cultures. In the Nubian Kerma culture (around 2000 to 1550 BCE) hundreds of people were placed next to deceased kings.[37] The same practice appears again in the Ballana culture in Lower Nubia (around 400 to 600 CE), where again servants were buried with their masters. In China during the Shang Dynasty (about 1550 to 1050 BCE) people were also buried next to kings and high officials, including royal women.[38] Later Chinese sources refer to this practice as "following in death."[39] The same is found at Ur in Mesopotamia, where in the burials of high-ranking persons other people were also buried, and were most likely killed for that purpose.[40]

In most of these societies the custom of killing people for the burial of a high-ranking person or king disappeared quite early on. In China and Egypt the idea lived on, but instead of real people, model figures were placed in the tomb. In China, terracotta, wooden, or straw figures were placed in many tombs.[41] The terracotta army of about seven thousand life-size soldiers for the emperor Qin Shihuangdi (259–210 BCE) is the most famous example. On a smaller scale these figures were common in many periods of Chinese history as burial goods. They often depict soldiers, but sometimes also officials or musicians. They represent the court of a high official or a king. In this respect they have a focus different from that of the Egyptian figures. Scenes of production are rather rare, but soldiers and officials appear. They might confirm the social status of a higher official by their wanting to be buried with his court. In Old Kingdom Egypt there were stone statues of single individuals shown working.[42] At the end of the Old Kingdom they were replaced by wooden figures, which are often shown in groups. These figures are still attested for the Middle Kingdom but disappear in the middle of the Twelfth Dynasty.[43]

At the end of the Egyptian Middle Kingdom shabti figures appear.[44] Originally these seem to represent the deceased, but in the Thirteenth Dynasty a spell was placed on them which reveals that they were helpers in the underworld and acted as stand-ins for the deceased when work had to be done.[45] Shabti figures are recorded in only a few tombs of the late Middle Kingdom and do not appear in any of the tombs discussed in this book.

Leftovers from Rituals

For Egyptian and other cultures, it is very likely that rituals were performed at tombs and for the deceased. Objects used in these rituals could be deposited with the burial. It is often hard to decide which objects placed in tombs belong to this category. Objects for certain rituals might have been placed in a tomb not because they were used in actual rituals but rather because the ritual should be performed with a view to all eternity. In this case the object could be something specially made for the tomb. There are indeed objects, however, where the indications are that they were really used in burials. In some tomb shafts of the Old Kingdom copper dishes were found, perhaps used in a ritual and then just thrown into the shaft after it was performed.[46] For Second Intermediate Period burials at Thebes it has been observed that the pottery shows signs of use in rituals.[47] In the court type burials of late Middle Kingdom princesses many staves and weapons were found (discussed in Chapter 1). Several of these were broken when discovered, as if they had been used in rituals and then placed in the tombs.

Objects from and for rituals have been found in many burials around the world but evidently vary with different burial customs. In the Bronze Age Aegean and on Cyprus burial equipment included specific vessel types—alabastra and stirrup jars. These might have been used in rituals and were for anointing the body and perhaps even garments.[48]

Guardians

Guardians were figures or burial goods protecting the tomb as a whole against living people, especially tomb robbers. Guardian figures are well attested for Chinese tombs, in some of which figures of monsters protecting the tomb have been found.[49] Another famous example from China is the army of terracotta soldiers found next to the tomb of China's "first" emperor.[50] Perhaps surprisingly, guardians in Egyptian burials are hard to identify with certainty. In the tomb of Tutankhamun two life-size statues depicting the king were found. They are often labeled "guardian statues,"[51] but their real function remains unknown. The same is true of figures of Anubis, the jackal god, the most famous of which was again found in the tomb of Tutankhamun. These Anubis figures are sometimes also labeled "guardians."[52] There is no hard evidence, however, that they are guardians. In Egyptian texts Anubis is often connected with burials, but not as a guardian.[53] The safety of Egyptian tombs was not secured by any "magical" objects or figures. Safety was mainly a question of the tomb architecture and sometimes of certain spells placed in the tomb.[54] Perhaps the four magical bricks with their spells belong to this category, though the related texts in the Book of the Dead (chapter 151) indicate that they were used in rituals at the mummification or burial.[55] The four magical bricks were found mainly in New Kingdom tombs and are inscribed with a short protective spell.

Protection

A wide range of objects was placed in Egyptian burials for protecting the deceased against evil spirits. Many of the objects for protection can be classified as amulets. Two types can be distinguished: amulets already used in daily life, and amulets especially made for the tomb.[56] To the first category belong fish pendants, lion claws, and perhaps even shell girdles, to name only amulets discussed in this book (Chapter 3). Amulets mainly made for the tomb are especially common in the Ramesside Period and later.

Personal Objects

Even in societies where it was not common to place grave goods in burials, it could happen that very personal items were still placed in them, such as pieces of jewelry always worn by the person in life. By personal objects I mean not only objects belonging personally to somebody but also those items with which the owner has a special tie, such as an heirloom or a gift from a beloved family member or friend. In cultures and periods when it was the custom to place objects from daily life in tombs, these objects are almost impossible to identify, as they are too similar to the other burial goods. The dividing line between personal objects and objects confirming social status or gender identity is very narrow. This is best seen in cases where personal jewelry is placed in the tombs discussed. Are these just social markers, or were at least some of them also selected because they might have been a favorite piece of jewelry of the deceased? Personal items are easier to identify in cultures and periods when most of the objects placed in the burial are of a funerary character and suddenly a more personal item appears. In ancient Egypt that might include certain objects in the Third Intermediate Period tombs at Tanis. In the Third Intermediate Period almost all objects placed in the tomb were made for the burial, such as the coffins, shabtis, and canopic jars. In the royal tombs at Tanis, however, and in the tombs of the highest officials buried there too, some objects from daily life were found, such as weapons and golden vessels.[57] Are these to be seen as personal objects?

The idea of having a personal, beloved item is well expressed in one of the tales in the Westcar Papyrus. Several girls are rowing a boat for the king. One of them loses her fish pendant, and so she stops rowing. The king is confused and asks her why she is not rowing. She tells him that she has lost her pendant. The king offers to replace it with another one, but she refuses. She wants her own pendant and not just a replacement, saying: "I love my object more than its copy."[58]

Preserving Social Identity

Preserving social identity seems to be one of the most important aspects of equipping the deceased and is found in many cultures around the world. Social and gender identity was an important part of the self-identity of a person and also important for the person's place in society. Social identity could comprise several aspects, notably the place of a person in the social hierarchy, the gender of a person, and his or her profession.

It has been shown that Egyptian burial equipment rarely contains objects related to the profession of the deceased. Most objects placed in burials can be explained in other ways.[59] The profession of the deceased is not visible in the tomb equipment. This is in contrast to several other cultures. Provincial Roman graves often contained objects related to the profession of the deceased. There are burials of dentists with their instruments,[60] others with potter's tools.[61] In the burial of a painter was found a set of small vessels still containing paint.[62] Other Roman burials contained different tools perhaps also relating to the deceased's profession.[63] Weapons in tombs of Celtic men might indicate that they were soldiers but might also relate to their social status in a "warrior society."[64]

Funerary Objects for Passages into a New Form of Life

Death is seen in many cultures as the critical passage from one form of life to another. To secure an uncomplicated transition, rituals were performed. In ancient Egypt these are the rituals around mummification, as well as the Opening of the Mouth ritual, which had the function of bringing back to life not only statues but also the mummy. Objects connected to these rituals might be placed in the tomb. In late Old Kingdom burial equipment a set of instruments for the Opening of the Mouth ceremony is sometimes included.

There were also other rituals. In late Old Kingdom burials, pottery ensembles were often found that appear again on stelae of the same period showing the stela owner being served food. This might be a ritual ensuring the eternal food supply. The ritual of placing these vessels in the tomb was performed with a view to all eternity, guaranteeing the food supply of the deceased.[65]

Communication with the Dead

Especially in some burials of the First Intermediate Period letters were found written on pottery vessels placed in the burial chamber. They contain messages from family members to the deceased.[66]

OTHER ASPECTS OF BURIAL

Funerary Objects

In this book, funerary objects are those objects that were mainly produced for the tomb or at least for related rituals. The most important object, and one still used today, is the coffin. It is also clear that other burial goods were made solely for the tomb. These include canopic jars, wooden models of food production, and certain vessels used in rituals, but also the funerary jewelry discussed in Chapter 3. It seems evident that model vessels were not used in daily life, although it might be argued that they were utilized in temples for votive offerings and are therefore not exclusively funerary. For other pottery the line between daily life and funerary is often hard to draw. Stephan Seidlmayer noticed that in Old Kingdom burials on Elephantine most items placed in the tomb were taken directly from life; only the pottery was specially made for the tomb.[67] The forms of pottery vessels placed in the burials were identical to those used in daily life, however, and these pottery vessels were also fully functional. They might therefore be better classified as daily life objects, but newly produced for a burial. For amulets it is often hard to decide to which category they belonged. Many First Intermediate Period burials often of modest size contained amulets, which it seems were worn in daily life as protection against evil spirits.[68] Amulets found in New Kingdom and Late Period tombs are often regarded as specially made for burial.[69] Again, this is not proven, and it might be argued that at least some of these amulets had already been worn in daily life. Another complicated case is jewelry made for the tomb. Mace and Winlock observed for the burial of Senebtisi that several of the personal adornments placed on her body were much too flimsy to have been used in real life (discussed in Chapter 3). Some of them did not even have proper clasps (Chapter 1). There are, however, other roughly contemporary court type burials where it seems that "real" personal adornments were placed on the body.

Models

A subgroup of objects of the funerary industry consists of models. Already in the Predynastic Period models were placed in Egyptian tombs.[70] Most often they simply replaced more expensive objects, but they were also smaller though still fully functioning versions of bigger objects. Object types where models are attested include the personal adornments found in many of the tombs discussed and the miniature pottery found in several of them. Models of bigger or expensive objects are known from the Old Kingdom, become less common in the Middle Kingdom, and then regain popularity in the New Kingdom. Of particular note here are painted models of stone vessels and small solid wooden models from the New Kingdom.

Models placed in burials are also known from many other cultures. Chinese models of servants have already been mentioned, but there are also models of houses and other items.[71] In the Middle Bronze Age Sappali culture (part of the Bactrian-Margiana culture in Central Asia) metal models of tools, weapons, household articles, and toiletry objects were placed in graves.[72] Models of weapons also appear in Iron Age burials of men in Italy, where it has been noted that real weapons appear too, more often spears than swords, perhaps because placing weapons in male tombs was seen as important but spears were less costly than swords.[73] This observation might confirm the impression that models are often a cheaper version of a more expensive original object.

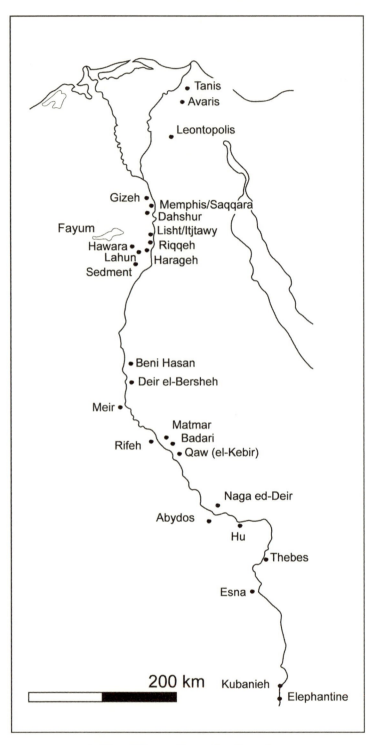

1. Map of Egypt. Drawn by the author.

CHAPTER 1

Court Type Burials

In this chapter the category of Middle Kingdom burials known as "court type" is discussed. The first two examples described are the burial of Senebtisi and the "treasure" from the tomb of Sathathoriunet. These two burials are discussed first because both were carefully excavated and the findings published in detail. Indeed, in terms of their documentation and publication, the excavations of these burials set the standard in Egyptian archaeology. Furthermore, it was in the excavation report on the tomb of Senebtisi that the term "court type burial" was first coined. The burials discussed after those of Senebtisi and Sathathoriunet are arranged in chronological order. The last two groups of jewelry discussed are those found in two disintegrated "jewelry boxes" recovered from a gallery tomb next to the pyramid of Senusret III at Dahshur. They appear at the end because only the jewelry in the boxes is preserved; the actual burials of the women in the gallery tomb were looted.

THE TOMB OF SENEBTISI[1]

The burial of the "lady of the house" Senebtisi ("the one who will be healthy")[2] is among the most famous tombs of ancient Egypt, at least for Egyptologists interested in the Middle Kingdom and funerary culture. There are three reasons for this: first, the tomb was found almost untouched; second, the excavation was very carefully recorded; and third, the excavation was fully published about ten years later. In the publication, Senebtisi's type of burial was labeled a "court type burial" because it was

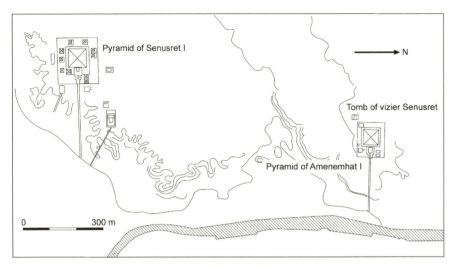

2. Map of Lisht. Drawn by the author.

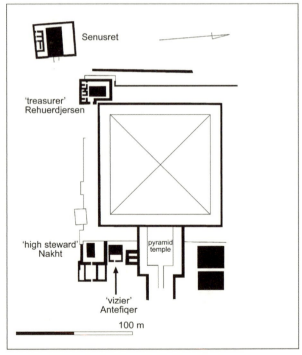

3. Plan of the pyramid of Amenemhat I.
Drawn by the author after Arnold 2008, pl. 114.

thought that the burial equipment was restricted to the royal court of the Twelfth Dynasty. Typical of court type burials are a set of staves and weapons, partly gilded coffins, and jewelry, all specially made for the tomb. They are mainly attested at the cemeteries at the royal court, but also at provincial cemeteries.[3] The best preserved examples belong to "king's daughters," although this type of burial was not restricted to women at the royal court.

The burial of Senebtisi was excavated in the winter season 1906–1907 near the pyramid of Amenemhat I beside the modern village of Lisht (Fig. 2). It was found within the burial complex of the vizier Senusret, who held office under Senusret I and Amenemhat II. In the Twelfth and Thirteenth Dynasties a huge cemetery developed around the royal pyramids. Many of the people at the court serving these kings were buried here, but the place also remained an important burial ground after this period, perhaps because it was the cemetery of the Middle Kingdom capital Itjtawy.

The burial complex of the vizier Senusret (Fig. 4) was already heavily destroyed when found. It consisted of two parts. There was an aboveground chapel, once decorated and perhaps accessible to everyone, or at least to the family of Senusret. The second part of the tomb consisted of the shaft and burial chamber, closed after the interment and, as usual, not decorated. The chapel of Senusret was found badly destroyed. Stone looters had taken all the stone blocks, and therefore little of the vizier's chapel survived. All that is left are small fragments of reliefs with the titles and name of Senusret, some fragments of scenes once decorating the aboveground part of the tomb complex, and fragments with portions of a biographical inscription. These few remaining fragments of the reliefs are of the finest quality. The inscriptions provide us with some of the titles of Senusret. He was "vizier," "overseer of the king's ornament," and "overseer of [all royal] works." The last title might indicate that he was involved in royal building works or even in planning the king's pyramid. As he is attested in the last years of Senusret I and in the first years of Amenemhat II, however, it seems unlikely that he was the major architect under Senusret I for his pyramid. The chapel of the complex for the vizier Senusret once measured about 12 × 26 m. Little has survived of its plan. It can be said with certainty only that there was a courtyard with columns at the front, with the cult chambers most likely at the back. Here was also the main shaft for the burial of Senusret, with the burial chamber at the bottom.

0   20 m

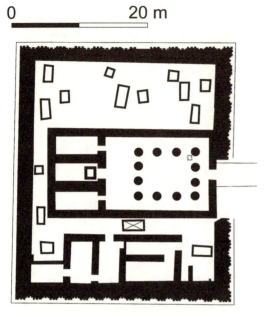

4. Plan of tomb of Senusret
(reconstruction). The shaft of Senebtisi's
tomb is marked. Drawn by the author
after Arnold 2008, pl. 147.

The chapel with the burial shaft stood within an enclosure wall of mud brick decorated on the outside with a palace facade. On the east side there was a building for funerary priests built of mud bricks. Within the enclosure wall were several shafts, most of them on the west side of the cult building. Here were most likely buried relatives of Senusret, or people belonging to his staff at work. Only three shafts were located on the east side of the cult chapel, one of them belonging to Senebtisi.[4]

The excavator Herbert Winlock recognized the importance of Senebtisi's tomb from the beginning and was very careful with his recording of its clearance. The main work was carried out with the help of Arthur C. Mace, a lesser-known figure of Egyptian archaeology but a very careful recorder, and in this area a pioneer. Later he was involved in the excavation of Tutankhamun's tomb, and the high quality of the recording there is also due in large part to his involvement.[5]

The burial of Senebtisi was found in a rock-cut underground chamber at the bottom of a shaft (Fig. 5). The shaft measured 1.38 m × 2.8 m wide and only 6.85 m deep. The mouth of the shaft was lined with bricks, perhaps to prevent sand fall. At the bottom of the shaft, on the west side, was the burial chamber consisting of two parts. The first was an almost square room with an opening in the north wall leading to a second, slightly smaller and longer burial chamber for the coffin. The first room was filled with pottery, while in the burial chamber were the coffins and three boxes. In the east wall was a niche for the canopic box. This box contained the canopic jars holding the entrails of the deceased body, which were removed after mummification and placed in four jars.

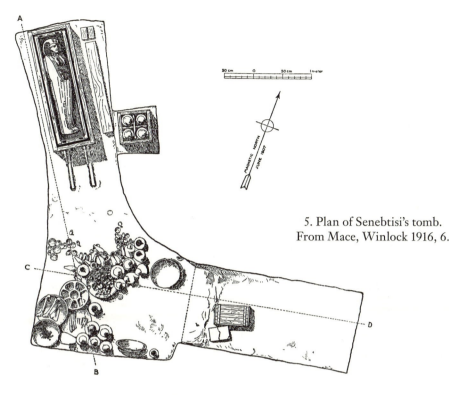

5. Plan of Senebtisi's tomb. From Mace, Winlock 1916, 6.

Senebtisi was placed in a set of three coffins. The outer coffin was made of a soft wood, most likely sycamore, and was badly preserved when found (Fig. 6). The excavators were just able to copy some of the inscriptions. The coffin was decorated on the long sides with four columns of text and a top horizontal text band. On the short ends were two columns and the top horizontal band. The front side of the coffin was further decorated with a pair of *wedjat* eyes. The lid was vaulted and had a single line of inscription down the middle. The coffin was painted red, perhaps in imitation of high-quality cedar wood. Although the inscriptions on the coffin were badly preserved, it seems clear that some of them are so far unique. Others are common for coffins of the late Twelfth Dynasty and contain short sentences spoken by different deities during the mummification.[6] The decoration of the coffin with the wedjat eyes, four text columns on the long sides, two text columns on the short ends, and horizontal text lines at the top is typical of coffins of the Middle Kingdom.[7] The coffin was not decorated on the inside.

Inside the outer coffin was placed the second wooden coffin.[8] It was better preserved, perhaps because it was made of hard cedar wood, which

6. View of Senebtisi's coffin as it was found.
From Mace, Winlock 1916, pl. Xa.

has a greater chance of survival. This coffin had only a single golden inscription band on the lid and was decorated on the outer side only with the wedjat eyes motif (Fig. 7). The edges of the coffin were ornamented with gold foil. The inscription on the lid is an address to Nut, the sky goddess: "Words spoken: Nut, you are glorious, you are powerful in the body of your mother Tefnut, before your birth, (when) she caused that the lady of the house Sathapy, justified, be the god, lord of eternity, that she may unite with the justified lady of the house Senebtisi in life, duration and power, that she may not die for eternity."[9]

Inside this second, middle coffin was the final inner anthropoid one. This human-shaped coffin was also badly decayed when found. At first the excavators thought that they had

7. The middle coffin of Senebtisi (194 cm long).
From Mace, Winlock 1916, pl. XVIIb.

8. The decoration on the chest of Senebtisi's anthropoid coffin. From Mace, Winlock 1916, pl. XX.

found a cartonnage (a mummy cover of plaster and linen) covering the whole mummy. That it was a coffin was recognized only when six copper clamps were found that had held the box and the lid of the coffin together. The anthropoid coffin was decorated on the chest with a broad collar inlaid with various materials such as faience and carnelian (Fig. 8). It was covered with fine gold leaf.

Senebtisi was mummified. Her body was wrapped in several layers of linen, all of which were badly preserved when found. The entrails had been removed through a 21 cm long incision on the left side of her body. The wound was stuffed with a yellowish material. The body itself was filled with linen. The heart had been removed, wrapped in linen, and then placed back into the body. The brain was not removed.[10] The entrails were placed in the canopic jars, where they were found treated with some kind of resin and wrapped in linen.[11]

Senebtisi was adorned with an array of jewelry. On her head was a golden circlet composed of gold wire. It was made of three separate pieces of wire forming a chain of loops connected at the back of the head by a simple gold wire fastener.[12] Ninety-eight golden rosettes remained from a hair covering that was once perhaps placed in or on the wig. They were made of gold foil beaten over a core. Two different molds were used for the rosettes, one with sixteen petals and the other with twelve.[13] Eighty-five rosettes were pierced with two holes so that they could be bound to

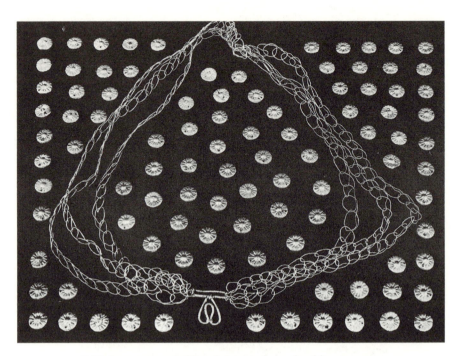

9. Hair ornaments of Senebtisi, circlet and golden rosettes.
From Mace, Winlock 1916, pl. XXI.

the hair or wig of Senebtisi. Thirteen had a small strip of gold at the back
to form some kind of attachment for the same purpose (Fig. 9).

Around Senebtisi's neck were three broad collars. Of these, one had
end pieces in the shape of a falcon's head (Fig. 10)[14] and another had
half-round end pieces (Fig. 11).[15] Both collars consisted of several rows
of tube-shaped beads. Along their outer edge was a row of drop-shaped
beads. The original arrangement of the beads is not fully certain, as the
strings had perished and the beads were found in considerable disorder.
The end pieces of the collars were made of plaster and then gilded. The
same technique was used for about two-thirds of the gold beads, while the
others were made of faience with gold leaf. The material of these collars
gives a strong impression that they were especially made for the burial and
never worn in real life. This impression is confirmed by missing holes in
the end pieces of the broad collar, which meant that no string could hold
them together at the back. The same is certainly true for the third collar.
It was made of copper and gilded with the decoration of imitation beads
incised into the gold leaf.[16]

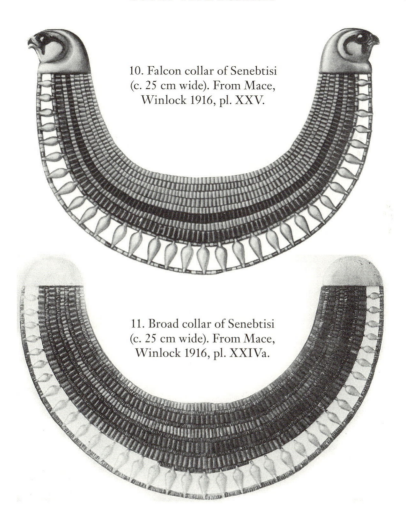

10. Falcon collar of Senebtisi
(c. 25 cm wide). From Mace,
Winlock 1916, pl. XXV.

11. Broad collar of Senebtisi
(c. 25 cm wide). From Mace,
Winlock 1916, pl. XXIVa.

Four necklaces were found. One consists of beads of various materials, including several sets of nine beads merged together to form one bigger unit. Twenty-five of these units were found interspersed with single beads in three rows. Hanging from this arrangement were twenty-five golden shells.[17] A second necklace consists of two strings of feldspar beads. Between these strings are twenty-one (tall) *sa* signs of different materials.[18] The *sa* sign is a hieroglyphic sign meaning "protection." A third necklace consists of a single string of beads in the shape of a long vase, called *hes* in ancient Egyptian (Fig. 12). The beads were made of different materials. This necklace has a pendant in the shape of a *shen* sign.[19] The shen sign was a popular motif, especially in the late Middle Kingdom but also

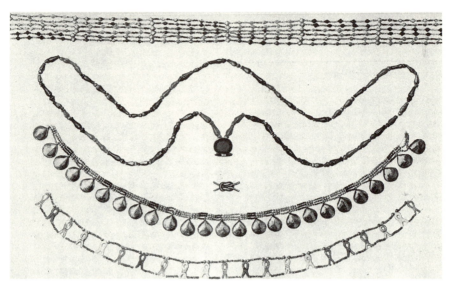

12. Necklaces of Senebtisi. From Mace, Winlock 1916, pl. XXIII.

13. Necklaces of Senebtisi. At the bottom is the sweret bead.
It seems unlikely that it was part of a bead necklace as reconstructed here.
From Mace, Winlock 1916, pl. XXVI.

in later periods. The exact meaning is unknown, but it may have offered some protection. As a pendant or amulet, it is indeed found in some late Middle Kingdom burials, almost becoming a standard object in the burial equipment of the period.[20] Of the fourth necklace, only one single carnelian bead was found, and it remains unknown what style of necklace it belonged to. Several further faience beads were found in the burial, and their exact function and position also remain unknown. The single carnelian bead is quite typical of burials of the time, and examples were found attached to anthropoid coffins. It is also known from its depiction on objects in pictorial friezes decorating coffins, and in that context is known as a *sweret* (Fig. 13).[21] The exact magical function of this bead is not known, but it appears as a single bead on a string around the neck of the deceased on anthropoid coffins and mummy masks.[22] "Sweri" is the Ancient Egyptian word for drinking, and there might be a connection. Perhaps the sweret bead was some kind of guarantee that the deceased would be able to drink (and eat) for all eternity. Others see it as protection against snakebites.[23]

The sweret bead is also sporadically depicted on the inside of coffins.[24] Early Middle Kingdom coffins are often decorated on the inside with long religious texts but also with friezes of objects. In these friezes are shown objects that also appear in some tombs as burial goods. The pictures have captions providing us with the names of many of these objects. Not all objects depicted in friezes are known as burial goods, however, and other objects were only sporadically found in burials. The coffin friezes of the middle of the Twelfth Dynasty, in particular, often show objects that also appear in the court type burials. These are mainly royal insignia. This might indicate that royal rituals were copied by private individuals.[25] It therefore seems that there were two phases for royal insignia in private burials. In the middle of the Twelfth Dynasty they were painted on the inside of coffins. In the late Twelfth Dynasty the insides of coffins were no longer decorated. Instead, a selection of these items appears as real objects in the burial chamber next to the deceased. The picture is certainly more complicated, however. Decorated coffins were mainly found in provincial cemeteries. The royal insignia were mainly found in cemeteries of the royal residence. Furthermore, royal insignia already appear sporadically in earlier burials, often those of local governors.

Around the pelvis of Senebtisi there was an apron or kilt (Fig. 14).[26] It is decorated with rows of beads hanging from it and with the lotus and the

papyrus at the upper ends. The apron therefore symbolized Upper and
Lower Egypt, as the lotus and the papyrus were the symbols of these parts
of the country. This type of kilt is also known from depictions of the king
and was therefore a royal garment. It is also often shown on friezes of objects on early Middle Kingdom coffins and was therefore an essential part
of a certain type of burial. On these friezes captions are also found, and
from them the Egyptian name of the apron, *besa*, is known.[27] In the center
of the girdle is a gilded wooden plate on which the name "Senebtisi" is
written in black paint. The wood had perished when it was found, and it
therefore remains unknown whether this piece once formed some kind of
clasp. At the back of the girdle were the remains of a decorative "tail." It
too was made of wood and decorated with beads. In the friezes of Middle
Kingdom coffins the tail appears as independent object and is called *men-
keret*.[28] A carnelian swallow is typical of this type of burial and was perhaps
once attached to the apron.[29] The swallow, often shown with a sun disk
on the back, also appears in the Coffin Texts and is there called *siat*.[30] This
type of apron with the swallow and the tail is a feature of several court type
burials, but certainly not of all of them.[31] Diana Graig Patch argued that
the apron was worn as a symbol for the sun god Re's daily birth. Indeed,

14. The royal apron of Senebtisi (c. 58.5 cm wide). From Mace, Winlock 1916,
pl. XXVII.

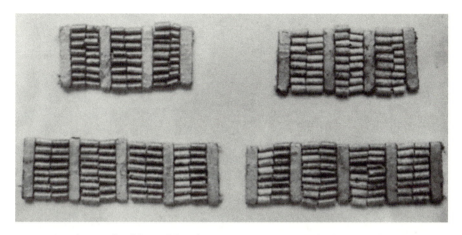

15. Armlets and anklets of Senebtisi. From Mace, Winlock 1916, pl. XXVIb.

a bead network, similar to the one on the apron, is visible on the solar barque of Re.[32]

Senebtisi was wearing two armlets[33] and two anklets[34] composed of gilded wooden bars with faience beads strung between them (Fig. 15). They were evidently made for the burial, since they were not long enough to go around the arms or legs and there was no means of fastening them together, so they were simply placed on the arms and legs of the mummy.[35] Several other smaller objects and many more beads were found, but their exact function and arrangement remain obscure.

Within the second coffin, but outside the anthropoid coffin, was found a set of staves and weapons (Fig. 16). These consisted of a double staff known as *pedj-aha* in ancient Egypt; a long *heqa* staff and a simple staff with a forked lower end called *abet*;[36] two *was* scepters, one wavy staff, and another more or less plain staff. Both *was* scepters had a stylized animal head on the top with eyes; one even had a broad collar painted under the head. This group also included two bows, a flail,[37] and a mace.[38] The flail was made of several conical beads attached to a wooden handle. The final object was a mace with a head made of aragonite (a type of stone). In the anthropoid coffin placed close to Senebtisi on her left side was also found a copper dagger,[39] placed within a partly gilded wooden sheath. The dagger was one of the most important items placed in certain burials of women in the late Middle Kingdom. In the Old Kingdom the dagger is already listed with other items also known from the late Middle Kingdom burials at the royal court.[40] The dagger was evidently seen as essential for a

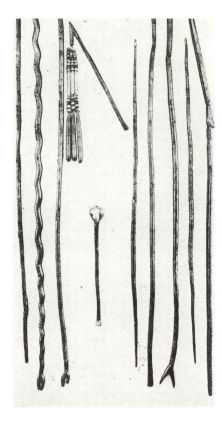

16. Scepters and flail. From Mace, Winlock 1916, pl. XXa.

certain type of burial. Its religious or ritual meaning still remains obscure.

Within the wrappings at the head of Senebtisi's mummy was found a round disk about 8 cm in diameter made of a dark resinous material (Fig. 17). Similar objects are known from the burials of the royal women discovered next to the pyramid of Amenemhat II. The function of this object is unknown.[41]

Next to the coffin on the left or east side was a long box once containing another set of staffs and scepters. These were badly decayed; only the stone head of a mace was well preserved. Next to the long box stood two small boxes or shrines, each about 20 cm high. These are both highly exceptional objects, not

17. Clay disk found under the head of Senebtisi's mummy. From Mace, Winlock 1916, pl. XXVIIIh.

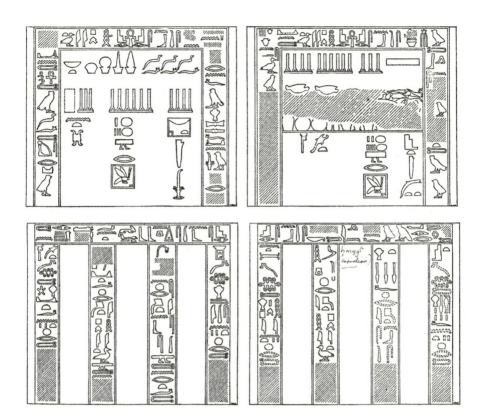

18. Inscriptions on the canopic box of Senebtisi. From Mace,
Winlock 1916, p. 37, figs. 19–22.

recorded in other burials of this type. One wonders what they once contained. All that was found inside was the remains of cloth, but its original
function could not be determined. There are several options. The shrines
were found next to the box containing the royal insignia. Often these royal
insignia are also depicted on coffins of about the same time or slightly
earlier. These depictions always include crowns. Is it possible that actual
crowns were placed in these small shrines? So far no such crowns have
been found. The depictions do not make it clear from what material they
were made, but it has been proposed that they were made of fur or some
other lightweight organic material.[42] According to this hypothesis, the
crowns depicted in Egyptian art are highly stylized and might originally
have looked quite different. This, however, is only a guess. Without further parallels these two boxes remain highly enigmatic. Another option is
that they served as receptacles for material left over from the embalming

19. The canopic jars of Senebtisi. From Mace, Winlock 1916, pl. XXXIIIa.

process. There are indeed several cases where the embalming material received its own "burial." This is always attested outside the tomb chamber, however, and not as close to the coffin as Senebtisi's boxes.[43]

On the east side of the coffin was a niche for the canopic box. The box was made of cedar, but like the coffins it was already badly decayed when found. The excavators were still able to copy most of the inscriptions, however. The box was inscribed on the east and west sides with short formulae that normally appear on canopic jars, while the texts on the north and south sides are without parallel on canopic boxes (Fig. 18). Within the box were four uninscribed canopic jars. The jars were made of stone, differing in color and size. In contrast, the heads atop the jars were made of wood and were painted.[44] These jars once contained the entrails of the mummy (Fig. 19).

Finally, the pottery from the tomb should be mentioned. Two hundred and six vessels were found (Fig. 20). Many of these were small model vessels perhaps specially made for the tomb. There were, however, also nine large dishes. Two of them still contained the bones of animals, evidently part of the eternal food supply or funeral meal for Senebtisi. Another dish was filled with many small saucers, and finally one filled with 125 small clay balls, perhaps imitating incense pellets. These dishes were perhaps normally used for serving food, especially meat.[45] They belong to the most common pottery vessels found in late Middle Kingdom tombs.[46] Other vessels found included a type of hemispherical cup that was most likely used for drinking water or other liquids and is very typical of the Middle Kingdom;[47] small plates that were perhaps for serving dried fruits;[48] and

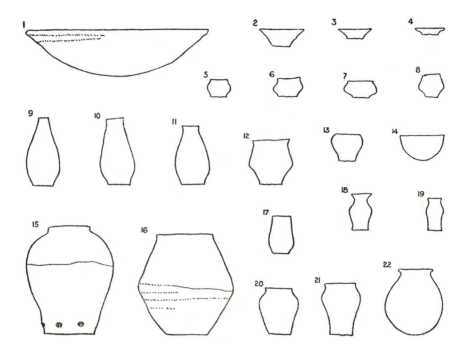

20. The pottery from the tomb of Senebtisi. From Mace,
Winlock 1916, p. 110, fig. 82.

taller beaker-like vessels once perhaps containing liquid or fat.[49] All these vessels were most likely important for ensuring the eternal food supply.

Other vessels found were used in rituals. These include four small jars,[50] perhaps of a type called *nemset*. They were important for purification and are mentioned several times in Pyramid Texts:[51] "You are cleaned with your four *nemset* and four *aabet* jars."[52] They also appear in the friezes of objects on the inside of Middle Kingdom coffins (Fig. 21).[53] Furthermore, eight examples of each of two different types of larger vessel were also found.[54] Susan Allen noted that the number four was important.[55] These eight vessels were either two sets of identical ritual vessels or four sets of vessels for rituals where the same form was used for two different functions. One option is that these are *senu* vases, placed under an idol of Osiris during the Khoiak festival.[56]

We shall see that the burial of Senebtisi has many points in common with burials of royal women in the late Middle Kingdom. The pottery is different, however, and has more in common with the pottery found in private burials, while burials of royal women most often contained so-

21. Two cultic vessels from the tomb of Senebtisi. From Mace,
Winlock 1916, pl. XXIV.

called "queen's ware," a pottery style typical of burials of royal women
of the late Middle Kingdom copying Old Kingdom fine tableware. This
comes as no surprise, since Senebtisi did not have royal status and was
most likely not part of the royal family.[57]

Who Was Senebtisi?

Senebtisi bears the title "lady of the house." On some items of her burial
equipment she is also attributed with the second name Sathapy, "Daughter of Hapy."[58] Beside this, nothing is known for sure about her. Senebtisi
is one of the most common names in the late Middle Kingdom, so any
identification with another woman of the same name known from other
monuments must be highly speculative. Also, to the best of my knowledge, there are no attestations on other monuments for a woman with the
double name Senebtisi Sathapy. Senebtisi therefore remains enigmatic.
It can only be said for certain that she was a lady of high social status, as
indicated by the high standard of her burial equipment.

The exact date of Senebtisi's tomb is disputed. Kim Ryholt identified
Senebtisi with the namesake grandmother of the Thirteenth Dynasty king
Neferhotep I, arguing that the burial is similar to one of the king's daugh-

ter Nubhetepti-khered and is close in style to royal court type burials.[59] However, court type burials are also well attested for nonroyal women. Furthermore, Senebtisi was not buried with "queen's ware," whereas most other king's daughters had queen's ware in the burial chamber. This seems to be another indicator that she was not royal, although this argument is weakened by the fact that the king's daughter Neferuptah was also not equipped with this type of pottery. Neferuptah was buried at the end of the Twelfth or the beginning of the Thirteenth Dynasty.

More recent research supports the view that Senebtisi most likely lived in the late Twelfth Dynasty. Her coffin is inscribed with complete hieroglyphs, while coffins at the royal residence in the very late Twelfth Dynasty and Thirteenth Dynasty bear incomplete hieroglyphs.[60] The pottery found in Senebtisi's burial is also more typical of the late Twelfth Dynasty,[61] although it is problematic to provide such a close date for a tomb via the analysis of pottery.

THE KING'S DAUGHTER SATHATHORIUNET

The first two kings of the Twelfth Dynasty were buried at Lisht, perhaps the cemetery of Itjtawy, the capital of the Twelfth and Thirteenth Dynasties. Amenemhat II, the third ruler of the dynasty, went north to Dahshur to build his pyramid, while the next king, Senusret II, instead went farther south, near to a place now called Lahun. Lahun is close to the Fayum, a river oasis connected to the Nile via a watercourse. The Fayum was originally a marshland not particularly suitable for agriculture. In the Middle Kingdom, however, the kings started to cultivate this region and built temples and other monuments there. Two royal pyramids were constructed close to the Fayum, one for Senusret II and another for Amenemhat III at Hawara, not far from Lahun.

Senusret II reigned for only about eight years. Perhaps he was already quite old when he ascended the throne. For that reason he might have chosen a small hill for his pyramid, so that less building material was needed to construct a pyramid of about the same scale as those of his father, grandfather, and great-grandfather. The pyramid measured 106 m at the base and originally rose to a height of about 48 m (Fig. 22). It was the first pyramid of the Middle Kingdom to be built mainly of mud bricks, although an inner "skeleton" of stone walls provided some stability and

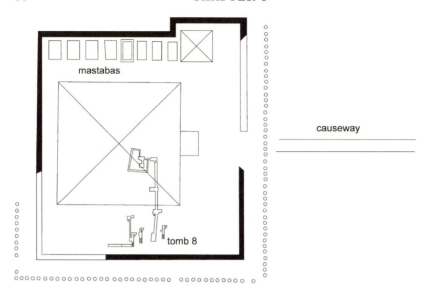

mastabas

causeway

tomb 8

22. Pyramid of Senusret II at Lahun. Drawn by the author.

the pyramid was clad with limestone slabs. Another innovation was to the entrance, which was no longer on the north side but in this case south of the pyramid.

In 1914, the pyramid and its complex were excavated by William M. Flinders Petrie and Guy Brunton. South of the pyramid they discovered four shaft tombs; one of them was the hidden entrance to the king's pyramid, the others most likely belonged to female members of the king's family. All the tombs were found heavily robbed, and the name of the owner could be ascertained for only one tomb, with the modern number 8 (Fig. 23). This was the king's daughter Sathathoriunet ("daughter of Hathor, of Denderah").[62] Her tomb was the smallest and had been robbed like the others, except for a niche that was found full of jewelry. The tomb consisted of a 6.6 m deep shaft. At the north end it opened into a small antechamber, about 1.5 m below the level of the shaft. A niche on the west side was found undisturbed, evidently overlooked by ancient robbers of the tomb. Next to the antechamber was the burial chamber, completely occupied by the big granite sarcophagus of the princess. At the southern end of the sarcophagus chamber, on the east side, was a further niche. Here was placed the canopic chest containing four inscribed canopic jars.[63] The texts on the jars provide the title of Sathathoriunet: "king's daughter." At the back on the east side is a further chamber, which was found looted but

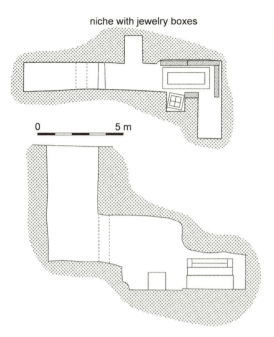

niche with jewelry boxes

0   5 m

23. Plan of burial chamber of
Sathathoriunet with niche with
jewelry boxes. Drawn by the author.

still contained some pottery
shards, beads, and an alabaster
and obsidian eye, perhaps from
an anthropoid coffin. The most
important object was a jar for
purification water, typical of
royal burials of the late Middle
Kingdom. It bears a purification spell and also mentions
Sathathoriunet (see Fig. 37 on
p. 45).[64]

As already mentioned, the
small niche in the first chamber
was found undisturbed. Water
had flooded the chamber, however, and so most of the organic material
had perished by the time of the excavation. Petrie and Brunton soon realized the importance of this find. They recorded the find spots of all the
objects in great detail and were able to reconstruct the contents of the
chamber and even the jewelry and boxes found there. Most of the jewelry
was bought by the Metropolitan Museum of Art in New York and today
forms one of the highlights of the collection.

Herbert Winlock, who worked for the Egyptian Department of the
Metropolitan Museum, had a further look at the tomb and the treasures
after they came to New York. He published a detailed study of this find.
In the following description of the treasure I follow his reconstructions.

Winlock counted fives boxes in this small niche. From two boxes several inlays survived, and so he was able to reconstruct them with some certainty. The box labeled 1 by Winlock was originally about 44.5 cm long,
31 cm wide, and perhaps 37 cm high. It was decorated on the outside with
ivory slabs showing stylized doors and *djed* pillars, six of the latter on the
long sides and four on the short ends. The lid was curved and decorated
with four Hathor heads with horns and a sun disk between them made of
thin gold sheet. Between the heads were three slabs of ivory with the throne
name, birth name, and Horus name of King Amenemhat III. The box was

24. Jewelry box of Sathathoriunet (reconstruction).
From Winlock 1934, pl. IB.

evidently crafted under the king and was perhaps a gift to the princess. It is among the most elegant examples of Middle Kingdom furniture (Fig. 24). Exact parallels have yet to be found, though some finds at Dahshur indicate the existence of similar boxes.

A second box was simpler but also decorated with ivory on the outside.[65] The long sides were decorated with most likely five stylized doors and the short ends with three. Inside the remains of this box were found alabaster jars for sacred oils. Boxes for such jars are more often of a different shape and much simpler, however, which suggested to Winlock that this box was originally made as a container for jewelry. A third box was perhaps decorated with gold foil and contained jars. This reconstruction again comes from Winlock, while Mace assigned the gold foil to the second box. Of a possible fourth box nothing survived, but it was reconstructed by Winlock, who believed that it once contained the crown of Sathathoriunet, not found in any surviving remains of a box or container. Made entirely of wood, the box had perished by the time the niche was excavated. The presence of a fifth box, although completely disintegrated when found, was identified from a pile of brown dust. Close to these faint traces were found copper nails without heads and others with golden heads. Some silver foil was also found in the same area. All this might indeed come from one box, which would have been the largest one in the niche. It was about 36.5 cm wide, 25.4 cm high, and at least 55 cm long. Within the remains of the box nothing was found, so one can only guess at its original contents, which must have been some organic material that decayed and left no traces. Brunton suggested that this box was for a wig.

The unique piece among the princess's items of jewelry was her crown (Fig. 25).[66] It is a golden circlet decorated with a uraeus at the front and with fifteen rosettes all around. It has an diameter of 19 cm. The band

25. The crown of Sathathoriunet. From Brunton 1920, pl. V.

of the circlet is 2.7 cm wide and about 0.4 cm thick. The uraeus is of gold with inlays of lapis lazuli (a semiprecious stone imported from Afghanistan), carnelian, and glazed material that had disintegrated to white powder when found. Attached to the circlet were golden "plumes." Under the crown were found 1,251 small golden tubes. These were originally most likely part of the king's daughter's wig or hair cover. Similar crowns are known from depictions in the tomb of the local governor Ukh-hotep IV at Meir.[67] In one scene, several musicians are represented in front of the tomb owner. They are each wearing a similar crown, but slightly simpler, with just one plume shown at the back of a circlet and going up. They are shown at a religious festival, most likely in honor of Hathor, who was the main deity of Qis[68] (Meir was the cemetery of Qis). The interpretation of the plume is disputed. Staehlin regards it as the symbol of Ukh, who was an important deity and symbol at Meir, which is written with a symbol similar to the plume of the crown.[69] The Ukh symbol was also closely related to Hathor.[70]

Another fine piece of jewelry found in the tomb is the pectoral with the throne name of Senusret II as the central element (Fig. 26).[71] Inlaid with carnelian, lapis lazuli, and turquoise, it is a masterpiece of ancient Egyptian gold work. The piece is a work of inlays set in a golden frame in cloisonné work, a technique whereby a gold foil outline shape is fixed to a metal base, forming cells that are filled with glaze or semiprecious stones.[72] In ancient Egypt, the technique reached its peak in the Middle Kingdom with these pectorals. The center is formed of the hieroglyphics for the throne name of Senusret II: Khakheperre. On either side is a Horus falcon with a sun disk on its head. Each falcon has one leg resting upon a shen ring, while the other leg is raised to the sign meaning "million years" in the middle of the composition under the cartouche. This sign consists of a man sitting on the ground and holding in each raised hand a palm rib, the sign for "year." Furthermore, from the right arm of the sitting figure hangs a tadpole, which is the hieroglyphic sign for one

26. Pectoral of Sathathoriunet with the throne name of
Senusret II. The picture shows the pectoral in the condition
in which it was found. Detail from Petrie Museum archive,
PMAN 1820.

27. Second pectoral of Sathathoriunet with the throne name of
Amenemhat III. From Brunton 1920, pl. VIIC.

hundred thousand. On each of the heads of the falcons is a sun disk with a
uraeus cobra. From the body of the cobra hangs an *ankh* sign, the symbol
for "life." Altogether, the pectoral can be read as: "The sun god is granting millions and hundreds of thousands of years of life and duration for
King Khakheperre." The back of the piece, though not visible when worn,
shows the details of the composition engraved into the gold and is again
of the highest quality.

A second pectoral[73] is an almost identical copy of the first one, but with

28. Motto pendants. Petrie Museum archive, PMAN 1802.

the throne name of Amenemhat III: Nimaatre (Fig. 27). It is again made of gold, with inlays in carnelian, lapis lazuli, green faience, and amethyst. Although the craftsmanship of this piece is still high, it has been noted that one generation after the first pectoral a certain decline is detectable. Semiprecious stones are replaced by glazed materials, and the falcons look slightly clumsy in comparison to those on the first pectoral.[74] Both pectorals were part of a necklace consisting of drop-shaped beads and simple ball-shaped ones, or at least these beads were found close to the pectorals.

These pectorals with their strings of beads are the only necklaces found in the treasure. All the other jewelry was for the arms, hands, fingers, and waist. Five motto clasps should be mentioned (Fig. 28). The function of the five mottoes is somewhat enigmatic. These are basically hieroglyphic signs making up short sayings (mottoes) executed as fine jewelry in gold with inlays in semiprecious stones. Two of them show

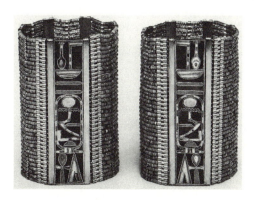

29. Armlets of Sathathoriunet with the throne name of Amenemhat III. From Winlock 1934, pl. X.

30. Lion amulets perhaps once used in armlets, modern reconstruction. Drawing by Paul Whelan.

a shen ring.[75] A third is composed of the hieroglyphs *aw* and *ib*, meaning "joy." The fourth shows two *sa* signs ("protection"), an *ankh* sign ("life"), and a *neb* sign ("all"), together reading "All life and protection."[76] The last one has the *ib* sign in the center ("heart"), two *netjer* signs ("god"), and the *hetep* sign ("satisfied") at the base.[77] This group reads: "The hearts of the two gods are satisfied." These motto clasps are quite small, the largest being just 2 cm high. On the back of each are two tubes, evidently for holding the mottoes on a string. No beads that might have belonged with these mottoes were found, however; they might have been strung on some kind of organic material and perished in the damp burial environment. Two rings adorned with a scarab were also found. Rings are not so common in the Middle Kingdom and are most often just a piece of wire with a scarab. Proper rings appear only later. One of the rings found here is remarkable

31. Bird claw, most likely a pendant from an anklet. Detail from Petrie Museum archive, PMAN 1820.

for the finely crafted scarab made of gold, lapis, and carnelian. The back shows a stripe pattern in blue and is in cloisonné work.[78] One scarab was found without ring and is made of lapis lazuli. It bears the throne name of Amenmehat III.[79]

The princess had two armlets and two anklets (Fig. 29). The armlets were made of beads with several bars holding them in place and a center-piece serving as the clasp with the titles and the throne name of Amenemhat III: "The good god, lord of the two lands, Nimaatre, may he live forever." The pieces are again composed of inlays set into a golden frame in cloisonné work.[80] Most of the examples for this technique were found in the burials of high-status women discussed here. This indicates that the technique was perhaps restricted to a small number of workshops or was at

32. Girdle with cowry shells of Sathathoriunet. From Winlock 1934, pl. VIII.

33. Elements of two girdles united for photographing. The photo was taken shortly after the excavation. Petrie Museum archive, PMAN 1801.

least quite expensive, so that only people at the royal court were able to afford it.

Almost identical armlets were found in the treasure of Mereret in Dahshur. The armlet itself consisted of thirty-seven rows of very small beads, with bars between them providing some stability. The two anklets of the princess were similar but without the richly adorned and inscribed clasps. Another armlet was adorned with two golden figures of lions.[81] This reconstruction, however, is far from certain (Fig. 30).

Two other anklets are simpler in design and consist of plain amethyst and golden ball beads with golden bird claw pendants (Fig. 31).[82] Winlock originally reconstructed them as one necklace,[83] but there are depictions in tombs of the period indicating that claw pendants were worn around the ankles.[84]

The princess had two girdles. One of them consisted of eight golden cowry shells (Fig. 32).[85] The other was a chain of seven double leopard heads, also made of gold, perhaps once connected by amethyst beads and further double, but smaller, leopard heads, most likely originally arranged between the larger ones (Fig. 33).[86] The cowry shell girdle in particular is also known from other tombs of royal and high-status women of this time.

Next to the jewelry several cosmetic objects were found. The first of

34. The mirror of
Sathathoriunet. From Winlock,
Lahun, pl. XV.

35. Razors of Sathathoriunet and whetstones.
From Brunton 1920, pl. X.

these was a partly gilded mirror with a golden Hathor head at the top of the handle (Fig. 34).[87] Two razors were found with two whetstones for sharpening them (Fig. 35),[88] and there were three cosmetic jars, all cylinder-shaped with a wider top part. These were made of obsidian with gilded rims; a fourth one is smaller but also with a gilded rim (Fig. 36).[89]

36. Examples of cosmetic vessels of
Sathathoriunet. From Brunton 1920, pl. IX.

A small saucer made of silver has the shape of a shen ring.[90] Two copper blades of two knives were also found.[91]

In a separate box were found eight similar vessels made of Egyptian alabaster[92] and not gilded.[93] They are described as not highly polished. The contents, a pinkish substance, was still visible in a few of the vessels. These eight jars are typical of high-status burials of the late

37. Vessel for pure water, from the tomb of Sathat-horiunet. From Petrie, Brunton, Murray 1920, pl. XXV, 7.

Middle Kingdom. In other tombs the lids of the jars are inscribed with the names of the seven sacred oils (compare the description of the burial of Ita, below).

Also found in the tomb was a jar made of alabaster inscribed with a magical spell connected to pure water (Fig. 37).[94] This type of inscribed jar is not common and is restricted to royal women and kings. The spell appears in later times as part of the second nightly hour of the "hour vigil."[95] This is the ritual in which Osiris was embalmed with the help of other deities. Whether the spell and the jar were already related to the hour vigil in the Twelfth Dynasty is not certain. It is possible that this spell is an important text in a purification ritual, later used in the hour vigil. Indeed, the purification of the body of the deceased was an important part of preparing the mummy in the purification tent.[96] The spell reads: "King's daughter Sathathoriunet, receive this cool water which is from the land that begets everything that lives, all those things that this land gives; indeed, it is the land that begets everything comes forth. May you live on them, may you receive upon them. May you live and revive upon them. May you live and revive upon this breath that is within it. It begets you, and you come forth. You live on all that is desired and perfect that is therein."[97]

Several pottery vessels were found in the burial of Sathathoriunet. They included large bowls, small fat-based cups, a beaker-shaped jar, a hemispherical cup, and a bottle.[98] The pottery belongs to a type most recently called queen's ware and most often found in burials of late Middle Kingdom royal women. It is made of Nile clay and highly crafted. It is covered with a red coat, but not so well fired, providing a somewhat patchy surface color. Altogether the pottery seems to copy Old Kingdom tableware known as "Meydum ware." The Middle Kingdom craftsmen, however, did not manage to match the Old Kingdom quality.[99]

Who Was Sathathoriunet?

Sathathoriunet is so far known only from her burial. The only title she bore was "king's daughter." Her burial place next to the pyramid of Senusret II might indicate that she was closely related to him and therefore perhaps his daughter. The name of the king was found on some objects from her tomb. Also found in her burial were more than one object bearing the name of Amenemhat III. This might indicate that she died under this king. In some publications Sathathoriunet is also called queen.[100] She did not, however, bear the title "king's wife." Her identification as a queen might go back to Brunton, who wondered whether she was a queen on the grounds that her crown was adorned with a uraeus.[101] There is so far no evidence that the uraeus was restricted to queens.[102] Indeed, there are examples where a king's daughter wears a uraeus. From the late Middle Kingdom comes the scarab of the king's daughter Nubhetepti, on which she is shown standing and with a uraeus.[103] Another example is a rock relief depicting the early Thirteenth Dynasty king Sobekhotep III and his family. Here too, the daughters are depicted with a uraeus.[104] The uraeus is the symbol of the goddess Wadjet, who was one the crown deities and therefore represented kingship. While it is possible to argue that Sathathoriunet was king's wife later in her life, being "promoted" after parts of her burial equipment were made, this argument does not work for the women on the scarab and on the rock relief, where the depictions and the titles belong together. From this evidence it is safest to say that Sathathoriunet was a daughter of Senusret II who died under Amenemhat III. She might not have been the youngest when she died, but there is no evidence that she was ever a king's wife.

BURIALS AT DAHSHUR

Dahshur is a modern village near Saqqara, about thirty kilometers south of Cairo (Fig. 38). In the Old Kingdom it was the location of the two pyramids of Snofru, first king of the Fourth Dynasty. There were also cemeteries of officials serving the king. After Snofru, Dahshur was no longer used as a cemetery for kings, though officials, perhaps not the highest ranked, were still buried there. All other rulers of the Old Kingdom were buried farther north, at places such as Gizeh, Abusir, and Saqqara. This

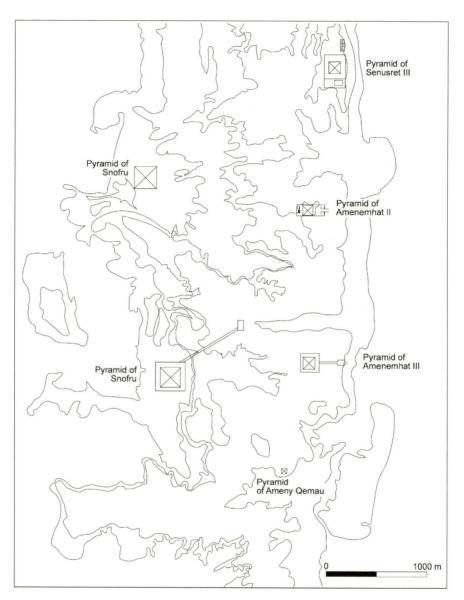

Pyramid of
Senusret III

Pyramid of
Snofru

Pyramid of
Amenemhat II

Pyramid of
Amenemhat III

Pyramid of
Snofru

Pyramid
of Ameny Qemau

0   1000 m

38. Map of Dahshur. Drawn by the author.

change is not necessarily as great as it may seem from the changing place
names, as the division between Dahshur and Saqqara is a modern one. In
ancient times, the region from Abusir in the north, down to Dahshur, and
even beyond to Magzhuna in the south formed one big cemetery, with
concentrations of tombs and mastabas around the royal pyramids.

In the Middle Kingdom the cemetery of Dahshur again became important. Amenemhat II, who ruled around 1900 BCE, was the third king of this dynasty. He built his pyramid at Dahshur. His son Senusret II was buried somewhere else, but Senusret III and Amenemhat III built their grand pyramids again at Dahshur. Most pyramids of the ensuing Thirteenth Dynasty have also been found at Dahshur. Excavations in recent years have also shown that there were huge cemeteries for officials of the Twelfth and early Thirteenth Dynasties at the site. They have not yet been explored, because Dahshur was for a long time a military zone and not available to excavate. This has changed only in the past few years with new American, German, and Japanese expeditions.

In 1894, however, the French archaeologist and director of the Egyptian Antiquities Service Jacques de Morgan excavated at Dahshur. Next to the pyramid of Amenemhat III de Morgan found two undisturbed burials. They were placed within a chain of burial shafts perhaps already built under Amenemhat III. It is unclear whether burials took place in his reign and were looted early on or the shafts were left empty and used only in the Thirteenth Dynasty. At present the latter option seems more likely, as there is no published trace of any Twelfth Dynasty use. Two burials belong to the Thirteenth Dynasty. One is that of King Hor, well known from his wooden statue now in the Egyptian Museum in Cairo and among its highlights; the other is that of the king's daughter Nubhetepti-khered. In the same campaign de Morgan also excavated at the pyramid of King Senusret III. Around the pyramid he found the tombs of royal women, and in two he discovered untouched jewelry boxes.

BURIALS NEXT TO THE PYRAMID OF AMENEMHAT II

In the expedition of 1894 to 1895 de Morgan excavated at Dahshur near and in the pyramid of King Amenemhat II (Fig. 39). The pyramid is so poorly preserved that even its exact measurements are not yet known for certain. It is sometimes called the "white pyramid" because the remains of the limestone cladding dominate the color of the otherwise shapeless rubble heap of pyramid remains.

West of the pyramid, de Morgan found three underground galleries, each of which contained two burials. In one gallery were the tombs of the queen Keminub and the "treasurer" Amenhotep.[105] Both were found

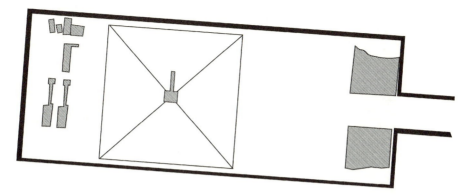

39. Amenemhat II pyramid complex. The undisturbed burials
are to the west. Drawn by the author.

disturbed. The burials belonged to the late Thirteenth Dynasty, perhaps around 1700 BCE.[106] Only inscribed fragments of the coffins were found, or at least these are the only objects mentioned and depicted in the excavation report. They provide us with the names of the tomb owners.

The other galleries were found undisturbed, still containing a remarkable set of objects. They belonged to Ita and Khenmet and to Itaweret and Sathathormeryt (Fig. 40). In each of these galleries two burials were found belonging to women, three with the title "king's daughter." For a long time it was assumed that they were daughters of Amenemhat II and buried during his reign, but the evidence of the pottery in the tombs indicates that they were most likely buried under Amenemhat III. In one of the burials a scarab was found with the name of Amenemhat III. The relationship of these women to Amenemhat II is thus unclear, though it is still possible to argue that they were daughters of that king, who died and were buried one or two generations later.[107]

In the first excavation season de Morgan documented the burials of King Hor and Nubhetepti-khered in some detail; the documentation of the other four tombs in the second season appears superficial, leaving modern researchers with many open questions. Only for the tomb of Khenmet did de Morgan present a plan and remark that all the burials were similar in layout.[108] However, it is easy to criticize the work of de Morgan today. Ideally modern archaeologists working in Egypt will photograph and draw all objects found, but in the nineteenth century archaeology was still in a phase of development. Excavations were often still seen as enterprises to acquire objects for museum collections. The publications

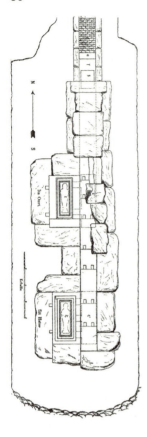

40. One of the gallery tombs found near the pyramid of Amenemhat II. They belonged to Itaweret and Sathathormeryt, as published by de Morgan. From de Morgan 1903, fig. 118.

are often very selective and concentrate on objects and architecture the excavators regarded as important. In Egyptian archaeology at that time this was more or less standard.

Each princess was placed in a set of three coffins. There was an outer stone sarcophagus and within it a wooden rectangular coffin, partly covered with gold foil. This wooden coffin was simply decorated on the outside with two eyes and gold foil, but without any inscriptions. Only on the inside of the coffin were there long religious texts, some already known from the pyramids of the Old Kingdom and therefore labeled "Pyramid Texts" by Egyptologists. Within this wooden rectangular coffin there must once have been an anthropoid coffin. All traces of any of the anthropoid coffins had already been lost when the burials were excavated, only the gold foil once covering their outsides and the inlaid eyes being preserved. De Morgan failed to recognize these anthropoid coffins, but their presence can be assumed from better preserved parallels and from the description given by de Morgan in the excavation report. Next to each anthropoid coffin was a set of royal symbols and weapons also often connected with royalty.

THE BURIAL OF THE KING'S DAUGHTER ITA

The first gallery excavated by de Morgan's team was found on 12 February 1895 and belonged to the king's daughters Ita and Khenmet.

The gallery consisted of a long corridor with the tombs of the women cut underneath. When found, the corridor was completely filled and blocked with stones. The tomb of Ita[109] consisted of two chambers, each just over 2 m long and 1 m wide and high. One chamber was fully occupied by the sarcophagus, while the other contained the burial goods. A small entrance, more a hole in the ground than a door, gave access from the corridor to the chamber for the burial goods, which is exactly under the corridor. The chamber for the sarcophagus was next to it and was entered via the roof, where there were the big blocks used to close it. The sarcophagus was most likely already in place when the whole complex was built; perhaps even the middle wooden coffin was placed here before the burial, leaving only Ita's mummy in her anthropoid coffin to be interred.

As already indicated, Ita's body was laid to rest in a set of three containers. The first was an outer sarcophagus in the form of a simple rectangular box with a vaulted lid with two raised ends. Then there was a partly gilded middle coffin (Fig. 41) inscribed only on the inside, and finally an innermost anthropoid coffin. The middle coffin was decorated on the outside with wedjat eyes and on the inside with religious texts written only in hieroglyphs in different colors.[110] Several of them are spells spoken by Nut and Geb.[111] The inner coffin was most likely made of thin wood with a fine plaster skin and overlaid with a substance described as bitumen.[112] The head had eyes inlaid with silver and a headdress in blue with golden bands. The breast was decorated with a broad collar, to judge from the beads of the collar described by de Morgan.[113]

The body of Ita was adorned with an array of jewelry and other objects. She had a richly decorated dagger, which stands as one of the masterpieces of Egyptian metalwork (Fig. 42). Its handle consists of three parts. The pommel (the end of the handle) is crescent-shaped and made of lapis lazuli. The handle proper is covered with thirty rosettes. The lower end of the handle is made of gold and frames the upper end of the blade. The sheath of the dagger was made of some organic material, with only

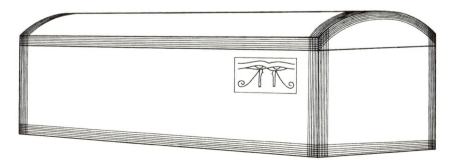

41. The middle coffin of Ita. From de Morgan 1903, fig. 109.

42. The dagger of Ita. From de Morgan 1903, pl. VII.

the mouth and lower end made of gold. It was most likely made specifically for the burial. The lower end of the handle was made of gold, a material too weak to support the pressure of the blade when used.[114] The dagger was found near a girdle with a silver fastener.[115] Daggers with a crescent-shaped pommel are of a type known from the Near East.[116]

Around Ita's neck was a broad collar with round terminals in silver and many beads of semiprecious stones, such as lapis lazuli, carnelian, and turquoise.[117] The terminals were simple and undecorated. Ita's body was adorned with several armlets and bracelets. There was a small figure of a swallow, perhaps once belonging to a girdle and not uncommon in this type of burial. From depictions it is known that such figures were attached to an apron. They also appear in the friezes of early Middle Kingdom coffins and are called *zait*.[118] Under the head of the mummy was a small disk of black earth of unknown function.[119] Ita was perhaps also adorned with a royal apron, but the short excavation report is not really conclusive on this point.[120] Placed on the left side of Ita were several weapons and royal insignia, including a flail, a mace, and scepters. Again, these objects were only briefly mentioned in the publication.

In the second chamber of the burial further burial goods were found. Under a big plate there was a set of bronze tools (Fig. 43). In the southeastern corner of the chamber was an uninscribed canopic box containing a set of four canopic jars, also uninscribed. The jars have human heads; three are shown with a beard, the fourth without. From the Middle Kingdom onward, canopic jars were placed under the protection of the four children of Horus: Amset, Qebehsenuef, Hapy, and Duamutef. In the Middle Kingdom Amset was a female deity, and therefore the canopic jar under her protection had a head without a beard, while the other three—all male deities—are shown with a short beard.

43. Tools of Ita. From de Morgan 1903, fig. 106.

The burial goods also included a box containing vessels for the "seven sacred oils."[121] In fact, it contained eight vessels, seven for the oils and a further one as some kind of placeholder. The lids of the vessels are inscribed with the names of the oils. The names are "best of ash-oil,"[122] "nekhenem-oil,"[123] "hekenu-oil,"[124] "iber-oil,"[125] "best of Tjehenu-oil" (perhaps best translated as "best of Libyan oil"),[126] "tuaut-oil,"[127] "sefetj-oil,"[128] "setji-hab" ("smell of the festival").[129] Only iber-oil does not belong to the classical list of the seven sacred oils. For most of the oils we just know the names and have only vague ideas about the plants or animals they were made from. The ash-oil came from the ash tree, not yet identified with certainty but often identified with the cedar tree. The sefetj-oil also comes from the same ash tree and was often imported from Syria. Hekenu-oil was perhaps made of peppermint and imported into Egypt.[130]

The seven sacred oils often appear in religious texts such as the Pyramid and the Coffin Texts.[131] This does not mean, however, that these texts appear on all coffins. The Coffin Text spell 934 mentioning all oils is attested on only two coffins of the early Middle Kingdom.[132] Nevertheless, the seven sacred oils are depicted on a high percentage of Middle Kingdom coffins with an inner decoration, quite often at the head end of the coffin, demonstrating the importance of the oils for the deceased.[133]

Another object was an incense burner or lamp consisting of a plate and a cover (Fig. 44).[134] These burners are well known from depictions in Old Kingdom tombs but are rarely found as original objects. In the tomb of Ita a set of tools was also found. Such tools are typical of Old Kingdom burials of the ruling class at the royal residence.[135] Is it possible that Ita copied—at least in parts—an Old Kingdom burial?

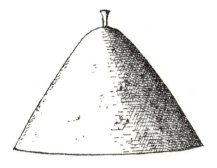

44. Incense burner of Ita. From de Morgan 1903, fig. 107.

Who Was Ita?

Ita is possibly also known from a monument outside her tomb. In Qatna (Syria), fragments of a sphinx were found and dated by style to Amenemhat II or even slightly earlier. On this monument Ita is called "member of the elite, beloved king's daughter of his body."[136] It remains an open question whether the princesses from the two monuments are one or two individuals. The Ita from Dahshur was most likely buried under Amenemhat III. This is about thirty years after the death of Amenemhat II, something that is certainly possible or even to be expected. As the daughter of the king, Ita was one generation younger than him and likely to have died one generation after him.[137] The name Ita, however, is not uncommon in the Middle Kingdom,[138] and the identification remains uncertain.

THE TOMB OF KHENMET

The burial[139] of the king's daughter Khenmet[140] was found next to that of Ita and was arranged along the same lines (Fig. 45). In her small burial chamber there was a sarcophagus made of quartzite. In this outer container was placed a wooden coffin that was not inscribed on the exterior but had texts written on the inside. These inscriptions are almost identical to those found on the inside of Ita's coffin. The innermost coffin was anthropoid, but it was heavily decayed when found. Again, de Morgan did not realize that the remains belonged to a coffin and described them as part of the mummy. The anthropoid coffin must have been similar to that of Ita's. Following the description in de Morgan's publication, the coffin was covered with a substance described as bitumen, and the head, or more likely just the wig, covered in blue and gold. The eyes were inlaid in silver.[141] Under the head was placed a clay disk.

On Khenmet's body were found several items of jewelry. They are described in the excavation report, and many of them are shown with photographic images. There are no drawings, however, of the exact find spots of these pieces. Furthermore, the reconstruction of single items is often highly problematic.

Around Khenmet's neck was a broad collar with falcon head terminals. The heads were made of hollow gold. The eyes were inlaid, while the eyebrows and the mouth were made of lapis lazuli. The collar proper was composed of 103 pieces in the shape of ankh, djed, and *was* signs.[142] These are made of gold foil and inlaid with different materials. The outer edge of

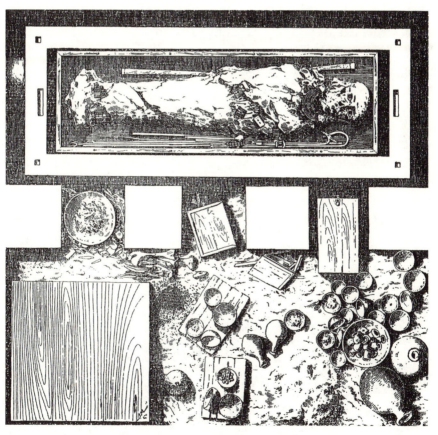

45. The tomb chamber of Khenmet. From de Morgan 1903, fig. 105.

the collar was most likely fringed with drop-shaped beads. Perhaps coming from a choker (see Fig. 49) are two smaller falcon terminals and an array of hieroglyphic signs, many of them connected with royalty, such as two vultures, each on a neb sign, two cobras on two neb signs, or two bees. Today they have been reconstructed as a narrower form of broad collar.[143] However, the small size of the terminals might better fit a choker.

On each arm Khenmet wore five bracelets. There were two clasps adorned with the sa sign from a pair of bracelets.[144] Furthermore, de Morgan mentions a massive undecorated gold bracelet and another consisting of beads of various materials. On the left side of the anthropoid coffin, a mace and several staves were found, typical of this type of burial, but again not described in detail. Outside the sarcophagus, on the southern side, were found a gilded wooden dagger and a staff, neither well preserved.

This was not the only jewelry to be discovered in the tomb; other examples were found in the small chamber next to the sarcophagus chamber. Here, there must have been a box with another set of personal adornments,[145] constituting one of the most remarkable sets of gold objects ever found in Egypt.

First of all are two crowns. One consists of a series of flowers each with four leaves. Each flower is connected via gold wires on which smaller flowers are attached.[146] The flowers were made of gold with inlays of carnelian, lapis lazuli, and turquoise (Fig. 46). The second crown is heavier and consists of a series of eight identical elements. In the middle are a rosette and two flowering rushes. Further rosettes connect these elements. On top of the rosette is again some kind of flowering rush, and there is

46. First crown of Khenmet (diameter c. 18 cm). From de Morgan 1903, pl. IX.

47. Second crown of Khenmet (diameter c. 20.5 cm). Cairo CG 52860. From Vernier 1925, pl. XXII.

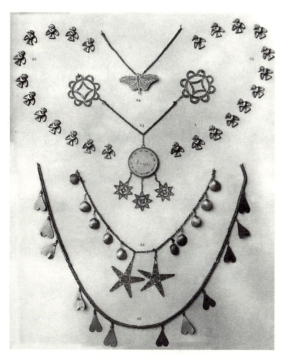

48. The "foreign" jewelry of Khenmet (medallion in the center c. 2.85 cm). From de Morgan 1903, pl. XII.

a royal vulture. All pieces are made of gold and inlaid with carnelian, lapis lazuli, and turquoise. On the front is a vulture made of gold leaf with inlaid eyes of obsidian. Attached to the back is a tree (Fig. 47).[147] Both crowns are dominated by the colors gold, red, and blue.

The most remarkable items in Khenmet's jewelry box were gold pieces of unknown function but perhaps belonging to a necklace (Fig. 48). These pieces appear un-Egyptian in character and were most likely produced somewhere in the Aegean, perhaps specifically on Crete.[148] With these pieces appears for the very first time in Egypt the gold-working technique of granulation, whereby small gold balls are attached to another gold surface. This technology was very common in antiquity but was forgotten in medieval times and only rediscovered in the twentieth century. It was developed in Mesopotamia and reached Egypt in the late Middle

Kingdom. The technology was only rarely employed in the Middle Kingdom, being more common in the New Kingdom.[149] The centerpiece of the group in Khenmet's tomb is a round golden pendant with glass inlays depicting a cow.[150] Perhaps attached to it were golden open-work rosettes fully covered with granulation.[151] There are two smaller rosettes and two bigger ones. Two stars are not open-work. The same is true of a golden butterfly.[152] All these pieces are covered with granulation. Other pieces in this set include several golden shells and several pieces resembling stylized flies. Finally, there are more than twenty small birds[153] and golden chains already broken and repaired in ancient times.[154] The birds in particular have close parallels with Minoan treasure found on the Greek island of Aigina, confirming the impression that this jewelry was not made in Egypt.[155]

Perhaps also of foreign workmanship are several ribbed beads that do not appear with any frequency in other Middle Kingdom burials but are found in the Near East and the Aegean, notably at Byblos and in the Aigina Treasure.[156] Other pieces of jewelry from Khenmet's burials include several motto clasps, similar to those found in the burial of Sathathoriunet (Fig. 49).[157]

49. Jewelry of Khenmet with choker at bottom.
Cairo JE 31113–16 (cat. 107). Photo: Juergen Liepe.

The other objects in the tomb include a set of canopic jars and a large series of pottery, most of it especially made for the burial. There was also a simple wooden box with the seven sacred oils. The box had a short inscription in hieratic (the cursive script of the hieroglyphs): "oil."[158] The vessels are inscribed on the lid and on the vessel proper with the names of the oils, similar to the ones on the vessels in the burial of Ita, described above. They still contain the remains of the oils, now mostly reduced to powder.[159] Many pottery vessels were also found. Among this group was a large beer or water jar typical of the late Middle Kingdom, which provides a rough date for the burial under Amenemhat III.[160] The other pottery vessels found and recorded include two large plates, model vessels, bowls, and bottles. The pottery likely belongs again to the late Middle Kingdom queen's ware also known from other burials of royal women.[161] Bones of cattle and birds were evidently the remains of a funerary repast or the symbolic eternal food supply.

The most remarkable find, however, is a wooden figure of a swan.[162] This is not a common burial object in the late Middle Kingdom or any other period of Egyptian history. Indeed, so far there are only two other published examples, both found in the nearby tombs of Itaweret and Sathathormeryt. Swans are not common animals in Egypt, and it seems that ancient Egyptians did not clearly distinguish between them and geese. Furthermore, a depiction of a swan or goose appears on a coffin excavated at Riqqeh dating to about the same time as the burial of Khenmet.[163] In the tomb of Senet, mother of the vizier Intefiqer, two geese fly in front of the Abydos boat transporting Intefiqer and Senet.[164] From the New Kingdom there is further evidence for such creatures. In New Kingdom royal tombs wooden figures of geese or swans have been found, as for example in the tomb of Tutankhamun.[165] In the Book of the Dead a picture of a goose sometimes appears apparently relating to a spell,[95] and in one instance this has the title "Spell to become a goose."[166] Another figure that often appears in the Book of the Dead is the "Great Cackler," also sometimes depicted in Book of the Dead papyri. In the Pyramid Texts the deceased king flies as a goose to the sky.[167] He flew there because it was believed that the king moved to the sky in order to become one of the imperishable or circumpolar stars in the northern night sky. These are the stars visible throughout the year and the entire night, while most of the other stars are visible only at certain seasons due to the movement of the earth on its axis around the sun. Evidently, this is again a religious belief taken from the royal sphere, not often attested in private contexts. Not surprisingly, on the coffin lid of Khenmet is a spell expressing the wish that she might become an imperishable star.[168]

Who Was Khenmet?

Not much is known about Khenmet. On her middle coffin she is called "king's daughter." On her canopic box she is "king's daughter" and "the one united with the white crown."[169] Nonetheless, no name is written on this box. This is strange, because it is rare for no proper name to appear on such an important object. It is possible that the title "the one united with the white crown" (Khenmet-nefer-hedjet) was indeed a proper name, as also suggested for some other women.[170] If so, Khenmet was perhaps just the short version of Khenmetneferhedjet. The name Khenmet appears within her tomb only on the coffin. Finally, a king's daughter with the name Khenmet is known from a cylinder seal and from a statue found in Ugarit.[171] All these objects might belong to the same woman.

Because of the crown with the vulture it has been assumed that Khenmet was a queen.[172] She does not bear the title "king's wife," and it might be on the safer side simply to say that she was a king's daughter, perhaps a favorite daughter of her father and therefore equipped with this amazing array of jewelry. However, the vulture is not yet attested for king's daughters with the exception of coffins and mummy masks.[173] The vulture might therefore indicate that Khenmet indeed became queen late in her life, after most of her funerary equipment had been made.

THE SECOND GALLERY AT DAHSHUR

The second gallery excavated at Dahshur,[174] west of the pyramid of Amenemhat II, belongs to the king's daughter Itaweret and a woman called Sathathormeryt. The description of these burials in the excavation report of de Morgan is very short, and it is therefore quite hard to get a clear picture of these tombs, although their layout seems to be more or less identical to those of Ita and Khenmet. The tomb of Sathathormeryt will not be described here, as the published excavation report for it is extremely short and lacking in detail. The other, and the first, burial in that gallery

50. Wooden swan from the tomb of Itaweret. From de Morgan 1903, fig. 123.

belonged to Itaweret,[175] who was placed in a sarcophagus of red granite, described as being of rare perfection. Within the sarcophagus was again found a wooden coffin, decorated only on the outside with gold foil and wedjat eyes. It was inscribed on the inside with texts identical to those on the coffins of the other women buried here. Inside this wooden coffin there must have been an anthropoid coffin. The mummy itself was adorned with anklets and armlets and with a broad collar with simple rounded terminals.[176] Next to the mummy were not only the expected royal insignia, such as a flail, a mace, and a bow, but also a hoe and other wooden objects described as gilded, but alas not depicted in the excavation report.

In the small chamber next to the sarcophagus chamber was found an interesting array of objects known from only a few burials of this period. These include a life-size wooden swan (Fig. 50),[177] round and rectangular tables, wooden gilded sandals, a board on which was found a mirror, a diadem made of beads, and four blades partly decorated with gold. Other objects discovered include an inscribed canopic box and a box with eight vessels for the seven sacred oils.[178] The eighth vessel served as a placeholder in the box, as was common with other boxes of this type.

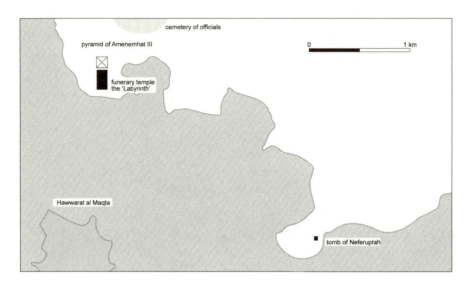

cemetery of officials

pyramid of Amenemhat III

0   1 km

funerary temple
the 'Labyrinth'

Hawwarat al Maqta

tomb of Neferuptah

51. Map of Hawara. Drawn by the author.

THE TOMB OF NEFERUPTAH

In 1936 the Egyptian Egyptologist Labib Habachi made soundings in the region of Hawara (Fig. 51) and discovered mud-brick structures. Habachi was at that time inspector of antiquities in the Fayum, but he was transferred shortly afterward to another inspectorate and was therefore not able to continue his work there. It was not until 1956 that the site was excavated by Nagib Farag, who was inspector for the Fayum at that time.[179] Farag found the undisturbed tomb of the king's daughter Neferuptah, a princess already known from other sources, and the remains of her burial equipment within the pyramid of Amenemhat III at Hawara.

The tomb of Neferuptah[180] was found in a region with a high groundwater level. As a result, all of the organic material had already perished by the time her tomb was opened. Even the body of the princess was gone; not even her bones survived.

The tomb of Neferuptah consisted of one big chamber separated by a huge block into two parts. In the larger room was the sarcophagus, decorated at the bottom with a palace facade and bearing a short inscription mentioning the titles and the name of Neferuptah (Fig. 52). This type of sarcophagus is known from several other royal tombs of the late Middle Kingdom.[181] Only a few of them have inscriptions, in particular several

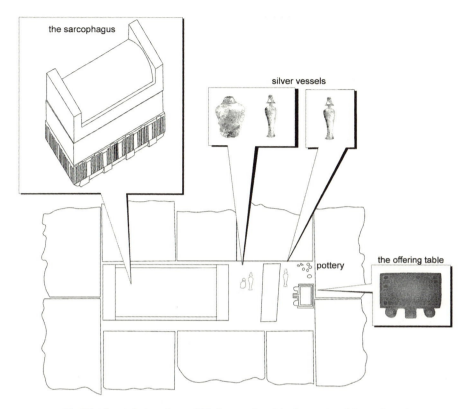

52. The burial chamber of Neferuptah with the main objects found (reconstruction). Redrawn by the author after Farag, Iskander 1971, fig. 6.

examples belonging to royal women buried next to the pyramid of King Senusret III at Dahshur. All the known sarcophagi of kings were uninscribed. The palace facade at the bottom of the sarcophagus is most likely a copy of the niche/palace facade of the Djoser complex at Saqqara, showing the same number of gateways on the front.

The sarcophagus of Neferuptah is the largest of its type. It measures 3.06 m long, 1.54 m wide, and 2.31 m high (including the lid). It is made of red granite.[182] The short inscription on the sarcophagus reads: "An offering given by the king to Osiris, lord of life, for the ka of the member of the elite, the great one of the hetes-scepter, the great one of honor, the beloved king's daughter of his body, Neferuptah, true of voice."

The inside of the sarcophagus was found full of water, but it is possible to reconstruct its contents to a certain degree. Within the sarcophagus was a wooden coffin decorated with bands of inscribed gold foil. The gold

53. The middle coffin of Neferuptah (reconstruction).
Drawn by the author.

foil was found only in small pieces, and there was little hope that the coffin
could be reconstructed. The few bigger fragments with preserved words
do not have any parallels in the corpus of inscriptions found on other
Middle Kingdom coffins (Fig. 53). However, recently it was possible to
identify parallels from the New Kingdom. The first sarcophagus made for
Queen Hatshepsut before she became king of Egypt offers some parallels
for the fragments on the coffin of Neferuptah.[183] One text line is fully preserved and was once most likely positioned at the head end of the coffin:
"Words spoken: we envelop your flesh, we order your limbs, Live! May
you not die!" Exactly the same phrase appears on royal sarcophagi of the
New Kingdom. Other texts on Neferuptah's middle coffin are preserved
only in small fragments. On one fragment the word "Nut" is visible. This
is the sky goddess, and spells relating to her are common on Middle and
New Kingdom coffins.[184] Other fragments of texts are small but indicate
that the coffin had a text program similar to that of the New Kingdom
queen Hatshepsut. The middle coffin of Neferuptah was evidently decorated with a text program still seen in the New Kingdom as relevant for
coffins of royal women. Even though no other Middle Kingdom coffins
with such texts are known, it seems most likely that this is due to a gap in
the archaeological record. It seems impossible that New Kingdom coffin
designers would have seen the coffin of Neferuptah. Maybe there were
other examples accessible to them, or they had access to papyri showing
Middle Kingdom coffin designs.

Placed on the coffin within the sarcophagus was most likely a box for
vessels containing the seven sacred oils. Indeed, ten vessels were found,

one still bearing an inscription on the lid, "nehem-oil." On another, the inscription was faded, but the word *aref*—packet—was still preserved.[185] Here also were found two sticks made of silver for applying eye paint. The placement of ten vessels is uncommon. In the tomb of Nubhetepti-khered eight were discovered, seven for the seven sacred oils and an extra one. Seven vessels each bore an inscription naming the oil. The lid of the eighth was uninscribed, and so it remains unknown what was placed in it, but one has the impression that the last vessel was just some kind of placeholder, as there was simply space left in the box for a further vessel. It remains unknown whether all ten vessels in the sarcophagus of Neferuptah's burial were once placed within a single box. The label of the vessel mentioning a packet recalls depictions on coffins of the Middle Kingdom where, next to the seven sacred oils, are shown two packets for eye paint.[186] On the only Thirteenth Dynasty coffin with decoration on the inside, which belonged to the "chief lector priest" Sesenebnef found at Lisht, the frieze of objects is reduced to a series of vessels and linen. The vessels include those for the seven sacred oils.[187] These oils were important for rituals connected with mummification. These items were evidently seen as essential in (at least some) late Middle Kingdom burials, while other objects typical of early Middle Kingdom burials disappear as objects from the tombs and from the depictions on coffins, such as wooden models of sandals and headrests.

Next to these ten vessels was a larger one, broken into pieces and lacking a lid. Its function is not certain. It contained a "mixture of powdered galena and a resinous matter."[188]

Beside these vessels, several insignia were placed in the middle coffin. Most were originally made of wood, although this is only known because some had parts made from other materials. These objects include a mace whose head was made of alabaster and another with a gilt cup head and a pair of small inlaid eyes of alabaster and crystal, most likely once belonging to a *was* scepter. There was also a flail of carnelian and faience beads.[189] It is not certain where within the sarcophagus these insignia were once placed. According to parallels from the tombs of Senebtisi, Ita, and Nubhetepti-khered, it seems most likely that they were once placed on the left side of the deceased, outside the inner anthropoid coffin but within the middle wooden coffin.

In the middle wooden coffin there must have been an anthropoid one, as inlays belonging to it were found. Only small indications confirmed the existence of this anthropoid coffin. There was a barrel-shaped bead made

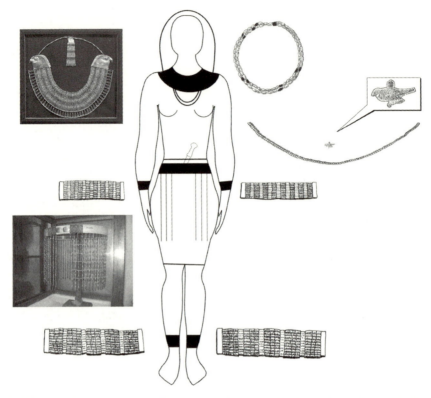

54. The jewelry equipment of Neferuptah. Drawing by the author; photo of collar by Jon Bodsworth (commonswikimedia.org); photo of girdle by Gianluca Miniaci.

of carnelian (a swertet bead), sometimes found on coffins of this type, and beads from a broad collar functioning as inlays and decoration on this coffin. Finally, there was a silver swivel that once held the lid and the coffin box together. This coffin was most likely made of wood and covered with linen followed by a layer of gesso (plaster), which was then gilded with fine gold leaf. Strangely, there were no inlays for the eyes. Most anthropoid coffins of this period had inlaid eyes made of (black) obsidian and a white stone. These elements are missing here, and it must be concluded that the coffin eyes were just carved into the wood. Another option is that they were made of glass. Glass is rarely attested so early in Egypt, but it does often completely disintegrate in damp soil.[190]

The body of the princess was richly adorned with jewelry. Around the neck was a broad collar with terminals in the shape of falcon heads (Fig. 54).[191] The counterpoise of the collar also had a falcon head at the top.

This counterpoise, hanging from the back of the collar, was needed to balance the heavy broad collar. The collar was made of gold, carnelian, and green feldspar beads. The dominant colors are gold and red. The lower edge of the collar was fringed with drop-shaped beads. The high quality of workmanship of the broad collar and the counterpoise might indicate that it had been worn in life.

The princess was also adorned with bracelets and anklets, one for each arm and leg. Around her hips, Neferuptah wore an apron. From the belt hung rows of beads, with the top beads in the row shaped as papyrus and the lotus plant, symbolizing Upper and Lower Egypt. Attached to the royal belt was a small swallow. In addition, the princess was wearing two necklaces made of carnelian beads.

Outside the sarcophagus further objects were found. On the west side were two silver vessels, both inscribed for Neferuptah. In the small side chamber was a further silver vessel, along with sixty-nine pottery vessels. Two silver vessels were shaped as a hes vase, a third one, slightly smaller with a high lid, was of a type well known from royal burials, including those of New Kingdom queens.[192]

The biggest object in the side chamber was an offering table made of dark granite, 61 cm long, 50 cm wide, and 35 cm high (Fig. 55). Its top was entirely covered with depictions of offerings, such as prepared birds,

55. Offering table of Neferuptah. Photo: Gianluca Miniaci.

several types of meat, and many vessels perhaps representing containers of further offerings. In the top corner were two long offering formulae for Neferuptah. On the front were two offering vases carved in three-dimensional relief. At the front of the table a water channel was provided for the libation that was once poured over the table. The table is very similar to one which was found in the pyramid burial chamber of Amenemhat III at Hawara and which also belonged to Neferuptah. Most likely both tables were made in the same workshop. One difference between the two tables, however, concerns the inscriptions: on the table found in the king's pyramid all the depictions of offerings are described in detail in the accompanying inscription. The materials are also different, this table being made of alabaster.[193]

There were three pottery jars of a form typical of the late Twelfth Dynasty and early Thirteenth Dynasty,[194] probably containers for water, beer, or even wine. There were seven dishes also typical of this period,[195] and fifty-nine small model vessels, consisting of bowls, hes vases, and cup-like vessels. The latter ones are also depicted on the two offering tables of Neferuptah. According to the captions on the almost identical offering table found in the pyramid of Amenemhat III, they contained different types of beer and wine, but also fruits. The captions for beer and wine appear on even smaller vessels, providing the impression that captions from offering lists were copied and applied randomly to different types of vessels. The table is therefore not very helpful in providing the function of these vessels.[196] The pottery in the burial of Neferuptah is different from that found in the burials of most of the other royal women discussed here. The vessels were made of coarse Nile clay and were red coated. There was no queen's ware so typical of the burials of the other women. Only the plates and model vessels have parallels in the other tombs.[197]

Who Was Neferuptah?

Neferuptah is the only king's daughter discussed in this book who is well known from sources beyond her tomb. She was the daughter of Amenemhat III, appearing in reliefs next to her father in the small temple of Medinet Maadi. Her tomb is also mentioned in a letter found at Lahun. On Elephantine, fragments of her statue were found. A headless sphinx bears her name and that of Amenemhat III. A fragment of a black granite statue comes from Darb el-Asfar and bears the otherwise unattested title "god's sister." A magical wand found at Lisht also bears her name.[198] Neverthe-less, it remains unclear whether the Neferuptah on the magical wand, and even on some of the other objects, might refer to a second woman with that name.

In 1892 Flinders Petrie excavated the pyramid of Amenemhat III at Hawara and found in the burial chamber not only objects with the name of the king but also objects with the name of a king's daughter Neferu-ptah, such as the above-mentioned offering table made of Egyptian ala-baster.[199] Amenemhat III is the last important and long-reigning ruler of the Twelfth Dynasty. He built two pyramids, one at Dahshur and another at Hawara, on the eastern edge of the Fayum, the great river oasis west of the Nile valley. The Hawara pyramid and the pyramid complex were al-ready famous in antiquity. The pyramid and its temple were known as the "Labyrinth" and described by several classical authors. However, already in Roman times it was being used as a quarry, and therefore little of it has survived. In the burial chamber of the Hawara pyramid were found two sarcophagi. One of them was most likely the sarcophagus of the king. The second was arranged between the sarcophagus of the king and the wall of the burial chamber. There were two stone slabs, one placed at the head end and one at the foot end, to form a second sarcophagus with a lid on top of the arrangement. Although neither of these mummy containers was inscribed, the second one is generally ascribed to Neferuptah. She is the only other person besides the king mentioned in the inscriptions of the tomb chamber. Evidently the king was buried in the main sarcophagus, or at least this is the impression given by this double burial.

Neferuptah evidently had two burials, one within the pyramid of her father, the other about two kilometers away. It is only possible to guess at the reason for this, but it can be assumed that the king prepared a burial for his daughter within his pyramid but died before her. The pyramid was closed, and there was evidently no chance to open it again.[200] When the princess died some time later, she was buried in her own tomb. Perhaps she died much later, maybe even in the Thirteenth Dynasty.[201] This is one possibility. Another option is that there were simply two daughters with the same name—not so uncommon in ancient Egypt. Indeed, there are some strange aspects of the burial of the princess within the king's pyra-mid, especially as her sarcophagus was secondary and somewhat make-shift, as already indicated. Normally one would expect to find a proper sarcophagus and not such a provisional-looking arrangement.

The burial of Neferuptah within the pyramid of her father had already been heavily robbed when found. The name of Neferuptah was discovered on several fragments of the burial equipment. An interesting observation concerns the treatment of the hieroglyphs. They are carved as normal signs, but later the legs of the birds were scratched out.[202] In the Thirteenth Dynasty, hieroglyphs on objects placed in the tomb chamber were often incomplete. The legs of birds are missing, the ends of snakes are not depicted, and human figures are avoided. The movement of living creatures was evidently seen as potentially dangerous for the deceased. The preparation of Neferuptah's burial in her father's pyramid evidently occurred at the time when these new hieroglyphs were introduced.

Neferuptah must have enjoyed special status, as her name was often, though not always, written within a cartouche, the oval denoting royalty. Indeed, she is the first royal woman whose name was written inside a cartouche. This suggests that not all of the sources listed above must belong to her. On the magical wand her name is not placed in a cartouche. There, she is only called "king's daughter." This opens up the possibility that the object belongs to another princess with the same name. In her tomb, however, the name on the coffin fragments is written without a cartouche, while on other objects in the tomb it is written within a cartouche. The absence of the cartouche is therefore no proof that the magical wand belongs to another woman.

At first sight, the burial of Neferuptah appears exceptional in several ways. Compared to the burials of Senebtisi and Khenmet, the provision of jewelry seems to be quite limited. There is only one broad collar, there are necklaces, there is the apron, and there are armlets and anklets. In general, the equipment of personal adornments is similar to that of Nubheteptikhered, also buried without a special jewelry box. From a technical point of view, however, the collars of Neferuptah and Nubhetepti-khered use elaborate cloisonné work, thus making them higher in quality and most likely more expensive than many of the collars found in the burials of the Dahshur and Lisht women, Ita, Senebtisi, and Itaweret. A further point might be that the production of funerary jewelry declined at some point toward the very end of the Twelfth or in the early Thirteenth Dynasty. Senebtisi had a full set of personal adornments specially made for the tomb. The jewelry in the tombs of Neferuptah and Nubhetepti-khered seems to have already been worn in daily life.

Furthermore, there was no pectoral in Neferuptah's burial. However, so far all the examples of pectorals in the burials of king's daughters were found in jewelry boxes of royal women and not on the mummy; tombs without jewelry boxes did not contain pectorals. This is true of the burials of Senebtisi, Neferuptah, and Nubhetepti-khered, and also for the burials of the women next to the pyramid of Amenemhat II. An exception is a pectoral found in a private tomb at Riqqeh, which was indeed placed on the body of the deceased. Although the person buried here was of high status, he (or she) was most likely only buried with "real" jewelry and did not have the resources for funerary adornments.

It seems that the custom of placing a jewelry box next to a woman stopped under Amenemhat III, at least at the highest social level at the royal court. This might be one reason no pectorals from the Second Intermediate Period are known. Cloisonné work is still attested in the Thirteenth Dynasty (the broad collar of Nubhetepti-khered), so technically the goldsmiths of the period were still able to produce pectorals. The next cloisonné-work pectoral comes from the very end of the Second Intermediate Period with the burial of Queen Ahhotep at Thebes.[203]

A further strange feature of Neferuptah's tomb is the absence of canopic jars. They are attested in all the other royal burials discussed, and so are missing only here. Canopic jars are in general not common in the Middle Kingdom and are restricted to a small number of people. One explanation is that Neferuptah had only a wooden canopic box without any pottery and stone jars. The box might have rotted away long before the tomb was opened, and therefore left no trace. Canopic boxes without jars are not uncommon in the Middle Kingdom, but it still seems strange for such a high-status burial. In the pyramid of her father, remains of canopic boxes and fragments of jars were found.[204]

THE KING'S DAUGHTER NUBHETEPTI-KHERED

The burial of the king's daughter Nubhetepti-khered[205] was found by de Morgan and his team on 19 April 1894 at Dahshur. It was placed within the pyramid complex of Amenemhat III on the north side (Fig. 56). There, a row of shaft tombs had been cut, perhaps during the reign of that king. Burials of the early Thirteenth Dynasty were found in only two of the tombs, however: the burial of King Awibre Hor and next to it the burial of Nubhetepti-khered. They are so similar in general features that they can

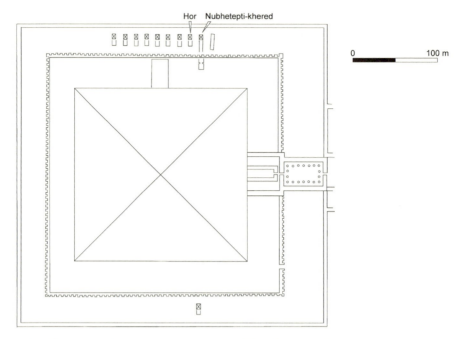

56. The pyramid complex of Amenemhat III at Dahshur. Drawn by the author.

be dated to about the same time. Nubhetepti-khered's tomb consists of a shaft with a 14.6 m long corridor on the south side (Fig. 57). After about ten meters the corridor widened out, forming a small chamber. Behind a wall made of limestone blocks was a further chamber, which was found undisturbed. A third chamber under the second one contained the coffin of the princess.

The first chamber was found empty and may never have contained any burial goods. The second chamber still contained two large dishes with many smaller model dishes, as well as a third dish containing a black powder, perhaps the remains of some funerary meal. Furthermore, there were eight pottery vessels and two rough bowls of the same material (Fig.

57. Plan of the tomb of Nubhetepti-khered. From de Morgan 1895, fig. 249.

58. Plan of the antechamber to the tomb of
Nubhetepti-khered. From de Morgan 1895, fig. 250.

58). The pottery has been published only as drawings without detailed description, but it seems that it is again queen's ware, also known from burials of royal women of the Twelfth Dynasty.[206] In the corner of the chamber
lay a long wooden box containing a mace, eight arrows, a wooden mirror
covered with silver foil,[207] and an object similar to the tall hieroglyphic sa
sign for "protection." Finally, several royal insignia were found in the box
(Fig. 59). There were two *was* scepters, a heqa scepter, and at least two
staffs or perhaps spears. There is also a *mekes* scepter not known from the
other court type burials described,[208] but that might relate to the bad publication of the other burials. The mekes scepter is a long staff with some

59. Box with staves and scepters from the burial of Nubhetepti-khered.
From de Morgan 1895, fig. 253.

kind of ring attached around the middle. It is well known from depictions
of kings.[209] From the published drawing it seems that several of these staffs
and insignia were already broken before or at the time of the burial. All
were made of wood. Of all the court type burials discussed, this is the best
preserved, with the best documented set of staves and royal insignia.

Next to this long box was a smaller one that contained eight alabaster
vessels (Fig. 60). The lids of seven of these were inscribed, and according
to these labels they contained the seven sacred oils: *hekenu*, *hat-en-tehenu*,
hat-en-ash, *tuaut*, *sefet*, *nekhenem*, and *seti-hab*.[210] All these vessels have the
shape of a cylinder, but wider at the top. The eighth one is smaller and
more rounded. This shape of vessel was often used for containing kohl, a
type of powder used for painting the eyes. The box with these oil vessels
was found sealed. The imprint of the seal belonged to the "true [?] king's
acquaintance" Senebtifi. Next to the box were several bones, perhaps the

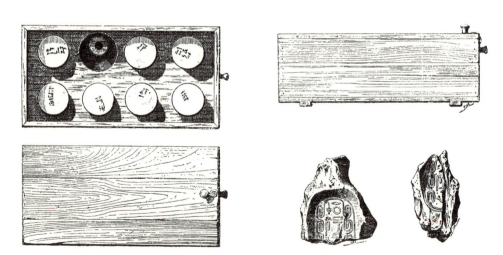

60. Box with seven sacred oils from the burial of Nubhetepti-khered.
From de Morgan 1895, fig. 258.

remains of the funerary meal, the meal for the journey to the underworld or the meal symbolizing the eternal food supply.

Under this chamber was another one containing the wooden coffin, canopic box, and four canopic jars of the princess. Indeed, the wooden coffin was placed in a narrow recess in the floor that itself formed a kind of sarcophagus. This type of sarcophagus was already common in the Old Kingdom. There are many examples where a recess was cut into the floor of the burial chamber to accommodate the mummy of the deceased or a wooden coffin box.[211] In the Middle Kingdom this type of container for the body was no longer so common, but is still well attested. Several examples from the Eleventh Dynasty are decorated on the inside. These include the sarcophagus of the vizier Ipi[212] and of the "overseer of sealers" Meru,[213] both officials at the highest social level. Fewer examples are known from the Twelfth Dynasty. The container of King Amenemhat II at Dahshur was of this type, however, forming a small chamber under the floor level of the main burial chamber.[214] In the Thirteenth Dynasty, this type became more popular again. Examples include the burial chamber and sarcophagi of King Khendjer and of individuals buried in a small pyramid next to those of the king, perhaps belonging to family members.[215] In particular, tombs of the Second Intermediate Period at Thebes often had a recess in the main burial chamber of just the right size to accommodate a coffin. This seems to be the Theban version of the same custom.[216] In both types of coffin recesses, a wooden coffin was placed inside (Fig. 61).

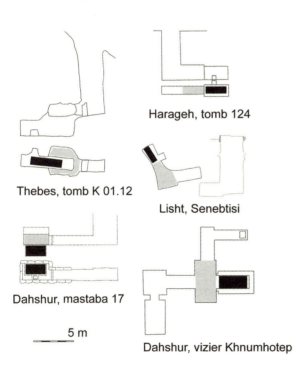

Harageh, tomb 124

Thebes, tomb K 01.12

Lisht, Senebtisi

Dahshur, mastaba 17

5 m

Dahshur, vizier Khnumhotep

61. Five examples of late Middle Kingdom tombs with separated chamber for coffin (black) and an antechamber (gray). Drawn by the author.

62. Coffin of Nubhetepti-khered. From de Morgan 1895, pl. XXXVI.

The architectural construction of Nubhetepti-khered's tomb was not examined by de Morgan in detail, and there is the possibility that she was placed in a sarcophagus similar to those found around the pyramid of King Khendjer.

At the southern end of Nubhetepti-khered's burial chamber, on the eastern side, was a niche where the canopic box was found. The wooden coffin of Nubhetepti-khered was placed in the sarcophagus chamber (Fig. 62). Inscriptions on it were incised on gold foil. The decorative scheme of the coffin had the standard layout for the Middle Kingdom coffins. There was a horizontal text line at the top of each coffin side as well as four columns on the long sides and two columns on the short sides. The lid was vaulted, with one text line down the middle. The inside of the coffin was undecorated. The texts on the coffin show a standard late Middle Kingdom text program. The four children of Horus are invoked to take care of the limbs of the princess. On the lid was a spell mentioning the sky goddess Nut. On the back appeared Anubis, protector god of the embalming, and on the front, east, side of the coffin was a spell to ensure that the "sight" of the princess was open so that she could see the sun god passing across the sky.[217]

Inside the coffin there must have been an anthropoid inner coffin, of which only fragments of the thin gold covering were found by the excavators. A uraeus and a vulture were found at the head end and might have adorned the face of the anthropoid coffin. De Morgan and his team did not recognize that there was an anthropoid coffin, but a careful rereading of his report with comparison to similar finds makes it very likely that this type of coffin was present.[218]

On the mummy were placed a broad collar with falcon head terminals and a counterpoise also with a falcon head (Fig. 63). Originally, the counterpoise was not recognized by the excavators as belonging to the broad collar. Instead, the falcon head was incorporated into the reconstruction of the flail that was found next to the body of the princess. With parallels from later discoveries in mind, however, it now seems much more likely that the falcon head was part of the counterpoise for the collar.[219] The collar itself was made of several semiprecious stones, with drop-shaped beads on the underside in cloisonné work.

The arms and legs of Nubhetepti-khered were adorned with armlets and anklets. Two of them were made of gold and carnelian, the other two of gold and green feldspar. Around the head was a silver diadem. Its back was decorated with a disk inlaid with a red stone and flanked by two lotus flowers. Surrounding this was an incised block decoration inlaid with a brown-colored stone. Sadly, the front part of the diadem was found totally decayed, and it therefore remains unknown whether it once had additional decoration. Furthermore, the description of the diadem in de Morgan's publication is very brief and leaves many questions unanswered, especially regarding the materials used as inlays.[220] So far, no similar diadems have been found in other burials of this period. At Byblos were found two gold bands of a similar design together with two uraei, perhaps once forming a similar diadem.[221] Furthermore, there are two diadems known from the Second Intermediate Period, about 150 years later, which are very similar to the one from the burial of Nubhetepti-khered. One perhaps once belonged to the Seventeenth Dynasty king Nubkheperre Intef, buried at Thebes.[222] It too has a disk flanked by two lotus flowers at the back, and the silver circle has an almost identical block decoration, though not inlaid. The king's diadem has a uraeus at the front, and at the back are silver extensions imitating the ends of a tie made of fabric. A very similar example dates to about the same period and is adorned at the front with two uraei, but the circlet is decorated with a "basketwork" design rather than a block pattern.[223] It might once have belonged to a queen, as two uraei appear sporadically for queens, but not for kings, before the Late Period. Both Second Intermediate Period examples are simpler and

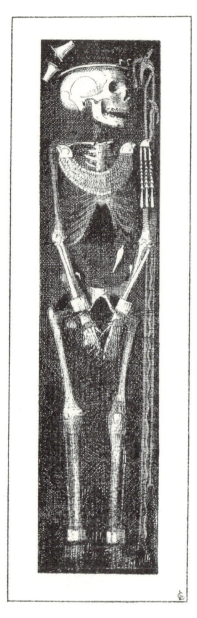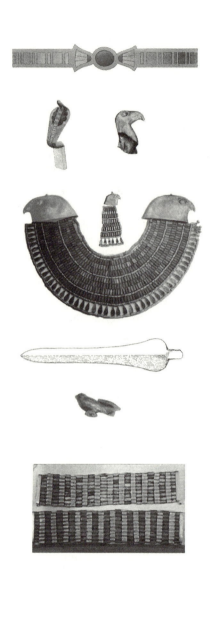

63. The skeleton of Nubhetepti-khered in its coffin, as published by de Morgan. On the right are some objects found with the princess: (from top to bottom) diadem; uraeus and vulture, both once perhaps adorning the anthropoid coffin; broad collar; blade of a dagger found at the pelvis; swallow, also found at the pelvis; armlets. From de Morgan 1895, figs. 264, 265, 267, pls. XXXVIII f, g; photos of armlets and counterpoise of broad collar by Juan R. Lázaro; photos of broad collar, vulture, and swallow by the author.

inferior in workmanship and quality to that of Nubhetepti-khered. The block decoration on the circlet is not inlaid, only incised. Nevertheless, the diadem of Nubhetepti-khered evidently represents a new type of jewelry that became popular in the following period. Comparable circlets are known from depictions in art, however, and were perhaps once made of an organic material.[224]

Next to the mummy several insignia were found. On her belly on the left side lay the blade from a golden dagger, the handle of which was no longer preserved.[225] There was the flail, already mentioned, made of several materials, and several staffs and scepters. In the drawing from the publication two *was* scepters and a heqa scepter are visible.[226] At the pelvis was a swallow made of carnelian. Finally, at the head end were two cylindrical cosmetic vases.

The swallow found at the pelvis is not depicted in the publication, but a similar one was found in the tomb of the king's daughter Neferuptah and other burials of this type, where it seems to be part of a girdle.

The canopic box next to the coffin was decorated in the same way as the coffin. It was made of wood, with inscriptions on gold foil. The preserved inscriptions on the horizontal lines mention three of the four children of Horus, Hapy, Duamutef, and Amset, and also Qebehsenuef. The spell is also known from Pyramid Texts but appears here only as a shortened version. The goddesses Neith, Isis, Selket, and Nephthys are mentioned on the vertical columns. These deities are known from several inscriptions on canopic jars and boxes as protectors of the entrails. The columns on the box are spells otherwise attested on canopic jars.[227]

Inside the canopic box were found the four canopic jars, again inscribed with typical spells for such vessels and naming the same deities:[228] "Words spoken by Selket: your arms are covering Qebehsenuef, who is before you; the revered one before Qebehsenuef, the king's daughter Nubhetepti-khered, true of voice."

The real meaning behind the spells remains obscure. The "covering" might relate to the mummification, while Selket (and the other goddesses) in these spells might speak to another goddess; "you" in this spell is the feminine "you" of the Egyptian language, which had different words for "you" when addressing men, women, or several people. It is unlikely that Nubhetepti-khered is addressed here. On the canopic box of King Awibre Hor, buried next to the princess, similar spells appear, and here again appears the feminine "you."[229]

Who Was Nubhetepti-khered?

Little is known about Nubhetepti-khered.[230] Her name means "The Gold is satisfied, the child." Nub, the Gold, is a common element of women's names of the Thirteenth Dynasty and is another name for the goddess Hathor.[231]

According to her teeth, Nubhetepti-khered died when she was about forty-five years old.[232] This estimate, however, should be taken with great reservation. Her skeleton was examined more than a hundred years ago. More recent research on human remains is cautious about estimating the age of the deceased. It is now realized that people age differently. Only for young people of less than twenty years of age is it possible to provide closer dates, as their bodies are still growing and there are indeed some common identifiable patterns.[233] Therefore, probably the best that can be said from this old account is that Nubhetepti-khered was certainly not young when she died. For a more exact date of her death, a new examination of her bones is needed.

At first, de Morgan believed that King Hor and Nubhetepti-khered were children of Amenemhat III. He thought that Hor was a coregent who died before his father. One indication for this was the use of a seal naming Amenemhat III in Hor's tomb.[234] Soon, however, Egyptologists such as Maspero, Wiedemann, Petrie, Weill, and von Bissing realized that King Hor is mentioned with his throne name Awibre in the Turin Canon (there as Awtibre).[235] The Turin Canon is an ancient Egyptian king list of the New Kingdom, today very much destroyed but still an important source for the sequence of Egyptian kings. According to this list, King Hor ruled in the early Thirteenth Dynasty. Nubhetepti-khered was buried next to this king, and her burial equipment is very close to his in style, indicating that they were buried at about the same time. It can be said therefore that Nubhetepti-khered dates to the Thirteenth Dynasty.

Nubhetepti-khered is so far not yet attested for certain outside her burial. However, there is a scarab seal of a king's daughter Nubhetepti,[236] and there are two queens with the same name. One of them bore the titles "king's wife" and "king's mother." The other bore the title "great king's wife, united with the white crown."[237] Both are known mainly from scarab seals, although the former lady's name is also preserved on a broken statue found at Semna, the Middle Kingdom frontier fortification in Nubia. Several questions surround these women. Nubhetepti-khered means

Nubhetepti-the-child. This indicates that there was another Nubhetepti of an older generation, perhaps even the mother of Nubhetepti-khered. If we accept this idea, Queen Nubhetepti was the wife of King Hor and the mother of Nubhetepti-khered.[238] A further Nubhetepti is known, the mother of a king Sobekhotep. She is known only from seals, where she appears as "king's mother."[239]

SATHATHOR AND MERERET

In 1895 de Morgan excavated the pyramid and pyramid complex of Senusret III at Dahshur (Fig. 64). The pyramid was built of mud bricks and measured about 107 m long (204 Egyptian cubits) at the base, with a height originally of about 64 m.[240] The pyramid stood within a complex containing a big temple on the south side, a smaller one on the east side, and three smaller pyramids of royal women on the south side. North of the pyramid of Senusret III were the remains of four more pyramids. De

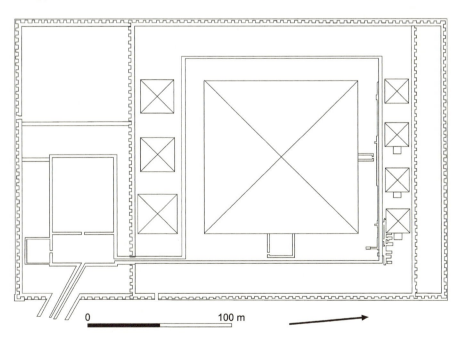

64. The pyramid complex of Senusret III at Dahshur. Most of the smaller pyramids belong to royal women. The underground gallery lies on the northeast side. Drawn by the author.

Morgan originally thought that these were mastabas, but more recent research by Dieter Arnold has identified them as pyramids.[241] The pyramids
on the north side of the pyramid had bases of about 16.80 m square, and,
with some caution, their height has been calculated to have been about
13 to 17 m.[242] Of the small chapels on the east side of each pyramid, only
some small relief fragments and foundations have survived, so that it is not
possible to reconstruct their plan, although it seems likely that they each
consisted of a single room decorated with reliefs.[243] The underground
burial apartments of these pyramids consist of several rooms. Each has a
burial chamber with the sarcophagus and two side chambers. The function of the latter is unknown, but one of these chambers must have stored
a canopic chest, and in the other most likely were placed burial goods,
such as jewelry boxes. The arrangement is similar to those found in the
tomb of Sathathoriunet at Lahun, mentioned above. The owner of the
first pyramid is unknown. A broken statue of the "high steward" Nesmont
was found there, but it seems highly unlikely that he was buried here.
Burials of high state officials in pyramids next to the royal pyramid are not
yet attested. In the burial chamber under the second pyramid was found
an inscribed sarcophagus naming the king's wife Nefrethenut. The third
pyramid belonged to the king's daughter Itakayet. Her name was found on
relief fragments from her burial chapel. The owner of the fourth pyramid
remains unknown. Only Itakayet is also known from sources outside the
pyramid. A king's daughter with this name appears on a papyrus fragment
found at Lahun. The fragment also mentions the king's daughter Nefret
and the king's son Senusret-seneb. Perhaps they were children of Senusret
II. This would make Itakayet a sister of Senusret III, generally thought to
be the daughter of Senusret II.[244]

    An unusual feature of these four pyramids is a gangway or gallery con-
necting the underground burial chambers (Fig. 65). Nothing similar is
attested for any other pyramid before Senusret III. Normally each burial
apartment under or within the pyramid of a queen or king's daughter
and located next to that of a king is a single unit, not connected to the
next pyramid. In addition, on the east side, this gangway led into an underground gallery with eight further burials, most likely all belonging to
royal women, as the few preserved names and titles indicate. These burials were placed in chambers open to the gangway. Two chambers have
additional niches for the canopic chest, while in the other chambers the
chest was placed next to the coffin. In general the canopic chest was al-

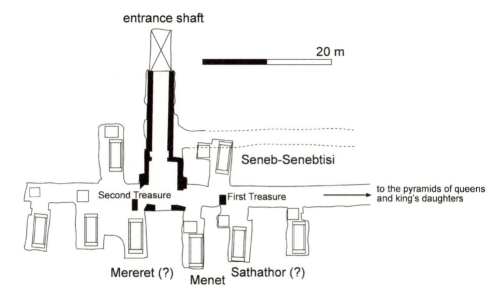

entrance shaft

20 m

Seneb-Senebtisi

Second Treasure   First Treasure   to the pyramids of queens and king's daughters

Mereret (?)   Menet   Sathathor (?)

65. Plan of the galleries of the pyramid complex of Sensusret III.
Drawn by the author.

ways placed south of the sarcophagus. Only two of the sarcophagi have an inscription. One names the "king's daughter, who is united with the white crown" Menet, the other the "king's daughter" Senet-Senebtisi. For Menet were also found two inscribed canopic jars. At present, neither of these two princesses is known from any other sources. In antiquity the gallery was entered by robbers, and all the sarcophagi were opened and looted. In the eastern gallery, however, de Morgan found placed in a hole in the floor two boxes filled with jewelry, overlooked by the tomb robbers. Evidently these were jewelry boxes belonging to two of the princesses buried there.

SATHATHOR

The first box was discovered on 6 March 1894 under the floor level close to burials 7 and 9.[245] According to de Morgan's description it was placed in a hole in the floor of the gallery. Recent excavations failed to find any such hole, however, and the circumstances of the find remain somewhat mysterious.[246] It is not clear who owned this jewelry, but the finds included a scarab with the title and name of the "king's daughter" Sathathor ("daugh-

66. Pectoral of Sathathor with the throne name of Senusret
II (5.2 cm high). Photo: Juergen Liepe.

ter of Hathor"), and so it has been assumed that this princess was buried here and owned the treasure. The possibility remains, however, that this princess presented the scarab to the woman buried here. She might have been her mother, sister, or daughter. The ownership of the treasure is therefore not really certain, though the king's daughter with the name Sathathor remains a likely candidate. The jewelry was found in a badly decayed wooden box that was partly gilded. It seems that these were adornments already worn in life, as they were much heavier than many of the thin items found on many mummies. Georges Legrain's description of the objects listed more than fifty pieces.

The outstanding masterpiece in this treasure is certainly a pectoral bearing the throne name of Senusret II (Fig. 66).[247] It is rectangular and takes the form of a shrine with a cornice at the top. In the middle are two names of the king: Neteru-hetep Khakheperre ("the gods are satisfied, may the forms of Re appear"). The latter name is written within a cartouche. On both sides a Horus falcon stands on the hieroglyphic sign for "gold." The name and the falcons can be read as "Golden Horus Neteru-hetep." The Golden Horus name is part of the royal titulary. Each falcon is depicted wearing the double crown of Upper and Lower Egypt. Behind the falcon on each side are a sun disk and a uraeus hanging from it,

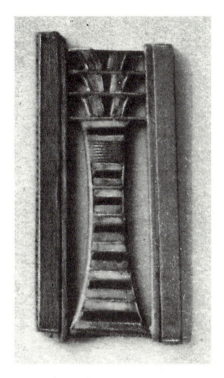

67. Fastening piece for a bracelet. From de Morgan 1895, pl. XVI, 2.

and from each uraeus hangs an ankh sign. The pectoral, 5.2 cm high, is made of gold, carnelian, lapis lazuli, and turquoise. The dominant colors of the piece are red and two shades of green. Both falcons and the name Neteru-hetep are inlaid with two shades of a green material. With the pectoral there was almost certainly once a necklace; indeed, de Morgan found many beads from it.

Other masterpieces from this treasure include two armlets with fastening pieces in the shape of a djed pillar (Fig. 67).[248] A similar armlet with fastening pieces in the shape of a djed pillar was found in the burial of queen Khenmet-nefer-hedjet-weret, wife of Senusret II, discovered in 1995.[249] The armlets were again made of gold, carnelian, lapis lazuli, and turquoise. The bracelets must also have consisted of several hundred smaller beads, perhaps with several gold spacer bars between them—at least this can be surmised from better recorded pieces found elsewhere. Although it is not certain, there were most likely also anklets. These tend to be simpler, however, without decorated claps and are therefore harder to identify if not found on mummies. Two golden bird claws[250] were found in the treasure, which are known to have been worn at anklets.

Two other bracelets were much simpler and made just of gold foil. There were also six golden lions,[251] which may have belonged to three armlets. Indeed, similar lions were found at Saqqara, where two of them formed part of an armlet. Similar lions were also found at Buhen, but there they belonged to a necklace. It seems that these lions could have had several functions and were not restricted to a particular type of personal adornment. Six bigger golden cowry shells might have belonged to a girdle.[252] In the Saqqara tomb just mentioned, they were found in exactly this position. About thirty-one smaller shells might have belonged to another girdle or to a necklace.[253] Sixteen knots made of gold could have come from a third girdle and were most likely arranged between beads. Another option is that they belonged to a bead arrangement used as a body chain. Hanging from one of the knots is a papyrus plant. Finally, there are other smaller examples of fine gold work whose exact function remains uncertain. A small motto clasp shows two netjer (hieroglyphic for "god"), an ib ("heart") sign, and a hetep ("peace") sign. It might have been a pendant from a necklace or from one of the girdles. Another fine piece shows two papyrus plants and the goddess Bat in the middle. Bat is shown as a cow, in frontal view, and is closely related to Hathor, who is also often depicted as cow. There are two cylinders, one made of gold. Both had a loop at the top and could therefore have been used as pendants. Five scarabs were found. One is made of amethyst and shows on the underside the throne name of Senusret III, Khakaure. Another is made of faience and names the "king's daughter Sathathor, lady of honor." Two scarabs show the Egyptian symbol "unification of the two lands," and the last scarab has no further decoration on the underside.

Next to the jewelry some cosmetic objects were found. There was a silver mirror with a partly gilded handle. There were eight vases made of alabaster, six of them tall open forms and two rather globular and short.

Some pottery was found with the burial assigned to Sathathor (tomb 9 in the gallery). The pottery indicates that the burial took place in the early years of Amenemhat III's reign.[254]

Who Was Sathathor?

Sathathor is known from a scarab seal found in the "first treasure" in the gallery tombs at Dahshur, next to the pyramid of Senusret III. On the scarab she bears the title "king's daughter."[255] The date and the position of this king's daughter are debatable. The find spot of the first treasure indicates that she was the daughter of Senusret III. This is far from certain, however. The scarab might be a present by a king's daughter to a member of the family. It is known that burials were still made under Amenemhat III within that gallery. Sathathor might therefore date under this king and be a daughter of his.[256]

Two king's names were found in the treasure of Sathathor: Senusret II and Senusret III. From these it might be concluded that the woman who owned it was the daughter or contemporary of the first king and died under the second. Other scenarios are also possible, however: for instance, she could have been the daughter of Senusret III and received the objects with the name of Senusret II as heirlooms.

The name Sathathor is one of the most common from the Middle Kingdom, and there are indeed other royal women with that name, but it is unlikely that they are identical with this princess. From the Thirteenth Dynasty are known a king's wife[257] and a king's sister with that name (the latter appears in an administrative document known today as Papyrus Boulaq 18). While there is the possibility that these two women are in fact the same person, who was first the king's sister and later became a king's wife, it seems rather unlikely that our king's daughter Sathathor, most likely dating to the Twelfth Dynasty, is related to them, principally because they date to the Thirteenth Dynasty. From about the same time comes a canopic jar of a king's daughter Sathathor. This object appeared several years ago on the art market. Its provenance is unknown, but Dahshur seems likely. It again seems doubtful, however, that this woman is identical with the princess known from her jewelry, as the canopic jar most likely dates to the very end of the Twelfth or the early Thirteenth Dynasty. The hieroglyphs on it are incomplete, which is more typical of the Thirteenth Dynasty. Another option for a possible identification comes from the inscription "member of the elite, king's daughter, beloved of Hathor, the mistress of myrrh, Sathathorduat." This appears on an alabaster vessel lid found at Tell el-Dab'a in the Delta.[258] In the Middle Kingdom people quite frequently had both a long and a short version of a name. Sathathorduat might be just a longer version of Sathathor. As already indicated, however, Sathathor is a common name, and there is also Sathathoriunet from Lahun with a longer name and possibly not identical to this Sathathor. Finally, it might be argued that they are identical and the scarabs in the treasure are presents of Sathathor to an unknown royal woman. Therefore, any identification should be made with great caution and can only be confirmed with further evidence.

MERERET

The "second treasure" in the gallery next to the pyramid of Senusret III at Dahshur was found on 8 March 1894 and contained an even greater num-

ber of personal adornments and cosmetic objects.[259] The two best-known
pieces of the treasure are again pectorals, one with the throne name of
Senusret III, Khakaure, and one with the throne name of Amenemhat
III, Nimaatre. Several scarabs in the treasure are inscribed for the "king's
daughter" Mereret, once written Meryt. Mereret is thus most often regarded as the owner of the jewelry.[260]

The following objects were found:

1. One pectoral measuring 6 cm wide and 5 cm high (Fig. 68).
   The frame shows a shrine with a lotus plant supporting the
   roof. In the middle is a cartouche with the name Khakaure
   (the throne name of Senusret III); above the cartouche is a
   vulture with outstretched wings protecting the scene under it.
   On the left and right are griffins, each with a feather crown,
   trampling two enemies of Egypt, one light skinned, perhaps
   an Asiatic, the other dark skinned, perhaps representing
   a Nubian. Blue and red are the dominant colors of the
   pectoral.[261]

2. A second pectoral is again framed by a pavilion (Fig. 69). At
   the top there is again a vulture, whose wings are spread over
   the whole scene. In the middle the name Nimaatre (the throne
   name of Amenemhat III) appears twice within a cartouche.
   Between the cartouches is written "the good god, lord of the
   two lands, beating all foreign lands." The main subject of the
   pectoral is the king, twice shown smiting an enemy with a
   mace. Behind the king an ankh sign is depicted with a fan. The
   enemies kneeling on the ground are identified by the label
   describing Amenemhat III's actions, "smiting Asiatics."[262]

While both pectorals from the treasure of Mereret are remarkable
objects, they are technically and in terms of composition inferior to those
from the treasures of Sathathoriunet and Sathathor. The scenes in the
pectorals of Mereret appear overcrowded. Every available space is filled
with figures and hieroglyphs. It has more than once been noted in discussions of these pectorals that this is an indication of a slight decline in the
goldsmith's art under Amenemhat III.[263] Indeed, this overcrowding can
be found on several object types under Amenemhat III and seems to be
a typical style of the period. One other example would be the offering

68. The "first" pectoral of Mereret, with throne name of Senusret III (8.5 cm wide). Photo: Juergen Liepe.

69. The "second" pectoral of Mereret, with throne name of Amenemhat III (8.2 × 4.7 cm). Photo: Juergen Liepe.

tables of Neferuptah found in her tomb and in the pyramid of her father, Amenemhat III, at Hawara.[264] Earlier offering tables always have depictions of a small selection of offerings on the main surface with wide space around them, whereas on Neferuptah's table there are literally about a hundred offerings depicted, closely packed side by side. Another example is the decorative layout of stelae produced in the reign of Amenemhat III. They display a type of checkerboard pattern, quite often with a large number of people shown side by side, often not distinguished by rank or status.

Further jewelry and objects found were:

3. A massive golden shell, with the top end pierced. The shell was most likely a pendant for a necklace.
4. A second golden shell, with inlays imitating a lotus flower.[265]
5. A third golden shell, once with inlays.[266]
6. A falcon in cloisonné technique. Each claw holds a shen ring. The figure is placed on a piece of gold with two loops.[267]
7. A row of ten golden cowry shells, once belonging to a girdle.[268]
8. A girdle with eight double leopard heads, identical to a girdle found in the treasure of Sathathoriunet at Lahun (Fig. 70).[269]
9. A necklace consisting of long beads.
10. A necklace with twenty-six golden shells.
11. Twelve small shells, most likely from a girdle or necklace.
12. A necklace with gold-framed beads.
13. Beads.
14. Twelve knots in gold, perhaps from bracelets or armlets.
15–16. Two terminals from bracelets, bearing the throne name of Amenemhat III: Nimaatre.[270]
17. Two simple golden bracelets.[271]
18. Two bracelets.
19. Four lions, perhaps from bracelets.[272]
20. Two bird claws in gold, probably from anklets (Fig. 70).
21. Remains of a mirror with a papyriform handle.
22. Remains of two handles from two mirrors, both with a leopard head at the top and a plant for the lower part.
23. A mirror handle with a Hathor head.[273]
24. Remains of a mirror box?
25. Two heads of Hathor, perhaps from a box?

70. Girdle and anklets of Mereret. The anklet in the middle is wrongly reconstructed as one necklace; once it must have formed two anklets. Photo: Juergen Liepe (JE 30879, JE 30923).

26–27. Two silver mirrors with remains of a gilded box, perhaps belonging to the handles mentioned above.

28. The lower part of a mirror handle.

29. A golden inlaid shen ring.

30. Three motto pendants with aw and ib signs, meaning "joy."[274]

31. A motto pendant with two netjer signs, one ib sign, and one hetep sign: "the hearts of the two gods are satisfied."

32. A motto pendant with two sa signs and one ankh sign, all surmounting a neb sign, meaning "all life and protection."

33–34. Two rings.[275]

35–54. Twenty scarabs, several with the title "king's daughter" and the name Mereret.

55. A golden cylinder.[276]

56. A second cylinder.

71. The two "foreign" rings of Mereret. Cairo CG 52238; CG
52239. From Vernier 1909, pl. XXII.

57. A small cartouche.
58–73. Fifteen vases, one made of lapis lazuli.[277]
74. A mace head.
75. A stone for sharpening razors (?).
76. Three razors.

The two rings (nos. 33 and 34) are of special interest (Fig. 71). They
are both made of gold. The larger one shows on the decorated face a
checkerboard pattern made in granulation, while the other shows four
spirals. The rings are made of one piece, while most Egyptian rings are
made of wire, with the decorated part most often a different piece of jewelry, such as a scarab. Granulation is very rare in the Middle Kingdom,
and on Egyptian jewelry it is usually restricted to late Middle Kingdom
cylinders. With some reservation it might be argued that the two rings
are not Egyptian but were made somewhere in the Middle East or even
on Crete.[278]

Who Was Mereret?

Three scarabs with the name of a king's daughter Mereret were found
in the second treasure at Dahshur.[279] A fourth scarab offers the writing
Meryt;[280] it too provides the title "king's daughter." There seems to be
a good chance that Mereret was the owner of the treasure, as the high
number of scarabs with the same name is possibly no accident. She was
perhaps a daughter of Senusret III, although conclusive proof of this is

missing. In the same treasure were found a scarab bearing the title "king's wife of the Lower Egyptian king,"[281] and another seal with the title the "king's wife, united with the white crown."[282] However, the latter scarab is perhaps to be translated "king's wife Khenmetneferdhedjet." Following the first translation it has been assumed that Mereret was also a wife of Senusret III. As no name is provided, this remains a guess. Therefore, in Egyptological literature, Mereret also appears as queen (king's wife).[283] This goes back to two scarabs from the same find. In Egyptology there is some discussion whether "united with the white crown" (Khenmetnefer-hedjet) is a proper name or just the title of a royal woman. The latter case would mean that on the latter scarab only the titles of a queen appear, not her name. This is not common in ancient Egypt, where the name is so important for the identification of a person. The scarab therefore more likely belongs to the king's wife Khenmetneferhedjet. Therefore Mereret was not a king's wife. The title "king's wife" is never connected with her name.

CHAPTER 2

Other Burials of Women

The most important undisturbed tombs of other women, not buried in court type style, are presented in this chapter in order to gain a better understanding of the burials of the royal and highest-status women buried in the court type style discussed in Chapter 1.

While the items of jewelry found in these other burials have many points in common with those from court type burials, it is striking that the other items of burial equipment are in general different, even though all the burials date from more or less the same period and many of these non-royal women are of high social status. Most notably, these tombs contain only a few objects produced by the funerary industry. A large amount, possibly all, of the jewelry had already been worn in daily life. The only other common burial goods were pottery and sometimes stone vessels. Further burial goods in the tombs presented in this chapter are rare. This might come as a surprise, as other grave goods of the late Middle Kingdom sporadically placed in tombs include faience figures of animals, most notably those of hippopotami, the so-called magical wands made of hippopotamus ivory and decorated with an array of deities and magical figures, the first "true" shabtis (those bearing the shabti spell), and heart scarabs. In a few tombs models of fruits made of faience were found.[1] There are sometimes also canopic jars and canopic boxes. Few of these objects appear in the following tombs with rich jewelry, however. This might be an accident of preservation, but it might also show that these objects were rare in the late Middle Kingdom, while tombs with rich jewelry were much more common. Indeed, all the objects mentioned appear sporadically and are not really typical of the period, belonging rather to exceptions relating to a higher social level. An average burial consisted of a coffin, some jewelry, and pottery vessels. Poor people were buried in shallow holes in the ground,[2] while wealthy people had a tomb chapel with a deep shaft and a burial chamber at the bottom.[3] Because so many tombs have suffered from looting, these conclusions should be made with great caution, but surely it is the jewelry that would be robbed first, so if jewelry was found, it seems highly likely that the other burial equipment is quite complete. As always in archaeology, though, a new excavation in a well-preserved cemetery might change this picture.

A common problem in archaeology is the sexing of bodies found in tombs. Most of the bodies from the tombs described below were sexed in the relevant publications, which means that the excavators were trained to make a quick judgment on the sex of the skeletons found. Often, however, these excavators were not trained as physical anthropologists.[4] In some cases inscriptions are useful for identification, but in many tombs of the level below that of royal and highest-status women no inscriptions are preserved, or they may not have been used on any parts of the burial equipment. For these reasons the sex of some of the people whose burials are described below must remain conjectural. The pattern of high-quality jewelry in connection with cosmetic objects in some tombs might too easily persuade the modern archaeologist to believe that these are all tombs of women. The reality may well be more complicated.[5]

HETEPET'S TOMB, TETI PYRAMID CEMETERY

The undisturbed burial (tomb 41) of the lady Hetepet was found at Saqqara near the pyramid of the Old Kingdom king Teti.[6] Around this pyramid a huge cemetery had already developed in the Sixth Dynasty, and it remained in use until the Late Period. This burial ground most likely served part of the population living in Memphis. Several of the tombs date to the late Middle Kingdom. The burials are of special importance for our knowledge of the period, not least because they are among the best recorded and published of all late Middle Kingdom tombs (Fig. 72).

The tomb of Hetepet consisted of a six-meter-deep shaft with a small chamber at the bottom on the east side. The chamber was blocked by three slabs of stone. Behind the slabs was a slim mud-brick wall, just one

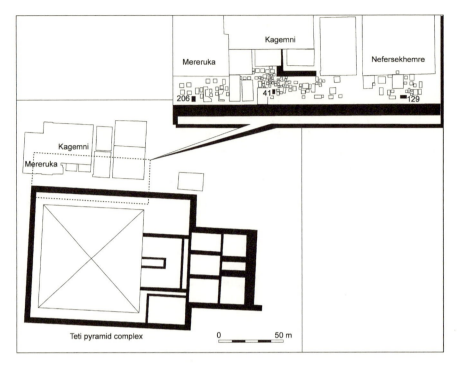

72. Plan of the cemetery north of the pyramid complex of the Sixth Dynasty king
Teti at Saqqara. Redrawn by the author after Firth, Gunn 1926, pl. 51.

brick thick. The chamber contained just the coffin and five identical vessels of red clay on its west side. The coffin of Hetepet was covered on the
exterior with pitch or a resin-like substance. It had a vaulted lid with raised
ends. In the coffin was found the skeleton of a girl placed on her back with
her head to the north looking to the west. The interior of the coffin was
painted or plastered white and had texts in vertical columns, sadly not well
preserved, so that the excavators were able to identify only the name of
the coffin owner.

The girl's body was richly adorned with jewelry, some of it helpful for
reconstructing the examples found at Dahshur, as here they were recorded
with greater precision by the excavators. The girl was wearing a girdle
of eight large cowry-shaped silver shells connected by a leather string.
Around her neck was a necklace of smaller gold shells,[7] and at her wrist
was an armlet consisting of beads with two small golden lions perhaps as
centerpieces.[8] There were also fragments of pink clay lions once covered

with gold leaf. They belonged to a bracelet with wooden beads covered with thin gold foil. Finally, there were three strings of carnelian,[9] garnet,[10] and amethyst[11] beads from one or several necklaces. The burial makes a simple, but certainly not poor, impression. Next to the personal adornments, the only grave goods were the coffin and the pottery jars.

TOMB 129, TETI PYRAMID CEMETERY

Another tomb found at Saqqara, close to the Teti pyramid, contained three burials (Fig. 73). It was again a shaft tomb, this time with three chambers in the southern side of the shaft. The whole burial complex was found undisturbed.

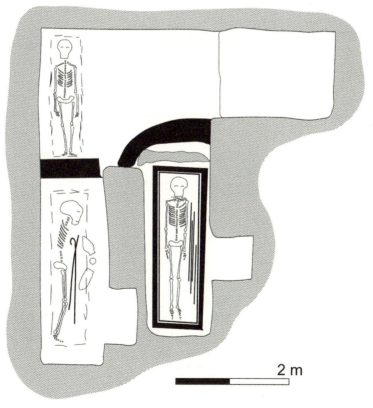

73. Plan of Saqqara tomb 129. Redrawn by the author after Firth, Gunn 1926, fig. 26.

The first chamber contained only a coffin with one female skeleton. No burial goods were found. South of that chamber was the second chamber, with a second burial. Here a large wooden coffin with a vaulted lid, painted black with a substance described in the excavation report as bitumen or resin, was discovered. The coffin was uninscribed. Within it was a second one of fine cedar wood. This coffin had blue wedjat eyes painted on the outside and was partly gilded. The edges of the coffin were also painted blue. In the coffin were found the remains of a woman placed on her back. On the left side of the coffin were four sticks, already broken in antiquity and repaired. There was also an alabaster vase with a separate neck. The woman's only jewelry was a collar of faience and gold cylinder beads with black stone pendants. Finally, the third burial contained the remains of a coffin, two decayed sticks, and three pottery vessels.[12] The arrangement of the second chamber seems to be quite similar to those burials of royal women found next to the pyramid of Amenemhat II at Dahshur. Here and in Dahshur there was an outer coffin or sarcophagus, entirely undecorated, and a second coffin sparingly decorated with gold foil and wedjat eyes (compare Chapter 1). The jewelry found in the Saqqara tomb is much simpler; presumably the women buried there did not have access to the resources available to the royal women buried at Dahshur. Any sign of Osiris (royal) regalia was also missing.

TOMB 206, TETI PYRAMID CEMETERY

Tomb 206 was the burial of a child placed in a simple shaft within a coffin, again found next to the pyramid of Teti at Saqqara. The child was placed on the right side with the head to the north and looking to the west. This is exceptional, as most often the deceased faced east. The only burial goods were again a small set of jewelry items. There was a necklace of gold beads with shell-shaped pendants also of gold, a series of gold plaques in the shape of the hieroglyphic sign *khenti*, and some beads of gold and carnelian.

SATIP'S TOMB, DAHSHUR

At Dahshur, next to the pyramids of the Twelfth Dynasty kings, not only the tombs of the king's daughters and queens but also burials of other individuals belonging to the royal court were excavated. The mastabas of viziers, treasurers, and other high state officials were unearthed. Most of these tombs were found looted, with little of the original burial equipment remaining. There are some exceptions, however. One of these is the undisturbed burial of Satip[13] close to the pyramid of Senusret III, excavated by de Morgan's team. The burial was found in a chamber at the end of a shaft about 6.8 m deep. The door of the chamber was blocked by mud bricks. Directly behind them stood the coffin of Satip, which was found badly decayed. Originally it was inscribed on the inside with long religious texts, but only parts of the inscription could be copied by the excavators. These were the Pyramid Text spells 247 to 258. These spells are not yet attested in this full sequence on any other coffin, but they appear in two tomb chambers of the Middle Kingdom: that of Senusretankh, buried at Lisht perhaps under king Amenemhat II, and the tomb chamber of the vizier and treasurer Siese, who was in office under the same king, perhaps at the end of his reign. In both cases, it seems that the tomb chambers were recreations of Old Kingdom royal tomb chambers, especially those of King Unas. On the coffin of Satip only parts of the west side were preserved, and it is quite likely that the whole coffin had originally been decorated with a more complete set of Pyramid Text spells, similar to those found in the burial chambers of Senusretankh and Siese.[14]

Next to the coffin several pottery vessels, globular vessels, and bowls were arranged. The mummy was found badly preserved. Around the neck beads from a broad collar were discovered, and over the face was a mummy mask, of which only the inlaid eyes survived. Some further objects were found, but they are not described or depicted in de Morgan's publication.[15]

Although the excavation report for this tomb is very short, it is still possible to gain a picture of the burial. Perhaps with the exception of the pottery, all of the objects in the tomb were specially made for it, but it is not a court type burial, because the royal insignia are missing. It is hard to judge Satip's social status. She did not belong to the richest level of society, as no golden jewelry is recorded from the tomb. The only personal adornment was the collar around her neck. However, she was placed inside an inscribed coffin, indicating access to some resources that she must have had in life. Most of the tomb equipment was specially made for the tomb but does not contain the Osiris (royal) regalia typical of the court type burials.

HARAGEH

Harageh is a large, wealthy burial ground at the entrance to the Fayum excavated in 1913 by Reginald Engelbach for the British School of Archaeology. Burials here date to the Predynastic Period, the First Intermediate Period, the late Middle Kingdom, and the New Kingdom.[16] In most periods it seems to have served small rural communities in the region. Only in the late Middle Kingdom does it seem to have served the pyramid town of Hetep-Senusret, now more often called Lahun after a small modern town in the region. Hetep-Senusret was a substantial town where many affluent people certainly lived. It seems that especially the richer people of the town were buried at Harageh. Most of the tombs were found heavily looted, however, although they still contained a rich selection of objects. Altogether the place provides a good idea of late Middle Kingdom burial customs in a cemetery mostly used by a wealthy community (Fig. 74).

Because of its full publication, Harageh is the essential cemetery for building a more complete picture of burial customs in the late Middle Kingdom, and so I shall provide a short survey of the tombs of this cemetery.

About 258 tombs at Harageh date to the late Middle Kingdom or Second Intermediate Period. Based on the burial equipment, I distinguish three burial types:

1. Ten tombs were most likely court type burials. In some of them were found the typical beads of a flail,[17] so far attested only in this type of burial. Other finds in these ten tombs support the observation that they were most likely court type burials belonging to people of highest social standing. In tomb 280 was found the inscribed canopic box of the "lady of the house" Imayt, one of only two recorded inscribed canopic boxes in the whole cemetery. Finally, tomb 608 was one of the very few in the cemetery paved with limestone slabs; almost all the others were simple shafts and chambers carved into the rock.

2. The second group consisted of about seventy tombs. Here were found remains of burial equipment belonging to products of a funerary industry.[18] These are decorated coffins,[19] mummy masks or anthropoid coffins,[20] and canopic jars or canopic boxes.[21] Burials with broad collars also seem to belong to this group,

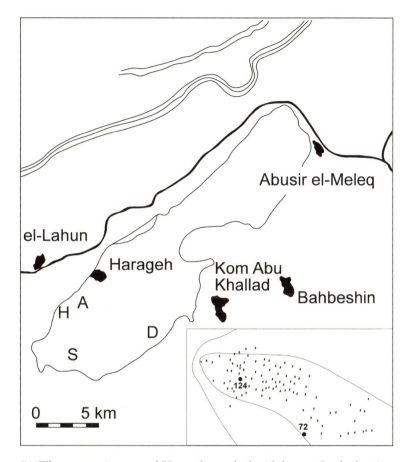

74. The cemeteries around Harageh, marked with letters. In the box is a plan of cemetery A. Drawn by the author after Engelbach 1923, pls. II, III.

most of them most likely products of the funerary industry.[22] The burials of the second group evidently continue a tradition of the early Middle Kingdom in which a similar range of objects was placed into the tombs. In many early Middle Kingdom burials there were, however, also wooden models of food production, of boats, and of carpenters. These are absent in the late Middle Kingdom. Furthermore, in the early Middle Kingdom coffins are often decorated on the inside, something also absent in the late Middle Kingdom. Similar types of burials are known from Lisht, where there were many burials in uninscribed coffins, with a gilded plaster mask on the mummy and the remains of jewelry,

most important of which were collars, armlets, and anklets. The
evidence from Lisht is not yet fully published.[23] In these tombs,
alongside objects of the funerary industry, appear other items
most likely already used in daily life. Tomb 271 had a canopic
box, but also a papyrus with an administrative or literary text.[24]
Tomb 353 most likely had a canopic box and a mummy mask,
and a cow and a frog made of faience were found. Tomb 399
most likely also had a canopic box, and wands or clappers and
an animal figure in faience were found.

3. Finally come the bulk of burials at this cemetery, which do not
contain any objects of the funerary industry. This might partly
relate to the heavy looting of the tombs or bad preservation
conditions, but there were some burials that were undisturbed
and indeed equipped only with objects of daily life, sometimes
even including gold jewelry. There are faience figures and other
objects such as stone vessels. The bulk of these tombs, however,
contained only pottery and jewelry.

This classification of tombs at Harageh should be regarded with some
caution. The heavy looting and bad preservation conditions mean that
a large number of wooden coffins may not have been preserved. Furthermore, the dimension of time was not taken into account. Some types
might be more common in some periods than in others. Finally, the graves
of the poorest were not published by Engelbach. The tombs published
seem all to belong to a higher social level.

Some of these tombs, although found disturbed, should be described
in detail to provide a clearer overall idea of the cemetery.

Tomb 96 was a simple shaft with one chamber at the bottom. The
tomb was found robbed; not even the remains of a skeleton were left, or
at least were not recorded. A range of pottery was found. Most interesting were the remains of a falcon collar; its terminals in faience, typically
shaped with a falcon, survived. In addition, there were fragments of gold
leaf and small buttons with grooves. These are known from other contexts
as belonging to the wig of an anthropoid coffin.[25] From this evidence the
burial must once have been quite rich, provided with an anthropoid coffin
and a falcon collar, both products of the funerary industry. The anthropoid coffin was almost certainly once placed in a rectangular coffin of
which nothing survived, since all the evidence from the Middle Kingdom

indicates that anthropoid coffins were invariably enclosed by an outer rectangular coffin. The first anthropoid coffins not so enclosed are the *rishi* coffins dating from the middle of the Thirteenth Dynasty to the early Eighteenth Dynasty.[26] These are anthropoid in shape and covered with a feather decoration (*rishi* is the Arabic word for feather).

Tomb 154 was again a shaft tomb, but this time with two chambers, one on the north and one on the south side. The tomb was found partly destroyed: parts of the chamber ceiling seem to have collapsed. There was no pottery, just a range of jewelry, including three golden shells, two ribbed beads with gold foil, a string of amethyst beads, and a string of garnet beads. Exceptional among them are two gold crocodiles, a golden turtle, and seven small wedjat eyes cut from a sheet of gold.

Another burial (tomb 357) consisted of a shaft with just one chamber on the south. Here were found the remains of a skeleton of a man. The burial had been robbed. Burial goods include some pottery vessels. No coffin was found, but there was a pair of painted limestone eyes,[27] perhaps from a mummy mask or an anthropoid coffin. Finally, there were elements of a broad collar. Broad collars were found in several tombs at Harageh, most often in the burials of women; this is one of the few examples of one from the tomb of a man. There is always the chance, however, that the skeleton was not properly sexed, or that it belongs to a later intrusive burial or simply to the burial of the woman who once wore the broad collar but whose remains did not survive.

The burial in tomb 72 (Fig. 75) was found in a chamber within a larger burial complex.[28] There was a shaft with two chambers in the northern side and one chamber in the south. The northern chambers were placed one above the other. All three chambers were found heavily robbed when excavated. In the southern chamber, however, a further shaft led down to another chamber, which was found undisturbed. In the publication report, Engelbach wondered whether a coffin had originally been placed over the entrance to this further shaft, so that robbers missed the burial it contained.

In the lowest chamber was found the burial of a child around ten years old. It was originally placed in a coffin, which was found totally decayed. The body was once wrapped in linen and placed on the back with the head to the north. Here were found many beads, often of semiprecious stones such as turquoise, lapis lazuli, and carnelian, some even decorated with gold foil. Silver cowries might have once formed a girdle, although

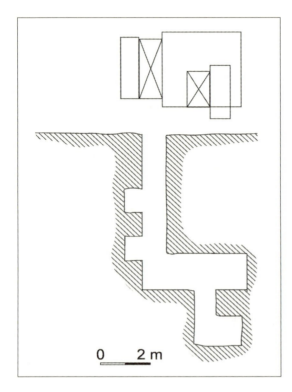

0   2 m

75. Plan and section of Harageh tomb 72; information taken from the description in the publication and from the tomb cards. Several points are uncertain, such as the exact positions of the chambers in relation to the shafts. Drawn by the author.

the publication mentions only that this type of shell was found. The masterpiece found in the tomb is a solid-gold fish (Fig. 76); next to it were found four other gold fish of less high quality workmanship.[29] The fish is 4 cm long and apparently of solid gold, though there may be a core of a different metal. Fish amulets were popular in the late Middle Kingdom. The ancient Egyptian name for this type of jewelry is *nekhau*, and it has been proposed that it was worn as protection against drowning.[30] Elisabeth Staehelin connects them with Hathor. Indeed, one fish pendant is mentioned in the Westcar Papyrus and is described as made of turquoise. Hathor was the "lady of turquoise."[31] An image in a Middle Kingdom tomb at Meir shows that it was worn on a side lock of hair, and some statues of young girls are depicted wearing the same amulet in exactly the same position.

Tomb 124[32] (see Fig. 61 on p. 75) was found disturbed but still contained a range of important personal adornments and toilet objects that make it one of the most important late Middle Kingdom tomb assemblages after those of the royal women. The tomb consists of a shaft with two chambers. The chambers are placed one behind the other, the second being smaller and perhaps mainly for the coffin. This seems to be typical of late Middle Kingdom and Second Intermediate Period burial apartments of the ruling class where the coffin often had its own small coffin-sized chamber. There is also a niche for canopic jars. The jewelry excavated

76. Fish pendant from Harageh tomb 72 (4 cm long). Photo:
Petrie Museum archive, PMAN 1050 © University College
London. Now in the Royal Scottish Museum, Edinburgh, reg.
no. 1914.1079.

includes one pectoral in silver, badly decayed when found. A reconstruction of this has proved to be problematic. It bears the throne name of Senusret II: Khakheperre. There are wedjat eyes at the top and two lotus flowers framing the scene (Fig. 77).[33] A Horus falcon and neb signs came from a second object. Engelbach describes the workmanship of these as

being of not very high standard, especially when compared to the pectoral found in the tombs of the princesses at Dahshur. However, an exceptional piece of jewelry found here was a bee made of silver, of the highest quality and so far without parallel in the Middle Kingdom.

77. The remains of the pectorals from tomb 124 at Harageh. Petrie Museum archive, PMAN 1055 © University College London.

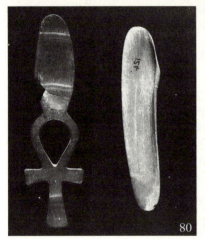

78. Shell girdles from Harageh tomb 124. Petrie Museum archive,
PMAN 1056 © University College London.

79. Mirror and razor from Harageh tomb 124. Petrie Museum archive,
PMAN 1058 © University College London.

80. Two cosmetic spoons from Harageh tomb 124. Petrie Museum archive,
PMAN 1058 © University College London.

81. Examples of cosmetic vessels from at Harageh tomb 124. Petrie Museum
archive, PMAN 1060 © University College London.

Other jewelry found in this tomb includes five scarabs and many gold and
carnelian beads. Also found were silver shells, perhaps once belonging to a
necklace, and cowry-shell-shaped pendants in silver, most likely once belonging to a girdle (Fig. 78). Other objects include three mirrors, several
razors (Fig. 79), and two nicely carved spoons, one with a handle in the
shape of an ankh sign (Fig. 80). At least twenty-two alabaster vessels were

found (Fig. 81). These were most likely cosmetic objects. Also discovered in the tomb was a stela naming the "lady of the house" Iytennebet. It remains uncertain whether the stela belongs to this tomb or ended up in this burial by accident.[34]

TOMB 124, RIQQEH

Riqqeh is a cemetery about twelve kilometers south of Lisht with burials dating to almost all periods of Egyptian history;[35] many date to the Middle Kingdom. Tomb 124 has a shaft with a chamber on the south side.[36] The roof of the chamber was found collapsed, which had saved the burial from looting. In the middle of the chamber were the remains of a wooden coffin. In the coffin was the body of the deceased adorned on the chest with a pectoral. The pectoral had two wedjat eyes at the top, two birds on the hieroglyphic sign for gold, and between them the *sekhem* ("power") symbol.[37] Also on the chest was found a shell inscribed with the throne name of Senusret III: Khakaure.[38] Another piece of jewelry, perhaps a pendant, is so far unique: in the middle is the hieroglyph *kha*, with two lotus flowers on either side and two hard to identify objects over the flowers.[39] At the neck was a small figure of Min, the god of male fertility. The Min figure and the shell were once most likely pendants of necklaces. Around the neck were found many beads belonging to a broad collar. In the publication the deceased is identified as a man. However, the pectoral and the shell are rather typical of burials of women. It cannot be discounted that the body was sexed wrongly by the excavators,[40] although the Min figure supports the skeleton's sexing as a man.

THE BURIAL OF SENEB, BENI HASSAN, TOMB 487

Beni Hassan in Middle Egypt is mainly famous for its decorated rock-cut tombs of Middle Kingdom governors. There are also many other smaller burials, however, belonging to the people working for these governors, including burials of family members of the governors and of the lower officials.[41] In 1902 to 1904 John Garstang together with Harold Jones[42] excavated parts of this cemetery. The excavations uncovered many tombs that still contained a large number of important objects.

The cemetery and its publication[43] still provide one of the most important records for burial customs in the first half of the Middle Kingdom. Garstang only presented a summary of his work in his book, however, leaving many questions open for a modern researcher. He also found several undisturbed tombs. Most of them are described in the publication, although again the record is not as detailed as we would like to see it today. A large number of the eight hundred tombs found at Beni Hassan date to the late Eleventh and first half of the Twelfth Dynasty. The latest dated inscription in the decorated rock-cut tombs of the governors mentions the sixth year of Senusret II. It occurs in the last fully decorated tomb, which belonged to Khnumhotep (II). There is at least one later governor's tomb, though not fully decorated, showing that such burials continued for at least another generation after Khnumhotep (II). The following tomb[44] might belong to those dating to the later Twelfth Dynasty.

The burial of the "lady of the house" Seneb, "son [sic] of Ity"[45] was in a small chamber in a wooden coffin that was already heavily decayed when found. Her skeleton was only about 145 cm long, so Seneb was most likely a young woman or girl when she died. Her coffin was placed on the left side of the chamber. All the burial goods were found in front of the coffin. There were at least four beer jars and a dish. Also found was a heavily decayed box and three smaller boxes, which were better preserved and had perhaps originally been placed inside the larger one, although the brief excavation report is not really clear on this point. In these boxes were found cosmetic objects, including several hair pins, a palette with a pebble for grinding eye paint, and a shell most likely for holding eye paint. There were nine alabaster vessels, one faience vessel, and another cylinder-shaped vessel. Finally, two clay figures depicting craftsmen were found.[46]

On the body of Seneb was an array of jewelry. This included two fish pendants made of silver with tails of electrum. There was a scarab with hieroglyphic signs worn as a bezel on a finger ring and a golden cylinder decorated with a zigzag pattern. The latter was fitted with two golden end caps and contained a small piece of papyrus. There were also several necklaces of carnelian and jasper as well as a few gold beads. Sadly the position of the jewelry when found is not well recorded, and basic contextual information has therefore been lost.

TOMB 521, MATMAR

Matmar is the modern name for several burial grounds in Middle Egypt, excavated by Guy Brunton. Tomb 521 was a small shaft about 3.3 m deep containing the burial of a child, described in the excavation report as eight years old, in a wooden coffin. According to the short description, several dishes were found beside the body. Jewelry beads were found in the child's hair and some beads at the right elbow. With the beads in the hair was a small silver fish.[47] The only grave good besides the dishes and personal adornments was a single vessel found outside the coffin.

A GIRL'S TOMB AT RIFEH

Rifeh is a modern village in Middle Egypt with a number of extensive ancient Egyptian cemeteries in its vicinity. Excavations have brought to light several undisturbed tombs. One of them belonged to a young girl.[48] She was placed in a decorated coffin. The only burial good mentioned in the short excavation report is a golden shell pendant found on her body.

TOMB 108, ABYDOS

Abydos is one of the most important sites of ancient Egypt, with extensive cemeteries of almost all periods. The density of the cemeteries was such that tombs were often reused or older ones destroyed to make way for new ones. Furthermore, several large-scale excavations were conducted there very early in the history of archaeology. As a result, all too often we have just a collection of objects from a tomb, with little further information. One example is tomb 108, excavated around 1900 by Garstang.[49] According to Garstang's short description, it was a shaft tomb with a chamber on the south side. In this chamber was found a remarkable set of jewelry, but as I indicated, we know only about the finds, with so little additional information that it is not even certain whether all the objects found in the tomb are mentioned in the excavation report. The jewelry published is typical of many of the women's burials discussed here. There is a set of hollow beads in the shape of cowry shells made of electrum. They were most likely worn as a girdle. The beads contain pellets of metal and would make a rattling sound when the wearer was walking.[50] There are two bracelets of gold sheet with a wavy incised surface. One big shell made of electrum is described as a pectoral and so was perhaps found on the chest. There are two small fishes made of feldspar. They are of rather low quality and not comparable to other fish pendants found in other late Middle Kingdom tombs. There was also a golden cylinder similar to the one found in the treasure of Mereret. Several types of bead were found, most likely from different necklaces. There are three scarabs from this tomb group, one inscribed for the "royal sealer, keeper of the secret of the palace, treasurer, Hor." At the entrance to the tomb chamber was found an uninscribed statue showing a man in a long garment. Other finds include two mirrors and several stone vessels. The statue of a man raises the question whether this was the burial of a man. The jewelry found is so typical of the burials of women, however, that at least one woman was presumably buried here. It was not uncommon in the late Middle Kingdom (and in other periods) for a couple to be placed together, next to one another, and this might have been the case here too. The scarab with the name Hor might almost give the impression that this was his burial. Scarabs are portable items, however, and so can easily be spread around. The person buried here might be related to Hor or might have been in his entourage: Hor was one of the highest state officials, as his titles indicate.

TOMB W 32, HU

Hu, Hiu, or Hut-Sekhem, also known by the Greek name Diospolis Parva, was the capital of the Seventh Upper Egyptian nome. Here, Flinders Petrie and his team excavated a series of cemeteries covering almost all periods of Egyptian history. They do not belong only to the town of Hu but most likely belong to a series of settlements on the west bank of the river Nile. Tomb W 32[51] is again an example of a rich burial of a young girl. She was placed in a rectangular coffin in a small chamber with her head to the north. At the entrance of the chamber were found four dishes, one still containing dates. East of the coffin a further fifteen dishes and beer jars were found. Still on some of the dishes were dates, bird bones, and leaves.

The young girl was buried with jewelry typical of the late Middle Kingdom. There were two fish pendants, one of silver and one of gold.[52]

They were found at the head of the girl. In front of the body was a mirror. On the right wrist were three amethyst scarabs and several strings of carnelian and amethyst beads. From one of the carnelian bead necklaces hung a silver hawk.

The cemeteries around Hu include a high number of burials dating to the late Middle Kingdom and Second Intermediate Period. They were excavated much too early in history of archaeology, and their publication does not provide any details—just a summary of the finds. The excavation notebooks (Fig. 82), however, especially for the Second Intermediate Period burial ground, are preserved in the Petrie Museum of Egyptian archaeology. It is therefore possible to gain at least a vague idea of the tombs found. About 154 burials are datable roughly to the late Middle Kingdom and Second Intermediate Period.[53] Of these, about nineteen contained objects of a funerary industry. There are at least six burials with an inscribed coffin[54] and thirteen with a mummy mask.[55] There is no evidence of canopic boxes and canopic jars, however. The only other objects

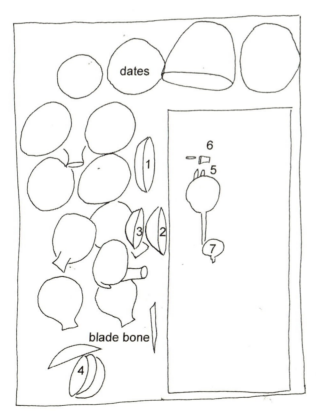

82. Sketch plan of burial W 32 at Hu. 1. dates; 2. bird bones; 3. white spotted pan; 4. white leaves; 5. two silver fishes above crown of head; 6. alabaster kohl pot and lid; 7. copper mirror. Drawing by author based on drawing in notebook.

specially made for burial are pottery offering tables and sometimes stelae or statues.

TOMB 15.L.1, KUBANIEH NORTH

Kubanieh is a village in the south of Egypt, some kilometers north of Elephantine. Here were excavated several burial grounds dating to almost all periods of Egyptian history. The most important graves belong to the Early Dynastic Period, around 3000 BCE, and to the Middle Kingdom. The graves are often simple, and many are those of Nubians. Evidently, the population of this part of ancient Egypt, although within the borders of the country, included many Nubians. Tomb 15.l.1 belonged to a young woman buried according to Egyptian traditions. She was placed in a shaft about 1.6 m deep. At the bottom of the shaft were found the remains of a coffin that was once plastered. The woman was lying slightly on the left side with her head to the north. On her head was found a simple metal object described as a diadem but more likely a torque.[56] A torque is a metal ring worn around the neck. At first glance these rings seem untypical of Egypt. Only about eight examples have been found in burials of the late Middle Kingdom.[57] They also appear in the Near East[58] and especially in Iran and Central Asia. It remains an open question whether this woman was from the Near East or an Egyptian woman who adorned herself with some kind of exotic personal adornment. This argument is weakened, however, by the burials excavated at Tell el-Dab'a, where many people from Syria and Palestine lived. In the burials at this site torques are not common. It is therefore an option that torques were a part of the Egyptian jewelry repertoire of the Middle Kingdom, perhaps influenced by Near Eastern models.

At the head were found many carnelian beads, and at the neck lay beads made of amethyst and carnelian. There was also a falcon figure made of lapis lazuli. At one hand beads made of amethyst were found, and a scarab. The young woman was buried with a cosmetic box as well, found in the region of her knees. The box[59] was inlaid with bone plaques, decorated with circles. In the box were discovered a cosmetic vessel made of a blue stone, its lid, and a cosmetic stick. There was a necklace of faience beads with a scarab made of carnelian as a pendant. Further objects found in the tomb were two stone vessels, a shell, and some rough small stones.[60]

TOMB K8, BUHEN

In Buhen, a fortress in Nubia, parts of a cemetery with several substantial tombs were excavated, most of them with several chambers containing several bodies. In tomb K8 one of the chambers was found undisturbed, containing a burial richly adorned with jewelry. The conditions for the preservation of organic materials are not very good at this site, and therefore almost nothing made of wood or textiles was found. In the small side chamber of tomb K8 were excavated the remains of a body lying on the ground with its head to the north and the arms on the pelvis. No coffin is recorded in the excavation report, but it may simply not have been preserved. Around the neck of the deceased was a necklace of beads made of gold and two lentil-shaped beads. Another necklace consisted of round amethyst and golden tube beads. The end of this necklace had two golden lions, lying on the ground. By the left shoulder was a green glazed steatite plaque inscribed with the Golden Horus name, Men-merut. This is a name of the Thirteenth Dynasty king Neferhotep I, and thus provides a rough date for the burial. On each forearm was a bracelet made of gold wires with a knot in the middle. On one finger of the left hand was a ring with a steatite scarab framed in gold bearing the name Nimaatre. This is the throne name of King Amenemhat III. On the face of the deceased was a gilded plaster mask.

Some other objects were also found in this chamber. On the south side was a large standing beer jar of a shape typical of the late Middle Kingdom, as well as a kohl stick, a shell, and a blue glazed bead. In the same tomb (but not in the same chamber) was found the statuette of the "gardener" Merer. In the published report the authors wondered whether Merer was the person buried in the tomb. This is uncertain, and it is not even clear whether the deceased was a man or a woman. In the publication, however, the person is identified as a man.[61]

CHAPTER 3

Types of Jewelry in
Late Middle Kingdom Burials

SOURCES

There are several sources from which it is possible to gain information on personal adornments worn in late Middle Kingdom Egypt. First of all there are the items found in tombs and to a lesser extent in settlement sites. They provide a firsthand view of Egyptian jewelry. However, they are not without problems. Jewelry found in tombs might have been selected especially for the burial, and so examples found there may not really reflect the jewelry worn normally in daily life or at least on those occasions when jewelry was usually worn, such as special religious or social events. An average farming man or woman might have had some jewelry but would not have worn it while doing daily activities in the house or in the fields. Jewelry was therefore most likely also event related, and this certainly applies to a burial. Death was a "special" event. This is most clearly visible in the high proportion of jewelry specially made for the tomb in the court type burials. The deceased was especially well equipped with jewelry for the underworld, at least in these burials.

Another problem with burials is inadequate recording and bad preservation. Beads are often found loose on the ground around the skeleton, and it remains pure speculation how to reconstruct their original arrangement. Beads at the neck might indicate one or more necklaces, but they might also belong to a choker. Beads on the chest might belong to a necklace, but there is also the option that they once formed a body chain. The order of different types of beads is very often lost, and too often the restringing of beads is left to the imagination and taste of a modern restringer.

A second source for ancient Egyptian jewelry is the range of depictions in art. Here we face different problems. Especially in reliefs and in large sculptures in stone or wood, women and men are shown with a quite narrow range of personal adornments. In the case of women these are the broad collar, armlets, and anklets. In contrast, most of the finds in tombs excavated show a quite different range of jewelry, indicating that the types known from art are jewelry for special occasions, perhaps seen as the most formal examples and important for scenes of religious self-representation.

Some tomb scenes from the late Middle Kingdom also show women with jewelry that differs slightly from the more standard examples shown in most tombs and on contemporary stelae. Examples include a tomb scene at Qaw el-Kebir showing women with body chains and tomb scenes from Meir with women wearing chokers;[1] both types of jewelry are otherwise not attested in tomb scenes or on stelae. These tomb depictions represent women with jewelry known from the finds in tombs. These images are rare, however, compared to the overwhelming majority of tomb depictions or pictures on stelae.

An important source for jewelry depictions is the corpus of objects known as "concubines" in Egyptology.[2] These are figurines of women often, but not always, shown naked. They are made of wood, clay, faience, and other materials. The function of these small-scale figures is disputed. Indeed, some Egyptologists have seen them as "dancing girls,"[3] others even as representations of the "divine mother."[4] Recently, E. A. Waraksa has argued that clay figures of women, at least in the New Kingdom, were used in rituals for medical healing.[5] S. L. Buddin regards them as figures promoting male potency and female fertility.[6] The New Kingdom figures are often roughly made clay objects, not comparable to many Middle Kingdom figurines, which are fully developed small-scale sculptures. What is clear, though, is that they were certainly not concubines, as they were found in tombs of women and children too. They might rather have a strong connection with rebirth in the underworld[7] and had the ability to "promote and protect fertility in daily life" and "to ensure the fertility of the deceased in the afterlife and/or to assist rebirth."[8] Here I will mainly discuss those made of faience and will refer to them as "faience fertility figurines."[9] They are most often made of blue faience and depict women, sometimes naked, sometimes fully dressed. They are always represented without feet. Even if they are naked, they wear at least some jewelry and are repeatedly decorated with tattoos. They are often shown

83. Faience female fertility figure found in the tomb of Neferhotep at Thebes (TT316), late Twelfth or Thirteenth Dynasty. From Winlock 1923, fig. 15 on p. 20.

with jewelry types not depicted in other sources and are therefore a helpful source for reconstructing how Egyptian jewelry was worn.

One example of such a figure is briefly described here. The statuette is now in the Egyptian Museum in Cairo (JE 47710) (Fig. 83), is of blue faience, and measures 13 cm high. It was found in the late Middle Kingdom Theban tomb of the bowman Neferhotep. The woman wears long hair, leaving the ears exposed. She is naked and without feet, her legs being cut off at the knees. She is shown with jewelry typical of such figures found in many late Middle Kingdom tombs. She has a necklace with a round pendant, perhaps representing a shell. There is a longer bead necklace, and over her body are crossing lines representing body chains. Around her hips she wears a girdle made of beads and shells. She wears two armlets, and her legs are heavily tattooed.[10] A similar source for depictions of jewelry are the so-called paddle dolls.[11] These are highly stylized figures of a woman reduced to a wooden board of very roughly human form without legs. Personal adornments and clothing are painted on the flat surface of the figure.

The following section describes the main jewelry types found in the burials, starting with the jewelry found in the tombs. As an aid in reconstructions, evidence from art is also used.

DIADEMS

Diadems and other types of head ornaments are known from the Early Dynastic Period and even earlier.[12] They appear in depictions of art, but there are also several examples found in tombs. From early on different types are known, ranging from simple metal circlets to those with attached flowers or attached depictions of birds. Some of the diadems are shown in reliefs with a knot at the back and streamers hanging down, perhaps representing examples in cloth.[13] Diadems with flowers shown in art might indeed represent examples with real flowers, which would have had little chance of surviving from the Old Kingdom. In Tarkhan a diadem was found with a circlet of linen and attached beads. This may be an object already worn in real life.[14] Other diadems found in Old Kingdom tombs are all most likely funerary examples, especially made for the tomb.

Middle Kingdom diadems are clearly a direct development of Old Kingdom examples. The diadem of Sathathoriunet is a simple circlet with attached golden flowers inlaid with colorful materials, similar to Old Kingdom examples but much more advanced in the technology of gold work. One diadem in the burial of Khenmet consists of gold wire again decorated with golden flowers. In contrast, the diadem from the tomb of Senebtisi consists of just golden wire. Most diadems were found in jewelry boxes, so they were perhaps worn in real life.

The diadem found on the body of Nubhetepti-khered is different, and seems to be a funerary example. It is made of silver and is a simple circlet with a knot at the back and streamers. This type becomes more popular from the Second Intermediate Period. One of the most important examples is the crown of King Nubkheperure Antef.[15]

OTHER HAIR ADORNMENTS

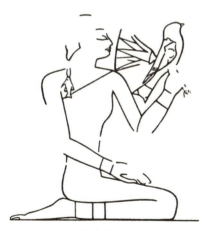

84. Girl shown with a fish pendant, painting in a Twelfth Dynasty tomb at Meir. From Blackman 1953, pl. XIV.

In the tomb of Senebtisi were found golden rosettes that had once adorned the hair. In the jewelry box of Sathathoriunet were golden tubes, which also perhaps once adorned the hair of the princess. This was the reconstruction proposed by Guy Brunton and Ernest Winlock, but other options for the use of these tubes are also possible. The depiction of a woman with golden ornaments in her hair is known from the head of a wooden statue found at Lisht.[16] Other ornaments for the hair include fish pendants, called *nekhau* in ancient Egypt. These were worn by young girls as a pendant at the end of a lock of hair. There are a few depictions showing this particular use (Fig. 84).[17]

BROAD COLLARS

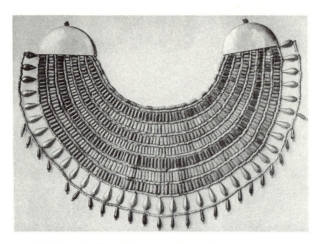

85. Broad collar of Itaweret, found in her burial at
Dahshur. From de Morgan 1903, pl. XIII

An important piece of jewelry found in many burials is the broad collar, one of the most typical items of ancient Egyptian personal adornment (Fig. 85). These are known from the Old Kingdom onward. One of the first depictions appears on the fragments of a shrine found at Heliopolis dating to the Third Dynasty under King Djoser. Here the god Geb is shown with a broad collar.[18] Another early example is found on the statue of Nefret, wife of Rahotep. Her statue and those of her husband were found in their mastaba at Meydum and date to the early Fourth Dynasty.[19] From this time on broad collars appear frequently in depictions of men and women. There is a social difference visible between the sexes, however. While in the Old and Middle Kingdoms women of almost all social levels are shown with a broad collar, only men at the highest level are depicted with them. In tomb decorations this is most often the tomb owner and his family members. In the Middle Kingdom tombs of the local governors, even the lower officials working for them were not depicted wearing broad collars in the tomb decorations.[20] This is especially remarkable, as the burials of these lower officials are also known, and there they are often equipped with broad collars, although most often these collars were made just for the burial.[21]

In writing, mainly as captions for collars in "friezes of objects" on Middle Kingdom coffins,[22] several names for collars (*wesekh* in Egyptian) are attested: "collar of green stone," "collar of lapis lazuli," "collar of gold," "collar of silver," and "collar of electrum." These names refer to the materials, while other names indicate instead power or magic, such as "collar, great of magic" and "collar of the lord of eternity." Royal collars had different names: "collar of Horus," "collar of Nekhbet," "collar of Wadjet," and "collar of the Two Ladies." It is often hard to relate these names to specific collars found in tombs, although the material already provides a clue.[23]

For the late Middle Kingdom two types of broad collar are attested in the archaeological record. There are falcon collars with terminals in the shape of falcon heads wearing head cloths, similar to depictions of deities, and there are simple collars with plain semicircular terminals. Both types of collar consist of several parts. There is the collar proper, most often made of tubular beads of faience or semiprecious stones. There are the aforementioned terminals, and also the counterpoise for the back of the collar. As a collar could be quite heavy it needed a counterpoise hanging from the other side to maintain balance, otherwise it would end up lying shapelessly on the shoulder of its owner. The top of the counterpoise was either a falcon head (for a falcon collar) or a round piece (for a simple collar).

Broad collars were not found in all of the tombs discussed. As a general rule they were placed in all those burials that contained a large number of products of the funerary industry, while those burials with objects taken from daily life (often just jewelry and some pottery) did not contain a broad collar, although they are often painted on anthropoid coffins and mummy masks. Based on this observation, it can be assumed that many of the collars found on the bodies of the women were funerary jewelry. This observation is in stark contrast to the depictions on Egyptian reliefs and statues. On these, the broad collar is the main personal adornment, after armlets and anklets, for men and women of some status. Another observation along the same lines concerns the jewelry boxes found in court type burials and burials of other women. The boxes seem to have contained jewelry worn in life. The contents of the boxes did not include broad collars. First of all, this clearly shows how the depictions in art differ in comparison to reality. A high percentage of the jewelry found in the boxes is rarely depicted in the tombs of the Middle Kingdom and equally rarely found on statuary. In terms of jewelry, images in art are almost identical to the physical examples of funerary jewelry but totally different with regard to jewelry boxes and burials of persons socially lower than those who received court type burials.

There are different versions of broad collars in terms of the technology of their beads and other materials used. The simplest examples were those found in the Dahshur burials next to the pyramid of Amenemhat II. They consist of rows of simple, mostly cylinder beads, while their lower edge consists of golden drop-shaped beads. Many type 2 burials (Chapter 2) contained the same simple broad collars. The two broad collars from the tomb of Senebtisi are both of similar, simple, workmanship, whereas the collars in the burials of Neferuptah and Nubhetepti-khered are much more elaborate. They have drop-shaped beads of cloisonné work as the lowest row of beads. This was most likely a very expensive gold-working technology and therefore not affordable even by some women at the highest social level. From this point of view, the rather simple-looking burials of Neferuptah and Nubhetepti-khered were perhaps in terms of their jewelry more costly than that of Senebtisi, despite her large selection of personal adornments; most of them were actually quite inexpensive funerary productions, and there were no examples of cloisonné.

A final type of broad collar clearly produced for a burial is that made of one piece of metal or wood, gilded and with the patterns of beads incised on the surface. An example was found in the tomb of Senebtisi; another comes from the burial of the "steward" Hapi Ankhtifi found at Meir;[24] and a third comes from the tomb of King Awibre Hor.[25]

NECKLACES

Necklaces are sporadically depicted in Egyptian art, though not as often as broad collars. By contrast, bead necklaces are very common in burials from almost all social levels. They are also well attested for men. They are sometimes present in the court type burials too, worn next to the broad collar. One example of necklaces in Egyptian art is in the image of Queen Aashyt from her funerary chapel in the mortuary temple of Mentuhotep II at Deir el-Bahari. Here, the queen is shown with a broad collar and three necklaces over it.[26] An almost identical set of necklaces was found in the burial of Mayet. Another example is a wooden figure of a woman, perhaps a servant, found at Asyut, shown with three necklaces.[27] In the late Middle Kingdom necklaces are regularly shown on faience fertility figurines and also on paddle dolls, while these figures rarely show broad collars.[28] Beads for necklaces are made of different materials. Amethyst was popular in the Middle Kingdom.

TORQUES

86. Torque found in tomb 345 A'07 at Abydos. Redrawn by the author from Snape 1986, 437.

Torques[29] are rings worn around the neck (Fig. 86). They are well attested in several Middle Kingdom burials. They do not appear in court type burials. All known Middle Kingdom examples were worn by women, though they appear again in the Late Period under Persian rule, when they were worn by men.[30] Torques as personal adornments are known from the Old Kingdom, when people were sometimes adorned with a wire band around the neck.[31]

SHELLS AS PENDANTS

Shells made of metal, often gold, were used mainly as pendants. Two types are known. In jewelry boxes, and also in non–court type burials, single big shells were found, sometimes richly inlaid and often made of gold (Fig. 87). In tomb 108 at Abydos a single pendant was found, perhaps on the chest of the deceased. A golden shell inscribed with a king's name was found in the region of the neck in tomb 124 at Riqqeh.[32] Other golden shells are smaller and were found as part of a necklace, as in tomb A/II-m/16 at Tell el Dab'a or in the tomb of Senebtisi.

87. Shell pendant from the jewelry box of Mereret, c. 4.6 cm high. From de Morgan 1903, pl. XX.4.

Single-shell pendants are perhaps also depicted on the friezes of Middle Kingdom coffins[33] and on the late Middle Kingdom faience fertility figurines. Although the figures are so small that details are lacking, several of them bear a round object depicting a pendant of a necklace.[34] Many of these figures wear jewelry found in the tombs under discussion, and here the only round objects regularly found are shell pendants. For this reason it seems likely that they are indeed represented with a shell.

PECTORALS

Pectorals are bigger pendants for a necklace worn on the chest with scenes or inscriptions. Excavated examples of Middle Kingdom royal pectorals have so far been found only in the jewelry boxes at Dahshur and Lahun. Two were found in the burial of Sathathoriunet, one in the jewelry box of Sathathor, and two in the jewelry box of Mereret. They are some of the finest examples of Egyptian gold work, using the cloisonné technique and many semiprecious stones as inlays. All pectorals found in the jewelry boxes of royal women bear a king's name, confirming the high social status of their owners and their close links to the king. It seems probable that they were gifts from the king and were produced in royal workshops.

There are only two burials of nonroyal individuals with pectorals, one at Riqqeh (tomb 124) and one at Harageh (tomb 124). Both pectorals are clearly lower in quality than those found in the tombs of the king's daughters, and were perhaps produced in a different workshop. Reginald Engelbach, who discovered both "private" pectorals, even wondered whether they are from the same "hand."[35]

There are two types of pectoral in terms of composition. Some are depictions of a shrine or naos, with the figures and inscriptions placed within a naos. Others place the composition just on a base. The depictions are always antithetical, often with the throne name of the king in the middle.

There are some rare depictions of pectorals in Middle Kingdom art, such as those worn by the daughters of a local governor buried at Deir el-Bersheh[36] and the statue of the king's daughter Nefret.[37] In both cases, the necklace holding the pectoral is a broad band, while in the modern reconstructions there are strings of single beads. The small loops attached to the back of them support the modern reconstruction.[38]

Only two further pectorals are known, both acquired on the art market, one of them with the name of Amenemhat III and one without a royal name but of high quality.[39]

CHOKERS

Chokers for women are depicted in reliefs and paintings in many periods of ancient Egyptian history.[40] An early example of a bead choker comes from the Fourth Dynasty tomb of Khufukhaf at Gizeh. Here the wife of the tomb owner is shown next to her husband. She has short hair and also wears bracelets.[41] In the Middle Kingdom, examples are depicted several times on women in the tomb of Ukh-hotep IV at Meir.[42] In general, however, there are not many depictions of this type of personal adornment in this period. This may not indicate that chokers were uncommon but rather may imply that they were not seen as canonical jewelry for depiction in formal art.

It remains difficult to identify chokers in the archaeological record. Examples made of beads would appear in excavations simply as a confusion of beads around the neck and thus virtually impossible to distinguish from a simple necklace. There is, however, a type of personal adornment found in some Old Kingdom tombs that was interpreted as choker. These are strings of beads with round terminals, very similar to the simple type of broad collar but with smaller terminals. A typical feature of these chokers is the use of spacers in the shape of the hieroglyphic sign for "water."[43] So far I have not been able to identify with certainty any example of a Middle Kingdom choker. One possible choker from one of the burials discussed was found in the tomb of Khenmet. It has two small falcon terminals and a row of amulets in between. Today it is reconstructed as a narrow collar (see Fig. 49, p. 58).[44]

ARMLETS AND ANKLETS

Like the broad collar, armlets, bracelets, and anklets belong to the main items of jewelry. They are depicted in art and found in many burials. Many examples found in the tombs of the royal women are made of rows of beads held together with several bars (Fig. 88). Luxury versions have bars with inscriptions inlaid in the cloisonné technique. These types are found on the mummies, but also in jewelry boxes next to them, and were therefore presumably also worn in real life. Bracelets are sometimes simple and undecorated and made of gold or other materials.

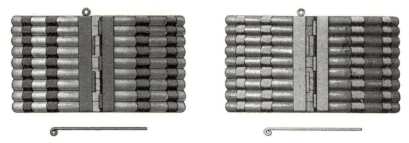

88. Armlets and anklets from the burial of Nubhetepti-khered.
From de Morgan 1895, pl. XXXVIII.

In the burials of individuals not belonging to the royal court, armlets and anklets are common too, but they are of different types. These are often just single strings of beads, sometimes with pendants, which are also found in court burials but are more often associated with the burials of lower-status women.

While in most depictions in art women wear just one armlet and anklet on each arm and leg, there are also depictions where they wear several of them. In the tomb of Djehuty-hotep at Deir el-Bersheh his daughters appear in certain scenes. They wear the broad bead armlets and anklets so well known from the late Middle Kingdom burials of royal women. Next to these appear simpler examples painted as one colored area but divided by fine white lines, perhaps indicating single strips of beads.[45]

Pendants are attested for anklets. In the First Intermediate Period these are often small legs shaped from carnelian, perhaps used for protection. A typical late Middle Kingdom pendant for anklets is an amulet in the shape of a bird claw.[46] In the tomb of the local governor Wahka (II) at Qaw el-Kebir is a depiction of this type of claw worn by a woman (Fig. 89).[47]

89. Dancer in the tomb of Wahka (II), reign of Senusret III. She wears anklets with bird claws and perhaps body chains. From Petrie 1930, pl. XXIV.

FINGER RINGS

Finger rings appear sporadically in the Middle Kingdom. They consist most often of a simple wire with a scarab as the bezel. Only in the Second Intermediate Period does the wire become thicker and full rings develop.[48] Nevertheless, in the jewelry box of Mereret two rings were found. They do not just consist of a wire and a scarab but are thick rings with a wider end. They are most likely foreign, as is also indicated by their design with spirals executed in granulation.

BODY CHAINS

Body chains[49] are well attested on late Middle Kingdom faience fertility figurines.[50]

Most often two chains are shown crossing over the navel or over the chest of the naked woman. A chain is represented by a dotted line; therefore it can be assumed that these chains were made of strings of beads. On two figures the chain consists of two strings of beads, not crossing over the chest but going parallel from the left shoulder down to the right hip.[51] They were not for covering the body but were clearly intended to "enhance the nudity" of the figure.[52] Body chains may appear on the wooden paddle dolls. Two almost identical examples found at Dra Abu el-Naga have necklaces shown as dotted lines.[53] One necklace hangs curved around the neck, while the other looks like a triangle placed upside down and might be a body chain where the lower parts of the chain disappear under the dress. A further possible example appears in a wall painting in the tomb of Wahka (II) at Qaw el-Kebir (Fig. 89). Here two women are depicted with chains of beads on their hands and arms.[54] Although the painting is much destroyed, it seems that these are not necklaces but rather body chains, since the strings of beads seem much too long for a necklace. One of the women also wears anklets with bird claw pendants, which is something often found in jewelry boxes but otherwise not often depicted in art. This indicates that the latter women are represented with jewelry that would be worn in daily life.

Looking at the archaeological record, these body chains are hard to identify. A well-recorded example is a child's burial in Sedment where five strings of beads were found over a dress, extending down from the top left shoulder to the right hip.[55] It seems unlikely that the body chains were placed on the body of the deceased in court type burials. Here most of the jewelry is funerary related and similar to the jewelry depicted in formal art. Therefore, the body chains should appear in the jewelry boxes or in those burials of rich women adorned with jewelry of daily life. There are so few examples of well-recorded (and published) burials of the latter type that it is not possible to reconstruct the exact place where beads and other items of jewelry were found. There are several burials, however, where mention is made of a large number of beads, and it seems possible that at least in some cases these beads were not just from necklaces but also from body chains. One rather vague example comes from burial 72 at Harageh where the excavation report states: "The body was wrapped in linen, and contained a large quantity of beads."[56] Body chains are attested in the New Kingdom. On an ostracon found at Deir el-Medineh a dancing woman is shown. She wears a short skirt, some jewelry, and body chains.[57] In general her dress and adornments are close to those of the faience fertility figurines, going some way to support the idea that these figures represent dancers. Another example dates to the late New Kingdom or Third Intermediate Period. A metal bowl found in the Twenty-first Dynasty burial of Wendjedbauendjed at Tanis shows on the inside three almost naked girls swimming. They are adorned only with jewelry, including body chains.[58]

Body chains are also known from other ancient cultures, such as ancient Greece. In Greece they were perhaps restricted to unmarried women.[59] Whether this is also true for ancient Egypt is unknown.

GIRDLES

Girdles were found in many of the tombs discussed. There are three main types. In the jewelry boxes and in the nonroyal burials there were girdles consisting of a chain of golden or silver cowry shells. Other girdles have, instead of the cowry shells, double leopard heads, also made of gold (Fig. 90). This type of girdle is also most likely shown on the faience fertility figurines,[60] although the details on these figures are often not clearly depicted. In the particular case of these figures it seems most likely that cowry shells are depicted.[61] Cowry shell girdles sometimes appear also on small-scale sculpture in other materials,[62] whereas leopard head girdles are so far only known from the jewelry boxes of the royal women and may be

90. Girdle from the tomb of Sathathoriunet; photo taken
shortly after the excavation. It is likely that there were once
beads between the leopard heads. Petrie Museum archive,
PMAN 1800 © University College London.

restricted to them. The cowry shells might have had a special function if it
was believed that they gave protective power to women, as the cowry shell
resembles the vulva.[63] They were still worn in recent times as girdles by
women in other parts of Africa.[64] In Egypt they are already attested in the
Badarian Period (around 4000 BCE) and were then often worn by men.[65]

A further type of girdle or apron was made especially for the tomb
and occurs only in court type burials. It consists of the girdle proper with
strings of beads hanging from it. These strings start at the top with beads
in the shape of lotus and papyrus plants and therefore represent Upper
and Lower Egypt, as these plants are the symbols for these parts of the
country. This type of apron is known from royal contexts and was most
likely a purely funerary object connected with the Osirification of the
deceased.[66] Such an apron is painted on an anthropoid coffin found at
Dahshur dating to the late Middle Kingdom.[67] It is also painted on the
anthropoid coffin of the "overseer of the troops" Sep, datable to around
Senusret II or Senusret III.[68]

COLORS AND MATERIALS

In the late Middle Kingdom a wide range of materials was used for personal adornments and other items of burial equipment. Some of these
materials were especially popular in the Middle Kingdom; others were
common in almost all periods of Egyptian history. Perhaps the most
common and most easily available material for personal adornments was

faience. It appears as beads and also as inlays for pectorals and other pieces of jewelry. It is most often light blue to green in color. Gold is the most commonly used metal, often as thin gold foil. Silver appears sporadically. Popular semiprecious stones in the Middle Kingdom and therefore also in the late Middle Kingdom were feldspar (microline; amazonite)[69] and amethyst (a quartz).[70] Both materials were mainly used for beads. Feldspar appears often within the beads of the broad collars, while amethyst was more often used for strings of beads in necklaces and girdles. Another popular material was turquoise.[71] It was again often used for beads, but also for inlays in pectorals and motto clasps. Lapis lazuli was imported from Afghanistan (via Mesopotamia) and was also popular. It is often dark blue.[72]

The colors used for jewelry evidently depend on the colors of the materials. These are mainly red and blue or green. Yellow seems to be completely missing but was most likely represented by gold. Black appears only sporadically. White or buff does not appear in the jewelry, but it does appear in other objects, such as the cosmetic vessels made of alabaster or the boxes containing ivory inlays. The broad collars of Neferuptah and Nubhetepti-khered were mainly made of carnelian, and their overall appearance today is bright red. This is in stark contrast to the broad collars of Senebtisi and Ita, which today are darkish green-blue in overall appearance. The dark color may, however, be a result of changes in the color of the faience over the past four thousand years, and the collars might originally have looked much lighter.

In general, it seems that stark color contrasts were used only occasionally. This is perhaps best visible on several cosmetic jars from the burial of Sathathoriunet. They are made of black obsidian, with bright gilding at the top and around the bottom. Other examples are jewelry with dark amethyst beads combined with golden elements, such as the girdles of Sathathoriunet, although these are reconstructed and there is no final proof that the amethyst beads went together with the golden elements. The same may apply to the personal adornments of Hapy at Lisht, also using dark lapis lazuli and golden elements.[73] Furthermore, amethyst is a transparent stone, which appears dark only under certain lighting conditions. The color contrast in other broad collars, for example those of Ita, appears today quite stark, with dark beads and bright gold. However, the dark color of the beads might not have been the original intention.

Mostly, stark contrasts were avoided. Where the materials used for personal adornments are semiprecious stones or gold, the colors today seem in general the same as in ancient times. From the evidence of the materials we might conclude that there was an evident general taste for bright, light colors, not contrasting dark colors with light. Instead, contrasts are subtle. In the pectoral with the name of Senusret II from the burial of Sathathoriunet, two shades of blue dominate, a darker against a lighter. A similar color scheme is visible on the pectoral with the name of the same king from the treasure of Sathathor at Dahshur. Here again different shades of green or blue are used. The broad collars of Neferuptah and Nubhetepti-khered show bright red against gold. Both are rather bright colors.

SUMMARY: DAILY LIFE AND FUNERARY JEWELRY

As we have seen, one can identify two types of jewelry in late Middle Kingdom burials. There are the adornments especially made for the burial, and there are those already worn in life. It has often been recognized that clothing and jewelry shown in ancient Egyptian art are different to those found in tombs. In this context Stephan Seidlmayer mentions a pleated tunic in his discussion of tombs of the local population on Elephantine. This type of dress was found in several tombs of the Old Kingdom but is extremely rarely depicted in art.[74] The same observation can be made of the burials discussed from the late Middle Kingdom. The jewelry on the mummies in the court type burials (and burials of type 2) is very close to that also known from contemporary art: broad collars, anklets, and armlets. Exactly these types of jewelry are by far the most commonly shown in sculpture, especially also on tomb reliefs and stelae. The jewelry found in the jewelry boxes and with women not buried in the court type style is different, however, and only rarely found in "high" art. Indeed, the only exceptions are the faience fertility figurines of the late Middle Kingdom, which depict other types of jewelry, many of them known from the jewelry boxes (Fig. 91). As I have already mentioned, these figures are known not only from burials but also from settlement sites such as Lahun.[75] They do not appear in court type burials, only in other burials of about the same time. On a formal level they are fully developed art objects and not comparable with contemporary clay figures of naked women and the stylized wooden figures called paddle dolls.[76]

In practical terms it is often not easy to separate funerary jewelry from

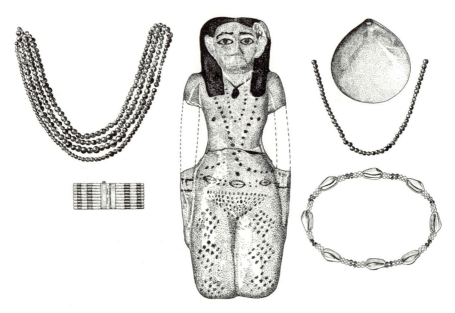

91. A faience fertility figurine adorned with jewelry with late Middle Kingdom personal adornments alongside. Drawing: Paul Whelan after de Morgan 1895, pls. XVI, XVIII, XXXVIII, Winlock 1934, pl. IX, Winlock 1923, fig. 15 on p. 20.

jewelry worn in real life. A closer look at each piece is almost invariably required, especially as older publications do not describe the personal adornments in complete detail. Funerary jewelry is often made of wood or plaster, only very thinly gilded. It is often flimsy, not at all suitable for use in real life.[77] This has been used to argue that it cannot have been used in real life. Much of this jewelry, however, seems to be related to ritual and would have been worn only on very special occasions, when it would not have had to be worn for a long time. The argument from weak material is therefore not really conclusive. Modern experiments have shown that broad collars are not at all suitable for wearing in real life, as they lose their shape very quickly and therefore would not look at all like the examples shown in art.[78] On the other hand, sometimes even the loops required to hold strings when worn for real are missing. Armlets and anklets in the burial of Senebtisi were not long enough to go around the arms and ankles. Other obvious cases of funerary jewelry are the personal adornments made of thin metal foil found in the New Kingdom burial of the three New Kingdom queens (Chapter 4) as well as those from the tomb of Senebtisi.

Funerary jewelry consists of a limited range of types. Foremost are broad collars, the royal apron, armlets, and anklets. The same is most likely true of many of the broad collars, armlets, and anklets in many other burials of the Twelfth Dynasty. John Garstang, however, in presenting his finds from the Middle Kingdom cemetery at Beni Hassan, mainly in discussing broad collars, had no doubt that the jewelry found was also worn in daily life.[79] In contrast, William Hayes was equally convinced that most jewelry found in Middle Kingdom tombs was specially made for the funeral.[80] Cyril Aldred also saw this type of jewelry as having been specially made for the tomb.[81] In discussing the broad collar of Itaweret, however, he argued that it was once worn in daily life and then adapted for use in the burial as it has a *menkhet* counterpoise, normally not found with funerary collars, which did not need them.[82]

All those buried in court type burials (burials of type 1) and many burials of type 2 were equipped with broad collars and often with armlets and anklets. Evidently these types of jewelry were seen as essential. Perhaps they were seen as the most prestigious forms and had some religious meaning. The broad collars and bead armlets and anklets are also exactly the items of jewelry shown in the majority of depictions in formal art, especially in representations in reliefs and painting. Here women often wear only a broad collar, armlets, and anklets. Clearly these were seen as essential personal adornments to be worn for all eternity. These types of jewelry are also often depicted in the friezes of objects on the inside of coffins of the early Middle Kingdom, and several of them are mentioned in the Pyramid and Coffin Texts.[83] For example: "Horus has placed gold on his eye, a gold collar" (Pyramid Text spell 742) and "O Osiris, the king, I make firm the Eye of Horus on your head, a headband" (Pyramid Text spell 744).[84]

The types of jewelry used as funerary jewelry were also worn in real life, perhaps just on special occasions, such as religious festivals or highly formal meetings. As I have already mentioned, in many burials, such as in the tomb of Senebtisi, they were especially produced for the tomb, but in other burials real examples were placed on the mummy, perhaps because these prestigious examples were available. Here an overlap between daily life and funerary jewelry is clearly visible.

Funerary jewelry was already in use in the Old Kingdom. Indeed, a possible Old Kingdom example is a diadem of gilt copper found in tomb 316 at Gizeh, which was too fragile and at the same time too inflexible to be used in real life. It would have broken very quickly if worn.[85]

Jewelry used in daily life was found in jewelry boxes[86] next to the burials of royal women, and sometimes also on their mummies and in non–court type burials. The types of daily life jewelry attested are clearly different to those used as funerary jewelry, with some overlaps.

First, special attention should be drawn to the personal adornments found in the jewelry boxes of Sathathoriunet, Sathathor, and Mereret. They contained pectorals, girdles, armlets, and shell pendants. Similar personal adornments were found in several private burials of the same time; many of these burials seem to belong to young women.

Similar in appearance to the personal adornments found in these jewelry boxes and several private burials are those depicted on some of the faience fertility figurines. Their personal adornments are often simple, but they are often different to those found in the depictions of reliefs and statuary. These figures are sometimes adorned with body chains and wear simple necklaces, sometimes with a round pendant, most likely a shell. Armlets are shown, but not the broad type depicted on many reliefs and statues. Many faience fertility figurines also wear a girdle, most likely made of cowry shaped elements, although the depictions are too small to enable one to identify the jewelry in detail.

As often pointed out, these figures represent women in specific cultic or ritual functions to promote fertility. This idea is supported by the jewelry depicted on them. Cowry shells are connected with female fertility in many cultures. The body chains enhance the naked bodies of the women. The tattoos shown on many of these figures have an erotic aspect and thus a connection with fertility.[87] I therefore wonder whether the jewelry found in some jewelry boxes and in several of the burials relates to the same function in some way, connecting these women with fertility. Another option is that these items of jewelry were typical of a certain phase of life. Here a relief depiction of Neferure, the daughter of Queen Hatshepsut, should be mentioned. In Deir el-Bahari she is shown almost naked, wearing only jewelry. This includes armlets and anklets, a broad collar, two necklaces, and a girdle, most likely of cowry shells. She wears a diadem with a uraeus. Over her chest are straps, placed rather like body chains.[88]

As these personal adornments are connected with fertility, they are also certainly connected with young women, and I wonder whether this was the typical jewelry equipment for a young unmarried woman. Indeed, from the sparse evidence for Middle Kingdom king's daughters it seems that these women were never married.[89] This conclusion should be made with some caution, however, to avoid circular reasoning. The burials of young women are often equipped with many different types of personal adornments. Therefore, almost any jewelry found can be seen as typical of young, perhaps unmarried women. Furthermore, a woman found at Qurna dating to the end of the Second Intermediate Period was buried with a girdle of cowry shaped shells, but also with a child. She might have died in childbirth, indicating that she was already married when she died.

As well as the jewelry mentioned, a wide range of other personal adornments is found in women's burials. It remains hard to find any clear pattern to these adornments. Certainly the personal choices and tastes of the women must have been involved. In the case of the foreign jewelry in the burial of Khenmet it seems possible that she was of foreign origin, but her jewelry may have consisted of presents from the king, who may have received them via gift exchange from a foreign ruler. Without further evidence every interpretation remains pure speculation.

An important observation is that there seems to be little difference between the jewelry of the king's daughters and that of high-status women. The personal adornments identified are almost identical. For both groups of women girdles of cowry shells, pectorals, armlets, anklets, and necklaces are attested.

The wide variety of crowns and circlets for adorning the heads of the women is remarkable. There are almost no two similar crowns. The diadem in the burial of Senebtisi consists of a simple wire arrangement. There are two crowns in the burial of Khenmet. One is an arrangement of wires with flowers in it. Despite its high quality, there seems nothing royal about this crown. A more complicated case is the other crown, with a vulture. In the Old, Middle, and New Kingdoms vultures were restricted to the king's mother and king's wife.[90] This might indeed indicate that this crown was specifically royal. All told, it seems hard to provide evidence that a certain type was restricted to royal women. For example, the crown of Sathathoriunet has parallels in paintings in the tomb of Ukh-hotep IV at Meir. Here women are shown with a similar crown, also with plumes, and these women are not royal.[91] These paintings include many royal symbols, however, and it is therefore arguable that the crowns shown are based on royal models.

The main difference between royal and private jewelry is the quality of the personal adornments and the materials used. Furthermore, some of the items found in the burials of the king's daughters are also adorned with royal names, most importantly the pectorals and the armlets. Together with the high quality of these pieces, this might indicate that they were produced in royal workshops, perhaps even workshops attached to the palace. Even the royal names, however, are not exclusively used in the jewelry equipment of the king's daughters. In tomb 124 at Harageh a pectoral, not of the highest quality, was found with the name of Senusret II. In burial 124 at Riqqeh a golden shell with the name of Senusret III was found. Shells worn in real life often bear the name of Senusret I.[92]

In comparing the personal adornments placed on the deceased in court type burials with those found in other graves and in jewelry boxes, there are several other observations to make. The daily life jewelry was more gender specific. The jewelry found in the court type burials and the jewelry specially produced for burial are more gender neutral. Necklaces with the shen sign, broad collars, and armlets are well attested for both sexes. Broad collars and armlets are also especially well known for men and are depicted in reliefs, paintings, and statues. In general, it seems that most types of personal adornment worn in real life could be worn by women, while men could wear only a selection of certain types.[93] The body chains, the cowry shell girdles, the bird claws, and the golden fishes are so far attested only for girls and women.

The types of jewelry attested for both sexes are those often produced specifically for the burial and placed on the deceased. This is an observation not only of the late Middle Kingdom but also of other periods of ancient Egyptian history, especially the First Intermediate Period.[94] This funerary jewelry included broad collars, necklaces, armlets, and anklets.

In this context it might be asked whether Egyptian women were treated as just "the sex object sought by all men and women"[95] or whether they put on jewelry for each other and for themselves. This is a question I cannot answer at the moment, as all of the literature that might provide information seems to have been written by men and would therefore reflect their view. The description of the rowing women dressed in nets for the pleasure of the king, described in the Westcar Papyrus,[96] might too easily support the view that women's jewelry and costumes were mainly sexual objects of men. In the same story, however, one of the women is very keen on getting back her own personal adornment after it has fallen into the water, and the story thus provides us with two different insights into how jewelry was seen by Egyptians.

CHAPTER 4

The Development of
Egyptian Burial Customs

In most periods of ancient Egyptian history burials include items from two types of objects—funerary and daily life—and the burial equipment of Egyptian tombs always represents interaction between them. In burials of the ruling class funerary objects are more common, while further down the social ladder in the graves of the broader population these funerary objects become rarer. In the cemeteries of the royal residence objects of a funerary industry are always common, while in many periods they are not so common in provincial cemeteries, even in burials of people of the highest social status.

The products of a funerary industry are often inscribed (e.g., coffins) and provide us with at least a vague idea of the concept of the afterlife and the next world as they were seen by certain people at a given time. It is much more difficult to gain a fair idea of whether the broader population had the same ideas or whether they had a different model for the next world. The different burial goods placed in the burials of the broader population in the late Middle Kingdom and also in other periods might indicate that they had a different model. In very general terms it seems unlikely that the broader population had the same precise views of the underworld as those articulated in the funerary literature of the ruling classes and visible in the court type burials. In his radical redefinition of folklore, Antonio Gramsci noted that the "subaltern classes" were not able to produce an elaborate concept of the world. They were too burdened to have the space and time to develop their own unified view of the world.[1] This might to a certain extent explain the high variability of objects in burials of the broader population. On the other hand, it might equally be doubted whether most members of the ruling class had a concrete and refined image of the underworld. They did, however, have access to funerary literature and to specialists with access to that literature. Therefore, they had people preparing for them everything needed for a proper transition into the next world, at least from the point of view of the specialists. This included the objects of a funerary industry. The specialist is the ancient Egyptian equivalent of Gramsci's "traditional intellectual,"[2] the member of society assigned the task of composing a worldview for those dominant in that society.

As a result, burials of the wider population often look very different from those of the ruling classes. They often do not contain many objects of a funerary industry, even in cases where the objects may have been affordable. Instead, in all periods up to the Ramesside Period objects that were close to the body during life dominate the burial assemblages of people of the broader population, and also burials in the provinces. These consist of jewelry and cosmetic objects for women and sometimes weapons and some jewelry for men.[3] Burials of the poorest often lack any grave goods.[4] Burials of the broader population also often look very different over the centuries, not because of fundamental changes in burial customs, but because the material culture changed and different objects were worn on the body in different periods.

In contrast, substantial developments are visible in terms of objects of a funerary industry. The objects most likely reflect changes in rituals performed at the funeral or around the mummy and perhaps also changes in beliefs in the underworld in general. The following brief survey of Egyptian burial customs provides an overview, with special attention to undisturbed burials of women. It also tries to place the burials of the late Middle Kingdom in context and to explain some typical features of these burials.

THE PREDYNASTIC AND EARLY
DYNASTIC PERIODS (3500–2700 BCE)

The graves in the Predynastic Period were often simple and equipped with objects already used in daily life. People were placed in holes dug into the ground; only a handful of more elaborate tombs are known. Proper tomb architecture on a wider scale is not known until the Early Dynastic Period, when at centers such as Memphis substantial funerary palaces were built.[5] In both periods, even in the burials of the poorest, grave goods were still provided and mostly consisted of pottery vessels. Women had some jewelry and cosmetic objects; in burials of men weapons and tools were sometimes placed. Confirming the social and gender identity of the tomb owner seems to be the most important point in these graves.[6] Richer burials could even contain furniture and games. Objects specially made for the tomb are rare and often not easy to identify. Coffins were certainly made for the burial. In this period the first signs of mummification can be found. Model vessels, model granaries, and model boats also appear, certainly products of an early funerary industry. They copy types of objects used in daily life.[7]

Two burials, perhaps both of women, bear describing. Abydos was of special importance already in the Naqada Period (4000 to 3000 BCE), with several hundred graves dating to this time. The Naqada Period was the most important Predynastic culture in Upper Egypt, in many ways paving the way for Dynastic Egypt. At Abydos one undisturbed burial of an adult woman was found in a small shaft, just about 1 m deep and about 1.2 m long. The woman was placed there in a contracted (fetal) position and covered with a reed mat. Near the head was found a flint knife. There were traces of copper or malachite and perhaps of lead. At the head and on the west side of the grave several pottery vessels were found. The most remarkable find, however, was a diadem at the head of the women. It is so far the earliest example of this type of personal adornment found in ancient Egypt. At the back of the head there was only a simple string of beads. At the front there were four strings of beads, once perhaps placed on a cloth. One wonders whether this was some kind of veil. The beads are made of gold, garnet, and turquoise.[8]

Naga ed-Deir is a site in Upper Egypt not far across the river from the better known Abydos. Here cemeteries were excavated, mainly dating from the Predynastic Period to the First Intermediate Period. Tomb 1532 belongs to the First Dynasty and was found intact, with the burial of a person, most likely a woman, richly adorned with golden jewelry.[9] The tomb itself consisted of five underground chambers built of mud bricks. The middle chamber was the largest, and here was found the body of the deceased. On either short end were two smaller storage chambers filled with pottery. The remains of the skeleton show that the deceased was placed in a contracted position with the head to the south and the arms in front of the face. Most personal adornments were found around the area of the head (the skull was not preserved). On the head was a simple golden diadem. The other jewelry found includes an array of necklaces. The beads were made of gold, garnet, and carnelian as well as white and black stones. There are twenty-four shells made of beaten gold leaf. Remarkable is a gazelle made of beaten gold and a bull made in the same way, perhaps both intended to be worn as pendants. A larger golden object was some kind of small container in the shape of a big beetle with the sign of the goddess Neith on it (a double beetle with two crossed arrows). The gold work is of high quality; nothing similar is known from the Early Dynastic Period or the Old Kingdom. However, some of the few other examples we have of high-quality personal adornments of about the same time were discovered in the tomb of King Djer at Abydos and should be mentioned in this context.[10] Four bracelets were found attached to an arm. They are made of pieces of lapis lazuli, turquoise, and gold. It had been argued that the arm belonged to the mummy of a woman.[11] Looking at the high number of personal adornments on the mummy of Tutankhamun, however, there seems no problem assigning the arm to King Djer.[12]

THE OLD KINGDOM (2700–2300 BCE)

In the Old Kingdom, a stark contrast is visible for the first time between burials of the ruling class at the royal residences and those of the rest of the population. The burials of the ruling class contained a selection of objects of a funerary industry: the coffin or sarcophagus, the four canopic jars, model tools, and model vessels. This is clearly visible in the Fourth Dynasty burials at Gizeh, excavated and published by Hermann Junker. These burials belong to the highest state officials of the Fourth Dynasty. They contained many dummy vessels and model tools.[13] The body of the deceased was adorned with only a small selection of jewelry, at least some of which was specially made for the tomb.[14] Burials below that highest social level often contained only very few objects, some pottery vessels and perhaps some jewelry.[15] A large number of tombs were devoid of goods, containing only the body of the deceased, perhaps wrapped in linen; this type of tomb can be found even for people of some standing.

Burials of the ruling class in the provinces also contained only objects taken from daily life and are therefore markedly different from those of the ruling class at the royal residence.[16]

Inscriptions were rare in burials of the classical Old Kingdom. They were restricted to the aboveground mastaba and the chapels of rock-cut tombs where the cult of the deceased was performed.[17]

The mastabas of the ruling classes in the cemeteries of the royal residence, and also in the provinces, were often decorated with reliefs or, less often, with paintings. They show the tomb owner in front of an offering table. This was the most essential decorated part of a mastaba, and tombs with little other decoration were at least adorned with this depiction. Where the tombs had more decoration, these further scenes show the tomb owner and his wife in front of offering bearers, and other depictions show the production of food and craftsmen working. Evidently, the eternal food supply and the supply of material goods were seen as essential and were guaranteed by placing scenes in the aboveground chambers of the mastabas.[18] The underground parts of the tombs were in contrast less important and often simply contained the body of the deceased.

There is evidently a break in burial customs at the beginning of the Fourth Dynasty. Before this period graves were filled with objects from daily life. In contrast, in the Fourth and Fifth Dynasties there were almost no burial goods at all in most burials of the broader population. If social identity was still the most important point in these burials, an impression emerges that a large part of the population had become extremely poor. Indeed, some researchers have argued that this poverty relates to the pyramids being built at this time, with all resources of the country being transferred to the royal cemeteries.[19] As we have seen, however, there are not many burial goods in the burials of wealthy people either. The restriction of burial goods was therefore not a sign of poverty but a deliberate choice.[20]

Next to these burials of the highest ruling class were those of the wider population. They did not have a decorated tomb chapel, and it remains a matter of speculation how these people secured their eternal sustenance. Possibly certain rituals even for the poorest were performed (by family members?) or certain burial goods such as vessels normally used in rituals were placed next to the deceased. With such vessels these rituals were at least symbolically performed for all eternity.[21]

Gizeh is the location of Egypt's greatest pyramids, dating to the Fourth

Dynasty, and it is the site of an extensive cemetery of about the same period. Here were buried the officials serving the kings who had their pyramids at this place. Here too, however, are many tombs dating to after the
time of the great pyramids. The cemetery was still important, although
kings after the Fourth Dynasty were buried somewhere else. Within the
mastaba complex of the important Fifth Dynasty official Rawer, excavated
by the Egyptian Egyptologist Selim Hassan, were many shafts, most likely
belonging to people related in some way to Rawer. Shaft 133 is 14.75 m
deep, clearly indicating that the person buried here was of some higher
social standing. Many other shafts are just a few meters deep. At the bottom of the shaft was a small chamber with a rough limestone sarcophagus.
Within the sarcophagus were found the remains of a woman, aged by the
excavators at about twenty to twenty-two years old. Her burial was found
untouched. The only burial goods found were her items of jewelry. She
was wearing two collars with round terminals and spacers in the shape of
the hieroglyphic sign for water, holding the beads. These might be broad
collars, but another option is that they are parts of a choker, well known
from Old Kingdom tomb reliefs but hard to identify in the archaeological
record.[22] The only other pieces of jewelry found were armlets and bracelets
made of strings of beads. The beads used were of expensive materials—
gold, lapis lazuli and faience—and confirm the high status of the woman.
No other burial goods are reported for this tomb.[23] The burial equipment
is restricted and not comparable to the goods placed in the Early Dynastic
tomb at Naga ed-Deir. Here the trend of reduction is clearly visible, typical of the classical Old Kingdom in the Fourth and Fifth Dynasties. It is
hard to say whether the personal adornments were products of a funerary
industry or whether they had already been worn in daily life. The same is
true for tomb 294, evidently belonging to a woman of the highest social
level and dating to the classical Old Kingdom.

   Tomb 294 was an undisturbed shaft within an Old Kingdom mastaba
at Gizeh. It too was excavated by Hassan, in his 1930–1931 excavation
season. The burial chamber of the mastaba contained a large number of
pottery and stone vessels, most of them dummies or models. They were
either far too small to have been of use in real life or, in the case of many
stone vessels, were not really hollowed out, being just stones in the shape
of a vessel, but otherwise solid. There were two larger, bottle-like, real
vessels, and finally there were two vessels of Palestinian origin. In a niche
in the southern wall of the burial chamber were found five bowls made of

fine red clay, of a type called "Meydum ware" because this type of pottery was first documented at the pyramid site of Meydum. It was the finest pottery produced in the Old Kingdom and was perhaps some kind of fine tableware, but it was also often found at temple sites and therefore used in the temple cults.[24] South of the sarcophagus were the bones of a bull and of a bird, evidently some kind of funerary meal. Next to these was found an alabaster offering table with remains of food and offerings still on it. Inside the rough and uninscribed sarcophagus was found a collection of Old Kingdom jewelry. The woman buried here, preserved only as a skeleton, had a golden diadem on her head. It measures 3.8 cm wide and 25 cm in diameter and has three golden disks as decoration. The middle one is round and shows a floral motive or rosette. The other two are in the form of two papyrus flowers with two birds on top of the flowers. Around the neck was found a necklace consisting of fifty golden elements representing beetles. These beetles are perhaps related to the goddess Neith, and they placed the woman buried here under the protection of the goddess. They relate to the beetle found in the burial at Naga ed-Deir.[25] There was also a choker with two rounded terminals and spacers in between in the form of the hieroglyphic sign for water. On her left arm the woman wore a simple golden wire with one agate bead. On the right arm were two armlets, of which the two gold-covered clasps survived. Similar anklets were found at the feet. The whole body was found covered with beads evidently once belonging to a dress covered with a bead net, also known from other burials.[26]

THE END OF THE OLD KINGDOM AND THE FIRST INTERMEDIATE PERIOD (2300–2000 BCE)

In the late Old Kingdom more attention was given to the underground parts of the tomb. More objects were placed in the burial chamber, and the type of objects changed. Now there were a large number of funerary items, most likely made specifically for the tomb or used in rituals related to the tomb. These include meat containers made of stone, shaped as the pieces of meat they contained for the eternal food supply,[27] wood and metal offering tables, and model vessels of metal and pottery.[28] Personal adornments were found in several tombs, specially made for the burial. Some tombs contained model wooden figures showing the production of food and representing craftsmen. An important point is that these types of burial also now appear in the provinces and are no longer restricted to a small number of people buried around the king. In the late Old Kingdom, inscriptions and images became important for the burial chamber too. Coffins bore offering formulae, and some burial chambers were adorned with pictures of offerings and granaries as well as lists of offerings.

The burials of the broader population contained a large number of objects already used in daily life. Women were buried with their jewelry, men of some standing were sometimes provided with weapons (bows and arrows), not to indicate that they had been soldiers in daily life, but as status markers. Pottery vessels for the eternal food supply were still important. In these burials confirming and preserving the social identity of the deceased was important.[29] Evidently these burials continued a burial tradition already known from the Naqada Period and the Early Dynastic Period.

Tomb 1316 at Matmar dates to the beginning of the First Intermediate Period and seems to belong to a wealthy woman who lived in a provincial town or village. The cemetery was excavated by Guy Brunton in the 1930s. The burial was found undisturbed, most likely because the roof of the burial chamber had collapsed before a potential looter could enter the tomb. The tomb consists of a shaft about 14 m deep. At the bottom of the shaft there is a small niche where seven pottery vessels were found, all of them closed with mud. Next to them was the entrance to the burial chamber, closed by a brick wall. Inside the burial chamber were found the remains of a wooden coffin, with the skeleton of a woman lying on her left side with her hands in front of her pelvis. Under her head was a limestone headrest already repaired in ancient times and therefore most likely an object used in daily life. In front of her face was a quartzite grinder, perhaps for grinding cosmetic powder. On the coffin a cosmetic box must have once stood, but only some metal fittings were found. In the remains of the box were a mirror and two alabaster vases, the latter most likely for some cosmetic powder or ointments. The woman was richly adorned with jewelry. Around her neck were six strings of beads made of different materials. Also on these necklaces were several amulets made of gold representing a face, a hawk, two crowns, and a uraeus. An outstanding piece found here was a golden seal. Furthermore, the woman was wearing bead bracelets and at least one bead anklet, the latter with a carnelian leg pendant.[30]

Already visible in this burial are some elements found in later court type burials of royal women. Except for the coffin, all objects in the burial were most likely used in daily life. The placement of an additional box for cosmetic objects directly next to the dead woman is also common in the court type burials of the Twelfth Dynasty. Although this particular box did not contain personal adornments, there are other examples of about the same time containing jewelry. The mirror and cosmetic vessels are typical objects found in the boxes of the later tombs.

Qau, also known as Qau el-Kebir, was a town in Middle Egypt. It is well known for the monumental tombs of local Middle Kingdom governors.[31] In addition, it has many other cemeteries of almost all periods of Egyptian history. Many of them have been excavated and provide one of the most important sources for provincial burial customs. Tomb 1735 at Qau belongs to the end of the First Intermediate Period and was found undisturbed. The burial was placed in a small chamber at the bottom of a shaft. The remains of an adult woman were found in a badly decayed coffin covered with plaster. She was richly adorned with jewelry. At her neck was a long string of carnelian beads; there were blue ring beads and beads of other materials. There were also three golden amulets: an ibis, a wedjat eye, and a lotus flower. On her right wrist the woman wore an armlet of dark carnelian barrel beads. At her ankles were found anklets of dark glazed beads with carnelian pendants in the shape of legs. Two scarabs most likely once belonged to the necklace. Next to the coffin were just three vessels, two made of pottery and one of alabaster.[32] Small pendants often made of carnelian are typical of the First Intermediate Period and were found mainly in burials of women. They were parts of strings often attached to the body part they represent. They most likely had the function of protecting these parts and had already been used in daily life.

THE EARLY MIDDLE KINGDOM (2000–1850 BCE)

In the early Middle Kingdom the trends of the First Intermediate Period continued. In burials of the ruling class, the deceased wore a mummy mask and was adorned with jewelry specially made for the tomb. There was a broad collar and, anklets and armlets. There were further objects specially made for the tomb, such as wooden sandals, and in some burials royal insignia, such as staves and weapons.[33] This type of burial was quite widespread, although it is hard to define the lowest social level still able to afford this type of burial.[34] At a higher social level coffins were often decorated on the inside with depictions of offerings and burial goods, and also with long religious texts, some of them already known from the pyramids of Old Kingdom kings, others appearing here for the first time. They provide an insight into beliefs in the afterlife. Many of these texts were most likely spoken at rituals at the funeral. In these burials of the regional ruling classes were placed a large number of objects from local funerary workshops, such as fully decorated coffins and wooden models showing the production of food, pottery, leatherwork, and so on. Even in the early Middle Kingdom, however, there were burials without such wooden models. The two best-recorded examples are the burial of the lady Ankhet from Lisht and the burial of the "storeroom overseer" Wah from Thebes, which basically contained only the coffin, the mummified body of Wah, his jewelry, and a statue.[35]

The burials of poorer people changed little during the early Middle Kingdom. They were still equipped with daily life objects, especially jewelry for women and perhaps for men. There were some pottery vessels for the eternal food supply for both sexes. It is clearly the social identity of the deceased that is most important.[36]

From the Eleventh Dynasty comes the burial of a young girl named Mayet ("the cat") (Fig. 92). She was buried at the bottom of a shaft within the funerary temple of King Mentuhotep II at Deir el-Bahari. Her inscribed coffin does not bear any titles, but it seems clear that she was in some way related to the king and the royal court. She was placed in a sarcophagus adorned with funerary formulae mentioning her name. Inside the sarcophagus was a wooden coffin inscribed with similar types of texts. Mayet herself was wrapped in linen. Her head was covered with a plaster mummy mask. Her jewelry consisted of an array of necklaces. There was a string of hollow gold balls, a string of carnelian beads, one consisting of small golden disks, and two other necklaces consisting of silver, carnelian, green feldspar, and glazed beads.[37] The inscriptions on the coffin give an idea of what was seen as essential for Mayet's afterlife. On the front of her wooden inner coffin the inscription relates to the eternal food supply given by Osiris, consisting of a voice offering of thousands of bread loaves, bears, cattle, birds, and linen. On the back of the coffin Anubis is described as granting a "beautiful burial before the great god, lord of heaven." Finally, on the lid Anubis is described as providing access to the "beautiful ways in the necropolis."[38] The burial of Mayet was found next to the burials of five women, all with the titles "king's beloved wife," "sole king's

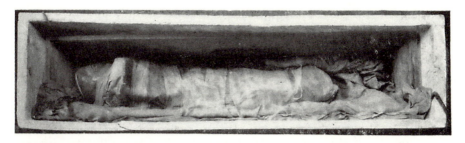

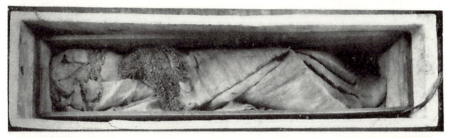

92. The coffin and mummy of Mayet as they were found.
From Winlock 1921, pl. 11.

ornament," and "priestess of Hathor." These burials were found looted, but that of Aashyt still contained beads from necklaces, shell bracelets, and two silver bead anklets. The impressions of her personal adornments were still found in the bandages that protected the mummy. Her burial is not yet fully published.[39]

Perhaps from about the same time comes the burial of a woman found at Sedment. Sedment is a modern village at the entrance to the Fayum where several burial grounds from the end of the First Intermediate Period and the New Kingdom were excavated. Burial 1512 is just a simple shaft, about 3 m deep. At the bottom of the shaft was the body of a woman with her head to the north looking to the east. Her head was covered with a mummy mask, but there were no signs of any coffin. The only burial goods other than the mummy mask are a broad collar made of faience beads and two anklets. The simple tomb architecture and the simple burial equipment stand in stark contrast to the woman's personal adornments.[40]

From the reign of Senusret I comes the burial of a woman named Ankhet, mentioned above. She was buried at Lisht, close to the pyramid of the king. Her tomb consists of a shaft about 5 m deep with a chamber, both roughly hewn into the rock. Ankhet, an elderly woman, was placed in a coffin decorated on the inside with long religious texts. The body was wrapped in several layers of linen. The outer layer of wrappings consisted of coarse linen, with the limbs not wrapped separately. Under that were nine layers of linen shawls and then several layers of fine linen shawls below them. After the mummy was placed in the coffin a black pitch-like substance was poured over the mummy. The brain was not removed from the mummy, and the body was treated with a salt solution and a dark oily unguent. The body of Ankhet was too badly preserved for us to be able to gain further information on the mummification.[41] Over her head within the wrappings was a mummy mask, and around her neck was a string of beads with 1,095 glazed disk beads. On her chest was a mirror and a wooden model of a hes vase, and there was a wooden headrest under her head. Next to the coffin were two jars and three cups.[42] The whole burial gives a simple impression. Many of the objects in the tomb, however, were most likely specially made for the burial. The exceptions are perhaps the necklace, the headrest, and the mirror, although headrests specially made for burials are well attested.[43] The pottery might also be taken from daily life. In some ways this burial is similar to that of Satip, who was also placed in a wooden coffin covered with religious texts and had most objects in her tomb specially made for the burial, none of them of any great value in terms of materials.

Another Middle Kingdom burial was found at Abydos and was numbered 1008 by the excavator Henry Frankfort. His report on the tomb is very short. According to it, Frankfort found the remains of a young woman with her head to the east and looking up. In the burial a mirror and several beads of silver, gold, garnet, and carnelian were found. There were also one silver and four golden cowry-shaped shells. These are all typical Middle Kingdom personal adornments. Remarkable is a metal wire in ring form for wearing around the neck, known as a torque.[44]

THE LATE MIDDLE KINGDOM (1850–1650 BCE)

The late Middle Kingdom saw a radical change in burial customs. Wooden models showing the production of food and other items are no longer present, and the coffins are no longer decorated on the inside.[45] At the royal residence, court type burials are common at the highest social level, while at all other places, for burials of all classes, not only of people of a lower social level, objects of daily life now dominate the tomb equipment. Next to these daily life objects, some wealthy tombs included products of a new funerary industry. These are the first shabtis, the first heart scarabs, and models of food.[46] Other objects, such as faience figures of animals and magical wands, appear sporadically in the tombs of the period.[47] These are most likely magical objects, already used in daily life and not specially made for burials.[48]

Because the burials of the late Middle Kingdom are the main subject of this book as a whole, they are not discussed in detail in this chapter. Instead, the most important objects placed in the burials of this period are presented, with brief discussions of their meaning in these burials. In order to gain a fuller picture, some tombs of the period belonging to men are also presented.

According to the evidence from Harageh (pp. 100–102), three major burial types can be distinguished in the archaeological record for the late Middle Kingdom. They range from the court type burials containing many products of a funerary industry to those with no such objects.[49]

Type 1: Court Type Burials

In the burials of royal and highest-status women, products of a funerary industry predominate. These objects were made specifically for the burial or for rituals related to it. The object types include weapons and royal insignia, but also often the jewelry and perhaps the pottery found in the burials. These women were most likely all properly mummified. Canopic jars and canopic boxes are always part of the funerary equipment. Court type burials of the late Middle Kingdom are attested only in cemeteries of the royal residence (Lisht, Dahshur, Hawara).

Court Type Burials of Men

Alongside the examples of women's burials of this type it should be re-
membered that contemporary court type burials are also well attested for
men and must be included in the discussion to provide a fuller picture
of the burial customs of the period. Few tombs of rich men were found
intact, however, making it hard to compare burials of men with those of
women. The most important example is the tomb of King Awibre Hor,[50]
a ruler of the early Thirteenth Dynasty. His burial has much in common
with the burials of the royal women discussed. The king was buried in a
stone-lined underground burial chamber at the bottom of a shaft next to
the pyramid of King Amenemhat III at Dahshur (Fig. 93). Alongside his
burial was found that of Nubhetepti-khered. Pyramids are still attested in
the Thirteenth Dynasty for kings, and so Awibre Hor presumably reigned
only for a short time and was not able to prepare a pyramid. The body of
the king was placed in a wooden coffin adorned with gold foil, which was
then placed in an undecorated sarcophagus. The coffin was almost identical to that of Nubhetepti-khered. The body of the king was not placed in
an anthropoid coffin but had a mummy mask, originally gilded. On his left
side were found the typical weapons and royal insignia. The mummy[51] was
adorned with a broad collar and some other personal adornments, such as
a wooden rosette, partly gilded and perhaps once belonging to a diadem.
He also had a royal apron.[52] Armlets and anklets are missing, possibly because the tomb was partly looted, but these personal adornments may
have been more typical for women. Next to the sarcophagus was a wooden
shrine with a wooden statue of the king, again with tools and weapons, and
two stelae, one inscribed with an offering formula and the other with Pyra-

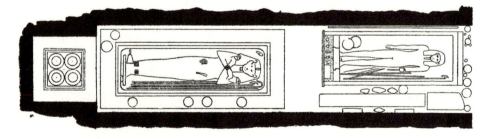

93. The tomb chamber of King Awibre Hor as it was found.
From de Morgan 1895, fig. 211.

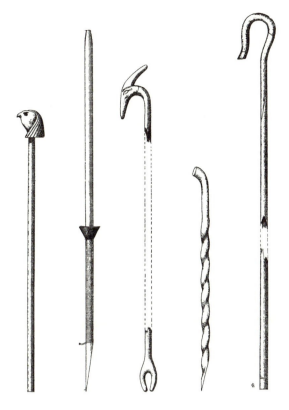

94. Some of the staves found in the tomb of King Awibre Hor. From de Morgan 1895, figs. 221–25.

mid Texts. There were also several pottery and wooden model vessels. In general, this burial seems similar to those of the royal women. Rich personal adornments are missing, but this might be due the fact that at one point robbers entered the tomb chamber. The burial is clearly a court type burial, as it was equipped with royal regalia (Fig. 94).

The burial of the "co-ordinator of the temple staff" Sawadjet was found at Riqqeh. He was placed in a set of three coffins, two outer rectangular ones and an inner anthropoid one. The outer coffin was richly decorated on the inside with friezes of objects, typical of coffins of the early Middle Kingdom. Next to the deceased on his left were two *was* scepters, a stick, and a flail. These were once gilded. The deceased was not adorned with any jewelry. There were many pottery vessels in the tomb.[53] The burial of Sawadjet is the only well-preserved court type burial of a nonroyal man. Although the burial does not have the full range of objects found in the burials of the royal women, there are several staves and a flail typical of court type burials. Sawadjet was placed in a set of three coffins, the outer one decorated on the inside with friezes of objects. The innermost coffin was anthropoid. Other court type burials of men are attested too, but most of them have been looted. One example is the tomb of the "chief lecture priest" Sesenebnef at Lisht. He was placed in two fully decorated coffins and provided with a canopic box containing canopic jars. He was also equipped with staves and royal insignia. Nothing survived of any personal adornments.[54]

Osirification

In court type burials certain objects seem to be, in a broad sense, related to ritual. This means that they were most likely used in rituals performed at the mummification. An account of one of the most important Egyptian myths is needed for an understanding of the rituals related to court type burials. In early times, Osiris was king over Egypt. He was married to his sister Isis and they had a son, Horus. Their brother was Seth, who was jealous of his brother and finally murdered Osiris as he wanted to become king of Egypt himself. He cut his brother's body into pieces and buried them all over Egypt. After the death of Osiris, Isis searched for his corpse and succeeded in reassembling it. Isis brought up Horus to avenge his father, and when Horus was older, he fought against his uncle Seth to punish him for murdering his father. Horus and other gods came to help Isis, and Osiris was brought back to life to become ruler of the underworld, while Horus followed his father and became ruler of Egypt.[55]

At the point at which Isis had reassembled Osiris, his corpse was placed in the embalming tent to be mummified. Several gods came to help in this process. The end of the mummification, the placing of the mummy in the coffin and the rituals around it, are known from Ptolemaic and Roman period temple texts as the hour vigil. In the twelve hours of the night and the twelve hours of the day, every hour a group of deities came forward to perform specific rituals of embalming. Many texts on Middle Kingdom coffins seem to refer to this.[56] Finally Horus came and brought Osiris back to life, a moment also known from many later depictions in burial chambers and on coffins (Fig. 95). Osiris is shown lying on a funerary bed with Horus in front of him placing at his nose the ankh sign (the symbol for life). The important point for this book is that a collection of crowns, staves, and royal symbols is always shown under the funerary bed. These items are identical to those found in the court type burials. From this depiction of Osiris it is clear that the deceased in court type burials was identified as, or at least treated like, Osiris,[57] most likely in the hour vigil. In this context, a depiction of King Merenptah on his sarcophagus lid found at Tanis should be mentioned (Fig. 96). It shows the dead king as Osiris adorned with many of the items also found in the court type burials. He wears a broad collar, a dagger, the apron, the *heqa* scepter, and the flail. The text next to this image starts with "Wake up!" and continues, "may you appear as Osiris . . . in your hand is the heqa scepter, in your hand is the flail."[58]

95. King Sheshonq III as Osiris on a embalming bed with Horus in front of him, bringing Osiris back to life. Under the bed are depicted royal insignia. From Montet 1951, pl. XXX.

Other objects placed in the burial chamber of the royal women relate to the hour vigil too. Among the relevant spells on coffins, the most important involve the four children of Horus taking care of the deceased's limbs and Isis and Nephthys taking care of the body. Other texts on coffins, however, are more concerned with the journey of the deceased to the sky and the correct placement of the deceased in the underworld.[59]

Some of the staves found in the court type burials are reported to have been found broken,[60] which perhaps relates to rituals performed around the mummy in the embalming tent at the hour vigil. The whole hour vigil was perhaps performed at the end of the mummification process or was part of it in the embalming tent. Therefore these staves can be regarded as leftovers from rituals as well as objects important for preserving the identity of the deceased's body as Osiris. The rituals around the burial of the deceased are quite well known from several depictions in tombs from almost all periods of ancient Egyptian history.[61] The hour vigil is not so

96. The figure of King Merenptah as Osiris on his sarcophagus (Cairo Museum, JE 87797B). Osiris is equipped with a flail and a heqa scepter. He wears an apron to which a dagger is attached. Drawn by the author after Montet 1951, pl. LXXVI.

prominent in these depictions, but it seems that it was seen, especially in the late Middle Kingdom, as an extremely important part of burial at the royal court. It was evidently the most critical moment for bringing the deceased back to life in the underworld.

Although these insignia and weapons are in other contexts associated with gender and in many cultures more typical for burials of men, they appear as ritual objects in late Middle Kingdom tombs of women. In this context they are not gender related[62] but confirm the identity of the deceased as Osiris, and clearly show that the deceased was treated as Osiris in rituals.[63] This treatment as the king of the underworld may be most visible in instances in the late Middle Kingdom where a private mummy mask was adorned with royal insignia, such as a uraeus[64] or a vulture,[65] normally part of a royal crown. The mummy mask with its decoration was evidently an object confirming the new identity of the deceased in the underworld.

Social Identity in the Court Type Burials of Women

In some of the court type burials of women jewelry boxes and cosmetic boxes were also found. They contained items of jewelry worn in daily life, and their main function was most likely to maintain the social identity of these women. As some of them were royal women, they had items with king's names, perhaps presents from the king but also status symbols confirming their link to a ruler. In some court type burials, however, no jewelry boxes were found. In the case of Senebtisi it seems possible that her personal adornments were placed next to the funerary adornments on the mummy. The necklaces and hair adornments on her mummy indicate that they were daily life adornments. For certain other burials, such as those of Nefruptah or Nubhetepti-khered, the evidence is not so clear. Their mummies were equipped with fewer personal adornments, but that might relate to the inadequate recording of these burials and bad preservation conditions.

It seems clear that jewelry was a display of prestige and power.[66] The materials used in much of the jewelry are exactly those described in texts of the late Middle Kingdom and the Second Intermediate Period as being the most prestigious ones: "O, yet gold, lapis lazuli, silver, turquoise, garnet, amethyst, diorite (?) our . . . have been hung on the necks of maidservants."[67] This passage comes from the "Dialogue of Ipuwer" where Ipuwer complains to the Lord of All about the inversion of the social order. Several precious materials are named with the complaint that they are in the hands of "common" people.

Protection in Court Type Burials

Few amulets were found in court type burials. It therefore seems that the protection of the deceased against evil spirits did not play any major role in equipping these tombs. Some of the jewelry in these burials, however, might have had the function of protecting the deceased or parts of the body. An example is the bird claw amulets found in several jewelry boxes. Their function is unknown, but perhaps they offered protection for the legs, most likely already in daily life but also in the underworld. The shen ring, often found as a pendant for a necklace in tombs of both sexes, was perhaps also an amulet offering protection, already worn in life.

There are a few other objects in the court type burials offering protection and most likely made for the tomb. In the burial of Nubhetepti-khered a sa sign was found. In hieroglyphs the symbol means "protection." The sa sign appears also in the frieze of objects on the coffin of Sawadjet and a few other coffins.[68] Indeed, the frieze of objects on Sawadjet's coffin is remarkable. It shows several items otherwise only found in court type burials, such as an apron, a figure of a goose or swan, and a swallow pendant. Finally, Senebtisi had a necklace made from different sa signs, offering her, in a very direct way, multiple protection. It is not clear whether the necklace was specially made for the tomb or was already worn in life.

Protection in the court type burials was therefore mostly a matter of the tomb architecture, best visible in the elaborate architecture of the burials around the pyramid of Amenemhat II and their placement without superstructure around the pyramid of Senusret II. Most other related objects in these tombs are better classified as amulets, many also providing protection for the living.

Type 2: Burials with Objects of a Funerary Industry

Below the court type burials belonging to people of royal and highest social status are burials of people of high social standing but perhaps not so closely related to the royal court. Their burials include a number of products of a funerary industry but lack the set of royal insignia (examples include tomb 129, Teti pyramid cemetery; Satip; and many burials excavated at Harageh).[69] These tombs contain decorated coffins, sometimes a mummy mask, and sometimes a canopic box with canopic jars. This indicates that these women were also most often mummified.[70] The jewelry found in these burials was again often made just for the tomb. These tombs are mainly known from the cemeteries in the Memphite and Fayum regions, but also from Abydos and Thebes. Examples from other parts of the country are rare, although the late Middle Kingdom is in general not well documented in cemeteries around the country. This is reflected in the fact that most decorated coffins of the period come from the centers mentioned, but not from the provinces.

Burials of Men

For comparison, two burials of men will be described. The undisturbed coffin of the "great one of Upper Egypt" Renseneb was discovered at Thebes within a disturbed shaft tomb with two chambers and several burials. At the time of the excavation, the tomb still contained an important collection of objects, notably a carved wooden box of an official called Kemni, shown in front of King Amenemhat IV. There was also a finely crafted gaming board, with gaming pieces consisting of pegs with heads of hounds and jackals. Most of the burials within the tomb were found heavily disturbed, and it remains problematic to reconstruct their original arrangement. The coffin of Renseneb, however, was intact, although badly decayed. It was inscribed on the outside. Within it lay the body of Renseneb adorned with a mummy mask. For jewelry, he wore a necklace consisting of ball beads made of a dark stone, each of them adorned with two golden caps and a pendant in the shape of a shen ring.[71] Other finds in the coffin were a mirror and the figure of a hippopotamus.[72] Further necklaces found in the tomb are not clearly connected with the coffin of Renseneb and may belong to the other people buried here.[73] A comparable but less well recorded burial was found at Abydos. It belonged to the "overseer of Lower Egypt" Nakht. Not much is known about this tomb, as only some of the objects found were published in the short excavation report. These included a necklace similar to the one found in the burial of Renseneb. There are faience beads, again with a cap on either side and a shen ring pendant. Two stone eyes indicate that there was once a mummy mask or anthropoid coffin. Further finds are one mummiform figure providing the name and title of the official and several alabaster vessels.[74]

In type 2 burials the deceased was still buried with objects of a funerary industry. The deceased has a decorated coffin and funerary jewelry, such as broad collars. Some of these burials also contained an array of personal adornments (such as Harageh tomb 124). These people, however, were not equipped with staves and weapons in the same way as the women and men in court type burials. Whether this is a deliberate choice or relates to insufficient resources must remain an open question. These burials relate closely to burials of the First Intermediate Period and the early Middle Kingdom, generally being similarly equipped[75] (compare the burials of Mayet and Ankhet). Here, then, there seems to be a continuous tradition going back to the First Intermediate Period. Evidently these women were also adorned as godlike beings, but the objects relating to the hour vigil are missing. The burial goods had the main function of protecting the body (the coffin and canopic jars) and maintaining the social identity of a godlike being (the mummy mask and funerary jewelry). Perhaps these women did not have the resources for the performance of an hour vigil while their body was being embalmed. The decorated coffins and other objects, however, show that they had some wealth. The two burials of men show a wider range of objects. Coffins, mummy masks, and the shabti are items of a funerary industry, but the personal adornments seem to be taken from daily life. The same is true of the box in the burial of Renseneb and the hounds and jackals game.

Type 3: Burials Without Objects
of a Funerary Industry

In the third group of burials (most burials of Chapter 2) presented here, most objects were taken directly from life. There are almost no objects of a funerary industry. The only exception is the coffin, always undecorated.[76] Personal adornments and cosmetic objects are often the only burial goods. There are many other burials of the same type with little or no jewelry, however. In this group the jewelry was most likely already worn in life. It seems remarkable that most of these burials concentrate on jewelry and cosmetic objects. Other object types such as faience figures and magical wands are known for contemporary burials but are rarely connected with expensive personal adornments. In the older literature[77] these items were regarded as typical of burials of the period, but they are in fact not all that common.[78] The expensive jewelry found indicates that the women had some resources. Therefore, the increased amount of jewelry in the burial equipment was a deliberate choice, and resources were not spent on funerary products. These burials do not have canopic jars or canopic boxes. It is thus uncertain whether these women (or men) were properly mummified or just wrapped in linen. Indeed, at least in the Middle Kingdom, mummification was most likely not essential for having an afterlife, as Harco Willems has argued.[79] This type of burial is known from all parts of the country.

In these burials the only point (at least the only one visible in the archaeological records) was evidently to maintain social identity in the next life. As I have already outlined, this type of burial is known from the oldest farming culture in Upper Egypt, the Naqada culture (around 4000 BCE) through to the New Kingdom and was always a common burial type for the broader population.[80]

Summary for the Late Middle Kingdom

According to the evidence from Harageh (and to a lesser extent from Hu), the three types of burials presented are certainly not as clear-cut as might at first appear. The borders between these groups are fluid. The types are essentially a spectrum of burial choices, from burials with a large number of objects exclusively made for burial to graves containing only objects taken from daily life. A burial with an array of jewelry already worn in daily life might also contain a large number of objects made for the tomb, specially coffins and mummy masks. This range might also reflect the social spread of mummification in the late Middle Kingdom. The deceased in burials with a large number of products of a funerary industry (types 1 and 2) were most likely also mummified. People having only daily life objects were less likely to be mummified. Furthermore, Harageh was the cemetery of a wealthy community, and it contains a high proportion of burials with products of a funerary industry. Other cemeteries provide a different picture. Objects of a funerary industry are much fewer in other cemeteries. In the Second Intermediate Period cemeteries at Qau and Badari there are hardly any, just some stuccoed coffins and perhaps one gilded plaster mask.[81]

Throughout the Middle Kingdom, the hour vigil was an important part of the rituals around the burial, and it is still well attested in later periods.[82] It is only in the court type burials of the late Middle Kingdom, however, that so many objects involved in the ritual were placed in the tomb, right next to the mummy. Court type burials are already known from the mid-Twelfth Dynasty. One example is the burial of the local governor Djehutynakht at Deir el-Bersheh, dating perhaps to Amenemhat II. In his burial were found staves, a mace, a flail, and the royal girdle.[83] Other burials of people belonging to the ruling class, such as the tomb of the "steward" Gemniemhat found at Saqqara and dating to the early Twelfth Dynasty, contain similar objects; but it is not always clear whether these objects relate to the hour vigil and are therefore part of a court type burial or whether they belong to other royal rituals.[84] These other rituals might relate to certain Pyramid Texts and are therefore most likely royal rituals. For example, Pyramid Text spell 221 is a prayer to the royal crowns.[85] Pyramid Text spells 742–756 are spells of rituals "presenting royal insignia to the king."[86] Whether this relates to the "hour vigil" remains unknown. In this context, important Pyramid Texts were also found in the pyramid chamber of Queen Neith, wife of Pepy II. In a ritual text several objects are mentioned, most of them also well known from court type burials.[87] They include royal insignia, a dagger, a blade, an apron, a tail, and a swallow, exactly the objects placed on the mummy in the court type burials. Evidently, the religious beliefs around these objects were already around at the end of the Old Kingdom. It is again uncertain whether the objects relate to the hour vigil or are items typical of a royal burial in general.

In this context it should also be mentioned that the burial of Tutankhamun contained many of the items found in the court type burials. The king was equipped with royal insignia: an apron and two daggers were found on the mummy.[88] In the Third Intermediate Period burial of Sheshonq II at Tanis were found an apron, an amulet in the form of a swallow, and a dagger. These are all objects typical of the court type burials.[89] From the slight evidence from the tomb of Tutankhamun and the sarcophagus of Merenptah (see p. 150 and Fig. 96), it might be asked whether court type burials are essentially royal burials but in the late Middle Kingdom used by a wider range of people at the royal court. The objects discussed seem to be the crucial elements of a royal burial, best visible not only in the court type burials but also on the sarcophagus of Merenptah.

In the court type burials (type 1 burials) but also in the burials of type 2, the deceased was buried as Osiris, or at least as a godlike being. This was the main aspect of these burials, and the social identity of the deceased is visible only through the jewelry boxes and cosmetic boxes and some additional items of jewelry placed on the body. In contrast, in type 3 burials the maintenance of the social identity of women and men was the most important consideration. There are no signs that the deceased was transformed after death into a godlike being.

In an article on burials in pre-Columbian American cultures Christopher Peebles describes the deceased with their burial equipment as the "fossilized terminal statuses of individuals."[90] Whether this is indeed the crucial point is still heavily debated in archaeology. There are certainly other factors complicating the picture for the interpretation of objects placed around the body in a burial. These objects were perhaps selected not only by the deceased but also by family members or by members of the community in which the deceased lived.[91] If so, they represent the image others had of a person's identity more than that person's self-image. There may not even be one single identity for a person. Indeed, Jan Assmann has distinguished three of types of identity. There is the "individual identity," characterized by the individual life of a person and unique to that one person. Second, there is the "personal identity": the roles and functions a society assigns to an individual. Finally, there is the "collective identity": the image a group of people develops for itself.[92]

It is hard to tell which of these identities are expressed in the late Middle Kingdom burials of women. The foreign jewelry found in the burial of Khenmet and in the jewelry box of Mereret might point to the individual identity. These are most likely pieces of jewelry owned by these women and presented to them. In contrast, the other items of jewelry found in the jewelry boxes often give a rather stereotypical impression. The personal adornments found at Lahun in the burial of Sathathoriunet and in the jewelry boxes of Mereret and Sathathor have many points in common. They seem to reflect the personal identity of these women. With these personal adornments they fulfilled a certain social and religious function at the royal court, evidently expressed by their jewelry, but also by their titles preserved on some of their monuments.

The different identities are much harder to identify in the burials of the broader population (type 3). Do their personal adornments give them a certain function in their society, or did these women buy or receive their jewelry because these items appealed to their taste, or were the items given to them on special occasions, such as festivals?

While in burials of types 1 and 2 becoming or being treated as Osiris was important, in the burials of the broader population (type 3) this aspect seems to be secondary, or is at least not visible. Only the eternal food supply plays a certain role at least in a number of these burials, discernible from the large number of vessels placed in some of the tombs. Other aspects might also have played a part, but the interpretation of certain objects often remains pure speculation. Magical wands most likely had the task of protecting mother and child at birth and might have had the same function when placed in the tomb. In a wider sense they confirmed the social identity of the deceased, as these people were equipped with exactly the objects they needed most in real life. Children were highly vulnerable in life and so needed special protection in both life and death. The meaning of many animal faience figures remains obscure, but their serving a magical function protecting the deceased seems possible.[93]

It is hard to detect social identity in the late Middle Kingdom tombs of men. Some objects placed in the male burials, such as gaming boards, writing equipment, and administrative papyri, seem to testify to this. These objects, however, have also been interpreted as equipment for a journey into the next world.[94] That would mean that some men were equipped for the journey into the underworld, while the focus for contemporary women was the maintenance of social and gender status. Perhaps the gaming boards are better explained as relating to the social status of the man, as somebody who had the leisure to play games, while papyri and writing equipment might indicate his status as belonging to the literate ruling class.

It is notable that a large number of the burials with an array of expensive personal adornments are those of rather young women. Stephan Seidlmayer observed a similar pattern for Old Kingdom and First Intermediate Period burials on Elephantine. Here too, the burials of young women were often richly equipped with jewelry, while burials of older women of the same social status or even higher—visible in the tomb architecture—were often not buried with jewelry at all. He wondered whether older women had already given their personal adornments to a daughter within their lifetime.[95] This might be confirmed by some of the burials discussed in this book, even for women at a higher social level. Ankhet buried at Lisht under Senusret I was an old woman when she died. Her burial equipment includes a range of high-status products of a funerary industry, including a mummy mask and a decorated coffin. She did not, however, have any elaborate or costly personal adornments, just one simple bead necklace. The evidence indicates that at a certain social level women were buried according to their social position when they died. This could mean without jewelry, or with only a little.

The placing of expensive jewelry in burials could be interpreted as a display of prestige and power, as has been argued for the jewelry in the court type burials.[96] This interpretation seems not to work in Middle Kingdom Egypt if we look at the burials of high-status women without jewelry. The social status of these women was most likely more important than prestige and power. They were buried without personal adornments, as though they did not have any expensive jewelry when they died. They belonged to a social level where it was perhaps affordable to include in the tomb jewelry other than that which was already the property of the deceased, but these women or their family decided not to do so.

The situation is evidently slightly different for the women at the royal court. The pectorals, in particular, were certainly high-status objects, and most of them are inscribed with a royal name. They were most likely produced in a royal workshop as objects of high prestige and would have announced for all eternity a link to the king.

The main bulk of the burials of the late Middle Kingdom contained objects from daily life (type 3 burials). The remarkable point is that these burials are now attested not only for lower levels of the society but also for women of some standing at the cemeteries of the royal residence and in the provinces. The situation is similar in the Early Dynastic period, but totally different to that in the early Middle Kingdom, when objects of a funerary industry are found all around the country. Evidently, the well-attested burials in the late Middle Kingdom with daily life jewelry and without objects of a funerary industry (type 3) belong to a tradition known from almost all other periods of ancient Egyptian history up to the Ramesside Period, and also well known from women's burials around the world, especially for women not of a high social level. In this tradition people were placed in graves with objects confirming their social identity (male versus female) and social status (often in tombs of men). In most other periods of ancient Egyptian history this burial tradition is typical of the broader population, while the ruling classes equipped their burials with products of a funerary industry.

It remains unclear why people of a higher social level suddenly adopted burial customs previously evident only at lower social levels.[97] There are several possible explanations. It might be argued that knowledge of certain rituals was no longer available to everybody and only people at the royal court had access to them. These developed together with the court type burials into a new funerary industry, while the rest of the country, including many people belonging to the ruling class, followed older models or were buried with a reduced amount of burial equipment (coffins, mummy masks, and so on). One might ask in this context: did the royal residence restrict the knowledge of certain rituals or even of religious literature to a small number of people? The main feature of the court type burials is the royal insignia, most often just made of wood and most likely not very expensive. Therefore it seems unlikely that these people could not afford to be buried in this style. The cost of the objects typical of the court type burials is evidently not the reason for not placing them in the tomb chamber.[98] It is also possible, however, to argue that the rituals around the court type burials were just too expensive and were therefore only used by a small select group who could afford them.

There is another possible explanation. The richness of some of the burials of the period, equipped with golden jewelry, seems to rule out the conclusion that the reduced burial equipment is related to poverty. Most of the women of type 3 burials presented in this book had substantial resources, but their burials include no objects of a funerary industry. Perhaps one reason for this relates to the centralization of the late Middle Kingdom.[99] After the reign of Senusret III most local centers became less important than they were in the early Middle Kingdom. No longer are there any grand tombs of local governors.[100] Local governors are still

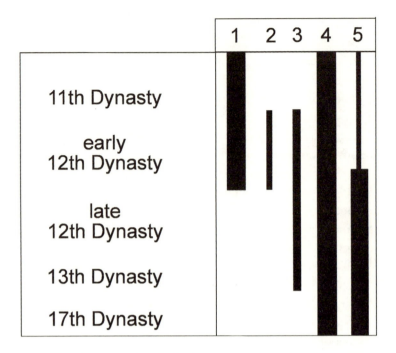

97. Burial types in the Middle Kingdom: 1. burials with wooden
models of estates; 2. court type burials in provinces (type 1); 3. court
type burials at the royal residence (type 1); 4. burials of the broader
population with mostly daily life objects (type 3); 5. burials
of the ruling classes with mostly daily life objects (type 3).

attested, but they had fewer resources. In the early Middle Kingdom there
were most likely workshops connected with the courts of the local governors. This is best visible in the tomb scenes in Beni Hasan.[101]

With less income for the local governors in the late Middle Kingdom,
there were no longer the resources to maintain funerary industry workshops at the local courts.[102] This funerary industry is now attested at only
a few places, such as at the royal residence (the cemeteries of Dahshur,
Lisht, Harageh, and Hawara) and to a lesser extent at Abydos and Thebes. Here, coffins were still decorated with longer religious texts,[103] and
the funerary industry produced the first shabtis and heart scarabs. There
were still wealthy people in the provinces, indicated by the women's burials with rich jewelry. Their number was not high enough to support a local funerary industry, however, and they were therefore buried according
to older traditions. Their jewelry may have been bought at the centers

mentioned above, but it was also produced locally, as indicated by the low quality of some of the items. The few decorated coffins found at provincial cemeteries may even have been produced elsewhere.[104] The same is true of some other funerary objects found in the provinces, such as shabtis[105] and mummy masks, although the latter seem still to be common in some places and might indicate that there were at least some local funerary workshops outside the main centers (as at Buhen and Mirgissa).[106] Workshops for stelae and statues are still attested in several provincial towns. Their products were not only used for tombs.[107] The evidence from stelae and statues still produced at some provincial places might even support the idea that knowledge of certain rituals was now restricted to a smaller number of people, excluding local officials, who were still able to commission stelae and statues but not elaborate objects of a funerary industry.

THE SECOND INTERMEDIATE PERIOD AND EARLY NEW KINGDOM (1650–1250 BCE)

Besides the coffin, objects of a funerary industry are rare in the Second Intermediate Period. It seems that the production of funerary jewelry and other funerary objects stopped almost completely, even at the level of the royal court.[108] At the end of the period only a small funerary industry remained at Thebes, producing coffins and canopic boxes. The rough stick shabtis[109] typical of this period are also products of a reduced funerary industry. Decorated coffins outside Thebes are extremely rare by the end of the Second Intermediate Period, the few examples being found at Abydos[110] and Saqqara.[111] It seems that these were the only other places in Egypt at least producing decorated coffins. This development evidently paved the way for the burial customs of the New Kingdom, which saw a high percentage of objects from daily life even in royal tombs. By the end of the Second Intermediate Period in particular, a shift is visible toward placing a wider range of daily life objects in tombs, including even small pieces of furniture.

Three burials belonging to Second Intermediate Period will be described here. Two examples from Upper Egypt confirm that the burial traditions of the late Middle Kingdom continued, while the first example is a burial from Tell el-Dab'a, where a rather different funerary culture developed. A large community of people originally from Palestine and perhaps Syria lived at Tell el-Dab'a. They followed the burial customs of the regions they came from. These included placing weapons in tombs of men, a practice not common in Egyptian burials in Upper Egypt dating to the late Middle Kingdom and Second Intermediate Period, although there are some instances.[112] Most of the jewelry placed in the tombs was Egyptian in type and production, however, although there are also several types not known from classical late Middle Kingdom cemeteries, such as diadems made of gold foil, which are otherwise well known from Palestine and Greece.[113]

One example of a rich burial, numbered A/II-m/16, contained the remains of three skeletons. One, mostly likely a woman, was richly adorned with jewelry. The most beautiful objects were two necklaces, each consisting of several rows of beads, many of precious materials such as gold, turquoise, and carnelian; some were made of faience. At the front of each necklace were perhaps several chains of beads held together in one case by special large beads with several holes for several strings. There was also most likely a row of golden shells at the front. A small figure of a lion was used as a clasp. Other personal adornments included two scarabs found at the left hand, perhaps once being part of two rings. There was a golden diadem found at the head and about eight hundred small beads. Other finds were a copper mirror next to the skull of the person buried there, a kohl pot, and thirteen pottery vessels.[114]

At Qurna, part of the Theban necropolis, the burial of a wealthy woman, dating to the end of the Second Intermediate Period or very early New Kingdom, was excavated (Fig. 98). The grave was set apart from any other burials and was just a shallow hole in the ground. Despite this simple arrangement, the burial itself makes a quite rich impression. The woman was placed into a partly gilded *rishi* coffin. On her body were found several golden personal adornments. There were two earrings, a necklace consisting of four strings of golden beads, golden armlets, and a girdle made of electrum beads, including twenty-six cowry-shaped beads between smaller, simpler ones. A scarab may have been used as a pendant. She also wore bangles. Other objects placed next to the coffin include several pottery vessels, some of them Nubian, and small items of furniture, such as a stool and a headrest. There was also a box next to the coffin containing the body of a child, most probably the child of the woman buried here. The young women herself was about twenty years old when she died.[115]

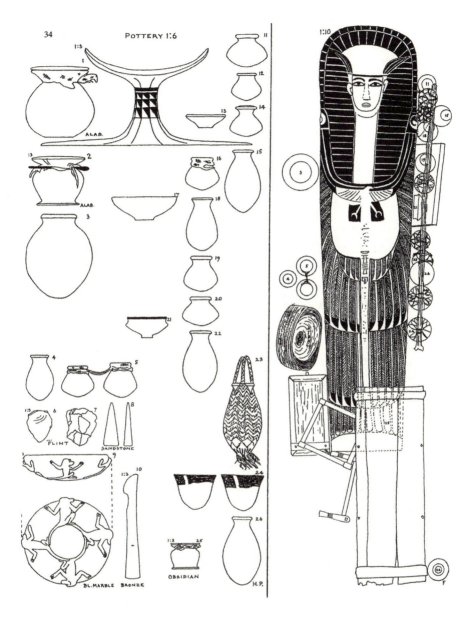

98. The burial of the wealthy woman at Qurna, as recorded and published by
Petrie. From Petrie 1909, pl. XXII.

The burial of Queen Ahhotep[116] was found in 1859 in Dra Abu el-Naga, which is the modern name for the northern part of the Theban necropolis[117] and was the royal burial ground in the Second Intermediate Period. The burial of the queen was found in a brick-lined vaulted chamber. In the chamber was a gilded coffin of rishi type. This type of coffin, which developed in the Second Intermediate Period, is anthropoid and covered with a feather decoration.[118] With the burial were found several items of jewelry, such as a pectoral, golden necklaces, several golden armlets, a broad collar, and bracelets of different types. The unexpected objects were a model boat in silver and another in gold, a dagger partly made of gold, two simpler daggers, and an axe, again partly made of gold, richly inlaid, and with the name of King Ahmose, the first ruler of the Eighteenth Dynasty and the founder of the New Kingdom. There are two further axes and several models of axes. These weapons need an explanation. They are not typical of burials of women of the late Second Intermediate Period and the New Kingdom. Daggers are well known from the court type burials, but all other objects typical of these burials are missing in this tomb, so it seems more likely that they had a different function here; indeed, it has often been suggested that these weapons refer to the political position of Queen Ahhotep at the end of the Second Intermediate Period when Egypt was fighting against the Hyksos in the north, and when Ahhotep might have played a part.[119] In this context also belongs a necklace with golden flies as pendants, as it is known that golden flies were given as an honor after military battles.[120]

The New Kingdom saw the continuation of the late Middle Kingdom and Second Intermediate Period trends. In the provinces at the beginning of the period there was almost no funerary industry. The tombs of the wealthy were now filled with objects already used in daily life, such as furniture, garments, games, weapons, and pottery vessels. Conserving the social identity of the deceased is still the most important aspect of burials at all social levels. Only at Thebes were found products of a funerary industry as well as objects of daily life. These consist of canopic jars and their boxes, shabtis, amulets, and the Book of the Dead.[121] It seems that in the early New Kingdom Thebes was the only place with a funerary industry, producing high-quality coffins, mummy shrouds with Book of the Dead chapters, and other objects (shabtis), although decorated coffins also appear sporadically outside Thebes.

From the mid-Eighteenth Dynasty comes the tomb of three women with foreign names (Menhata, Menuwai, Meruta), all with the title "king's wife" and therefore belonging to the same social level as the main burials discussed in this book. The burials of these queens were looted in the early twentieth century and most of the objects sold to the Metropolitan Museum of Art in New York. The preservation conditions for organic materials were not very good in the tomb, so only inorganic objects survived. These are mainly jewelry and cosmetic objects, including many stone vessels. The range of objects from these three burials is quite similar to that found in the royal tombs of the late Middle Kingdom. There was jewelry made for the burial, in this case a vulture, a falcon broad collar, covers for toes and fingers, and golden sandals. All these were made of gold leaf and are of rather simple workmanship. There was also jewelry most likely worn in real life. These include some broad collars, a diadem with gazelles, a cover for a wig, earrings, several armlets, and girdles. The cosmetic objects include mirrors and many stone vessels.[122]

Aniba, ancient Miam, was the capital of the Nubian provinces in the New Kingdom. A large cemetery has been excavated there, including the undisturbed burial of Weser and his wife Tanefert, who probably lived in the middle of the Eighteenth Dynasty. Their burial contained a number of important objects, including many pottery vessels and also metal vessels. The deceased were found in two heavily decayed wooden coffins, once black with painted yellow decoration. The mummy of Weser was not equipped with any jewelry, while the mummy of Tanefert was adorned with five rings, one of silver, one of gold. On her body was found a heart scarab, a mirror, a knife, a whetstone, and cosmetic spoons. On her coffin was found a box with several alabaster vessels, evidently a cosmetic box with cosmetic jars.[123]

THE LATE NEW KINGDOM (1250–1070 BCE) AND AFTER

Burial customs changed dramatically under Ramses II (c. 1279–1213 BCE). From around his reign onward, products of a funerary industry were placed in richer graves: coffins, canopic equipment, shabtis, the Book of the Dead, and sometimes amulets.[124] Daily life objects became rare, and personal adornments do not appear in many burials.[125] The display of the deceased's social identity becomes secondary in the burials or disappears completely, the main focus being the protection of the body

and the transformation of the deceased into a godlike being. This type
of burial, containing mainly products of a funerary industry, is attested in
the Third Intermediate Period, in the Late Period,[126] and into the Roman
Period; it is thus the dominant burial type for the whole first millennium
BCE. During the course of a thousand years some variations are visible:
new funerary object types appeared, others were dropped, and the decoration of coffins changed. Nevertheless, the general picture remained fairly
constant. Daily life objects appear sporadically, sometimes in the form of
personal adornments or a few high-prestige objects, perhaps confirming
the high social status of at least some of the deceased.

An example of a rich woman's burial of the Ramesside Period is that of
Henutmehyt. At some point in the nineteenth century its contents came
into the possession of the British Museum, and the burial was most likely
found undisturbed. There is a set of gilded coffins belonging to the finest
examples of the Ramesside Period, a Book of the Dead papyrus, a canopic
chest, the four magical bricks, and a shabti box with shabtis.[127] Although
the burial assemblage was not found in a proper excavation, it seems that
these objects represent the essentials for the burial of a woman of the
highest social level. Personal adornments were not seen as necessary.

In 1908 in the Valley of the Kings, however, a partly disturbed burial
(KV 56) was found, also known as the "Gold Tomb" and containing a
range of high-quality jewelry.[128] This includes a circlet, several finger
rings, two bracelets with the name and figure of Queen Tawesret standing in front of Sethy II (Fig. 99), golden earrings (Fig. 100), and a golden
necklace. There were also several alabaster vessels. The jewelry was found
at one wall of the chamber next to the remains of a coffin. The tomb
owner is unknown, but Cyril Aldred suggested that it was a royal child.[129]
The interpretation of the jewelry is complicated and seems to indicate
almost the opposite of what was previously thought. At first glance, all
the personal adornments seem not to be funerary jewelry but made to be
worn, indicating that there were always exceptions, perhaps particularly at
the royal court, where the display of prestige and power might also have
been an important aspect of burial. There is, however, the option that
most of the personal adornments were funerary. Most of them are made
of gold or silver, but without using inlays of other materials. Therefore
most of them look rather simple, although technically of a high standard.
Only a few items are clearly funerary, such as amulets[130] and silver hands,
perhaps once covering the hands of the mummy, and silver sandals.[131]

99. Silver bracelet with the name of Queen Tawesret.
From Davis, Maspero, Ayrton, Daressy, Jones 1908, pl. [10].

100. Earring. From Davis et al. 1908, pl. [7].

The burial of the king's wife Kama dates to the Twenty-second Dynasty, around 900 BCE. She was most likely married to one of the many kings of the period with the name Osorkon or Takeloth. The burial was found at Tell Moqdam, a place in the Delta known by the Greek name Leontopolis in ancient times. Kama's burial was placed in a small tomb complex consisting of two chambers for two burials. One chamber was found looted. The other belonged to Kama. The walls of the vaulted chamber are decorated with religious scenes. In the chamber was a granite sarcophagus, the lid being a reused stone from an older building, still showing parts of the old decoration. Next to the sarcophagus were four canopic jars, also once belonging to another person. There were a shabti and several alabaster vessels as well. The queen was richly adorned with jewelry. The main piece, and a highlight of Egyptian jewelry, is a pectoral made of gold and inlaid with several types of stones. It shows in the center a baboon sitting on a papyrus, with a deity on either side: Maat, and perhaps Hathor. The workmanship is superb. Although today most of the inlays are gone, the back shows the details incised in the greatest detail into the gold foil. Next to the pectoral there was a golden crown, several bracelets, many amulets, and a heart scarab with the name of the queen. Most of the objects in the tomb were made especially for the burial, but the main pieces of jewelry were most likely worn in daily life and underline the high status of the queen.[132]

One last burial should be described. It was in Nubia, to the south of Egypt, but is in full Egyptian tradition and perhaps no different to contemporary ones in Egypt.[133] It belongs to the king's wife Mernua and was found in Meroe in modern Sudan.[134] She lived in about the reign of King Anlamani to the reign of Aspelta (around 600 BCE), although a king's name was not found in her burial. Her royal husband remains unknown.[135] The queen was placed in a simple, undecorated chamber under a small pyramid. She was lying inside a set of at least three coffins preserved only in minor traces when found and recognized only by the three complete sets of eyes and eyebrows found. Her mummy was covered with a bead net, a set of jewelry, and a vertical silver band with an offering formula also naming the queen. Her face was covered with a silver mask, and her whole body with amulets. In the burial chamber a few pottery vessels and about eighty-eight shabtis were found. Evidently almost all objects in the burial were specially made for the tomb, although the vessels might have been used before in daily life. Unlike most of the other burials of women discussed in this book, there is no jewelry already worn in daily life. Around Mernua's neck was placed a broad collar in silver, but that was made of a single sheet of metal and is therefore in its general form a copy of a real broad collar, not at all comparable to the Middle Kingdom examples, which were still made of strings of flimsy beads. The beads on Mernua's collar are just incised on the silver foil and therefore highly stylized.

BURIALS OF RICH WOMEN
IN OTHER ANCIENT CULTURES

Certain common features can be found in burials of women around the world and in different periods. The main focus is often jewelry, some vessels, and cosmetic objects. Clear sex differences in burial goods are already visible in the Neolithic period. One early example can be found in burials in Catal Höyük (modern Turkey) around 6000 BCE where deceased women were often adorned with necklaces made of boar tusks. They also often had mirrors in their burials, while men were buried with weapons.[136] The mirrors recall those found in Egyptian burials of women. It should also clearly be said, however, that there are many cultures where women are not especially richly adorned with jewelry.[137] Indeed, in some cultures, female-related objects other than jewelry are placed in the burials of women. To this object type belong spindle whorls.[138] Weaving and preparing cloth is a task often related to women and therefore seen as part of their identity.[139] In Denmark there are many well-preserved late Bronze Age (around 1000 BCE) burials of men and women in oak coffins with amazing preservation conditions for organic materials, including costumes. The burial equipment concentrates on the costume, a few personal adornments, and some personal items. The equipment is therefore in a wider sense gender related. Women wear costumes different to those worn by men, and they are more often equipped with personal adornments. Several object types appear in burials of both sexes, however, although we might expect them to be found only in burials of one sex. These include daggers and combs.[140] From the Ukraine many burials are known in which women were buried with many objects related to their sex (mirrors and personal adornments) but also had weapons in their tombs, such as quivers, arrowheads, and spearheads. These burials belong to the Scythians, renowned in ancient Greek sources for their wars.[141] A similar range of objects was found in the undisturbed tomb of the Shang Dynasty queen Fu Hao, who lived around 1200 BCE in what is today China. Her tomb contained many jade and bronze objects, but few personal adornments. There were hairpins and mirrors, but also many weapons. From ancient texts it is known that Fu Hao led armies and fought against enemies of Shang Dynasty China.[142] In this respect she seems comparable to Queen Ahhotep, who also was involved in fighting against enemies of her country.

Indeed, there is always a danger that we will project our expectations onto ancient burials. Timothy Taylor noted that swords are sometimes found in Saxon burials in England. In examples where a sword is found in the burial of a man it is interpreted as a weapon; in cases where the same or a similar object is found in the burial of a woman it turns into a weaving baton.[143]

While there are many rich tombs of women all around the world from almost all periods of history, little comparable material is known from the Middle Bronze Age around the eastern Mediterranean, the period under discussion here. One example of this lack of rich personal adornment is several hundred burials excavated at Jericho, in southern Palestine. These burials were most often placed in small burial chambers with several bodies placed side by side. Burial goods include personal adornments, toilet objects such as combs, food and drink and the vessels for it, and even furniture. These objects were all taken from daily life, and there is little sign that anything was produced specially for the tomb.[144] The jewelry appears rather simple. There are beads, most often perhaps worn as necklaces, and there are many scarabs in Egyptian style, at least some of them produced in Egypt,[145] many in Palestine.[146] Only one tomb had some gold objects.[147] It remains an open question whether the poverty of these tombs, which are otherwise quite richly equipped with pottery and furniture, relates to local burial customs or whether the people buried here simply did not have the resources for richer burial equipment. Evidently, Jericho was not the seat of a rich and powerful court.

Similar and roughly contemporary burial customs are attested in Megiddo, about sixty kilometers north of Jericho. People were buried in rock-cut caves, often with several chambers, over a long period. Burial goods include weapons and inlaid boxes.[148] Some personal adornments were found, including many scarabs. Next to the communal burials there are also single burials reserved for one or a few people, most likely placed there at a single moment. One example is tomb 257, perhaps belonging to a woman and dating to the Middle Bronze Age. The deceased was placed in a small chamber made of rough stones and mud, lying in a slightly contracted position and holding a child, while a second child was placed at the feet. Seventy astragali (bones), perhaps of a sheep, were found at the head. There was also a simple golden earring. Other burial goods include three bowls and six jugs.[149] Organic preservation is not very good at Megiddo, so it is impossible to say whether the tombs were also equipped with furniture to the same extent as in Jericho. In general the burials make a slightly richer impression; perhaps Megiddo was a more important town.

There are few burials of women with rich jewelry dating to the Middle Bronze Age in Palestine or Syria. However, some important tombs were found in the Syrian city of Ebla. The city was a flourishing center in the third and first part of the second millennium BCE, capital of a city state. Important burials of the Middle Bronze Age were found beneath the floor of the "Western Palace," where the prince most likely resided. There were three underground burial complexes, two of which had been looted, most likely at the time the city was sacked by Hittites around 1650–1600 BCE. They still contained a range of important jewelry and objects, including an Egyptian gold-inlaid mace of the Thirteenth Dynasty king Hetepibre Hornedjheriotef. Only the so-called tomb of the princess was found untouched (Fig. 101).[150] It was built into a cave that had been enlarged and partly paved with stone slabs. The young woman buried here was richly adorned. There is a pin with its head in the form of star and a series of six golden bracelets made of twisted wire. A beaded band contains a rectangular central piece with a scarab-like object in the middle surrounded by paste in cloisonné work. On either side of the centerpiece melon-shaped beads are attached, one of them of amethyst.[151] The amethyst certainly came from Wadi el-Hudi in Egypt and demonstrates some trade contacts with Ebla, most likely via a third party, perhaps the Lebanese harbor town of Byblos. One round object made of gold is either an earring or a nose ring. It is made of two sheets of gold, curved and shaped into a circle. The sheets are covered with a pattern of triangles and lozenges in granulation.[152] Next to the remains of the women were several vessels, one of sardonyx (a semiprecious stone), one of alabaster, and a pointed faience vase with two handles. These vessels most likely functioned as containers for ointments. The tomb dates to around 1700 BCE and is therefore contemporary with the Egyptian late Middle Kingdom.

There are some tombs of kings found at Byblos that also cannot be ignored. These are tombs of local rulers from about 1600 BCE.[153] The tombs contained an array of Egyptian-style jewelry, and there is good evidence that the burial equipment included a large number of Egyptian-style objects, including wooden coffins, an example of which was found decayed in a stone sarcophagus.[154] Remains of wedjat eyes from the coffin attest to its Egyptian style in tomb I (Fig. 102). Tomb II[155] perhaps belonged to the "governor of Byblos Yepshemaib, begotten of the governor Ibi." His name was inscribed in hieroglyphs on a sword. The tomb contained an obsidian box partly covered with gold and naming King Amenemhat IV. The lid of a hard stone vessel also mentions King Amenemhat, without providing further information as to which Amenemhat it is. Another outstanding piece is a pectoral in Egyptian style but perhaps made by local craftsmen, as the workmanship is not very good (Fig. 103). It shows under a winged sun disk a falcon and two facing kings. Other objects found in the tomb

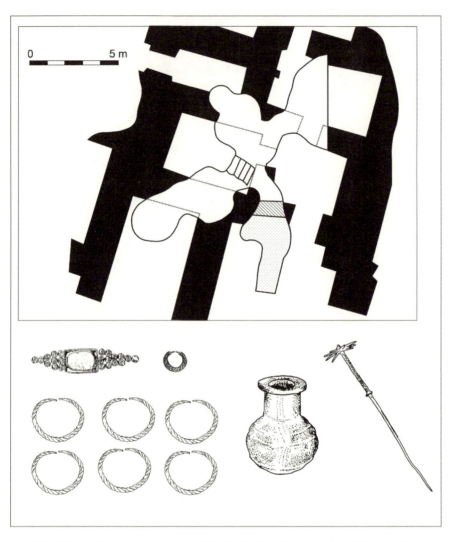

101. The tomb of the princess at Ebla in Syria with examples of the jewelry found there (drawing, 1/2). From Paolo Matthiae, *I tesori de Ebla*, Bari 1984, pl. 77 (needle), pl. 80a (sardonyx vase); Kay Kohlmeyer, "Bracelet," in *Ebla to Damascus: Art and Archaeology of Ancient Syria*, ed. Harvey Weiss (Washington, 1985), 237, color pl. on p. 180.

102. Egyptian-style burial (tomb I) at Byblos in Lebanon. The tomb chamber
contained a sarcophagus and most likely an Egyptian-style inner coffin made
of wood, which has only recently been identified. Only the inlays for the eyes
survived. Egyptian or Egyptian-style objects include an obsidian vessel, a mirror,
and a uraeus. (Reconstruction according to information published in Virolleaud
1922, Montet 1928, Schiestl 2007.)

include the remains of an Egyptian-style mirror. A golden shell with inlays
bears the name Yepshemaib. Bangles and silver vases were also found. The
types of jewelry in the tomb are known from the court type burials, while
other objects are atypical of Egyptian burials of the late Middle Kingdom,
such as the inscribed sword and silver vessels, though the sword recalls the
dagger of court type burials. They might indicate the influence of local
traditions. One wonders whether this also relates to at least some part of
the personal adornments that so far are otherwise attested in Egypt only
for women, most notably the pectoral and the shell.

Going back in time, an outstanding burial group of a high-status

103. Egyptian-style pectoral found in Byblos, tomb II (about 16 cm wide).
Drawing by Paul Whelan, after Montet 1928, pl. XCIV, 617.

woman of the third millennium BCE was excavated at Ur in Mesopotamia. It is the burial of Puabi, discovered by C. L. Woolley. Puabi was
found in a chamber lying on her back on the remains of a wooden bier
with her head to the west and hands placed on her stomach. Two women
were found next to her, evidently servants who had followed their mistress
into the next world. On the body of Puabi was an array of golden jewelry.
On her head were several diadems, some decorated with golden leaves
and in the middle a tree of some kind with six golden blossoms (Fig. 104).
The whole upper body was covered with beads of gold, silver, lapis lazuli,
carnelian, and agate. There was also a belt of beads, again made of gold
and semiprecious stones. On the arms were pins and several amulets. Ten
finger rings were also found. Next to the bier with the body of Puabi was
found a diadem decorated with many small gold ornaments shaped as animal figures, such as bulls, gazelles, and rams, as well as rosettes. Perhaps
this diadem was placed on a wig. This recalls the burials of the late Middle

104. Head dress of the queen Puabi. From Woolley 1929;
cf. Woolley 134, pl. 128.

Kingdom royal women, with a set of jewelry on the body but another set placed in a box within the burial chamber. Other burial goods were found, including many metal vessels, some even made of gold, as well as a pouring vessel that had been placed on the body of Puabi.[156]

Dating to the end of the third millennium BCE are burials on the small island of Mochlos on the north coast of Crete.[157] Here several burial complexes were found, partly disturbed but still rich in finds. The excavation and recording of these tombs face many problems common to excavations of many ancient cemeteries. Tomb II is one of the richest in the cemetery. It is a building positioned next to the rocks of the island. The structure was about 5.6 m long and about 1.8 m deep and had two entrances at the front. The tomb is not an underground structure but more like a "house" for the dead. Dead bodies were placed here over a long period of time, and it seems that old burials were just pushed aside when new ones arrived. The excavators therefore found a mixture of bones and many objects. Burial goods found include eighty-five golden ornaments, fifteen stone vessels, nine objects of copper or bronze, and sixteen objects of ivory, clay, or stone. Among the personal adornments were at least three simple diadems basically consisting of a broad strip of gold foil.[158] There are armlets and sprays of gold leaves, the latter perhaps once adorning the hair of the people living here. There are simple golden pendants, perhaps part of a diadem.[159] There are two pins representing a flower.[160] It is almost impossible to assign the jewelry to particular bones found. The arrangement of the personal adornments is only possible from parallels and is often just guesswork.

In Ashur, in northern Mesopotamia, an undisturbed woman's burial was found in an underground chamber within the city limits. The tomb was arranged within a house, a widespread practice in the Near East. The woman was placed next to the body of a man, perhaps her husband. The chamber was used for several burials, but this couple were the last to be interred. Both were richly adorned with jewelry. Especially notable were the adornments of the woman, who had several sets of earrings and must have had several necklaces. At least eleven hundred beads of semiprecious stones were found on her body, most likely from necklaces. Several pendants were found with a semiprecious stone in the middle and fine gold work around it. The figures of a carnelian mouse and a golden frog were most likely part of a necklace. Next to the body of the woman were vessels and cosmetic objects. These included several alabaster vessels and a comb made of ivory decorated with figurative scenes.[161] The burial dates to the Late Bronze Age, from around 1350 to about 1250 BCE.[162]

One burial found in Babylon serves as an example of many other similar interments. It is thought to date to around 1300 BCE. The person buried here was placed in the ground in a contracted position with the head to the east lying on the right side.[163] The sex of the skeleton was not examined but was perhaps that of a woman, as the burial was richly equipped with jewelry. She was adorned with eight gold earrings each consisting of a gold ring with a gold ball. They were found next to the skull. There were two needles made of bronze, perhaps as part of the dress, as well as many beads of gold, glass, and several other materials, perhaps once belonging to one or more necklaces. The only other burial item was the fragment of a vessel. The person buried here was certainly of some wealth, as is evident from the gold jewelry. All attention was placed on the jewelry and perhaps the dress. No other burial goods were found, although it is possible that some items made of organic material were there originally but had decayed long before the tomb was excavated.

CHAPTER 5

The King and the Women
Buried Around Him

The burials of kings with only women placed around them seem to be a significant feature of many Old and all Middle Kingdom pyramid complexes. Among them are the burial complexes of the Sixth Dynasty containing the smaller tombs of queens. The pyramid complex of Pepy II consists of the king's pyramid and pyramid temple, and around this pyramid the small pyramids of the king's wives.[1] There are no tombs of king's daughters or male members of the family. They must have been buried somewhere else, perhaps somewhat farther away. The same arrangement is found for the pyramid complex of Pepy I, not far from the pyramid of Pepy II. Here, recent excavations uncovered many pyramids of king's wives. In the pyramid complexes of the Twelfth Dynasty there were pyramids not only of queens but also of royal daughters, although the picture is patchy, as many of these complexes are heavily destroyed. It is possible to interpret this evidence on several levels. First of all, the king wanted to be close to his family, which included his wife, his daughters, and his mother, if she was not buried with her husband. One might ask, however, why there appear to be no burials of the king's sons or brothers, who are almost invisible in Middle Kingdom sources. Perhaps with adulthood they became high officials and dropped the title "king's son," and are therefore no longer noticeable in our sources. Death in childbirth and mortality of young children was high in all pre-industrial societies, and we could therefore expect a certain number of king's sons to have died young before entering any formal position. Nonetheless, even these are invisible in Middle Kingdom sources, while they are known from the New Kingdom, where objects

105. Relief fragment found at
Heliopolis showing King Djoser.
The female members of his family
are depicted in small scale next to
his feet. Drawing by the author
from photograph; cf. Curto 1988,
fig. 48; Ziegler 1999b, no. 7b.

of king's sons were found in
the royal tombs, indicating that
they were buried there.[2] Therefore, it seems that there was
some other reason why in the
Middle Kingdom only women
were placed around the king.

First of all, it should be
stressed that in almost all periods of Egyptian history, royal
women appear in texts and
depictions around the king.
The most famous examples
are the family "portraits" of
King Akhenaton. On stelae, in
tombs of officials, and in temples, Akhenaton is often shown
next to his wife Nefertiti and
next to some or even all of his
daughters. Sons are never shown. This has often led to the conclusion that
Akhenaton did not have sons.[3] Looking at the whole of Ancient Egyptian
history, however, it appears to be a common pattern that the king is shown
or placed within the circle of the female members of his family. The male
members of his family are not often represented, and only very rarely in
the same context as the king.[4]

One of the earliest examples of this depiction of the king and his female family members is the series of stelae found at the Djoser complex
at Saqqara. On these stelae king Djoser is mentioned by his Horus name,
Netjerikhet (the name Djoser is known only from later sources for this
king). Next to Djoser side by side on these stelae are the names of the

king's wife, the king's mother, and a king's daughter (who are not depicted).[5] There are fragments of a shrine or chapel of the same king in
Heliopolis.[6] Here the king is shown with, at his feet, the same women,
depicted on a much smaller scale. No king's son is present (Fig. 105).

From the rest of the Old Kingdom, no comparable representations
are preserved. In the mortuary temple of King Sahure, dating to the Fifth
Dynasty, the sons of the king, the king's mother, and the king's wife are
depicted several times.[7] Officials serving the king are also depicted here.
One wonders whether these reliefs had a different focus. The intention
was most likely to represent the whole royal court.

As we have seen, the Sixth Dynasty pyramid complexes are arranged
with special attention to royal women. In the middle of these complexes is
the king's pyramid, and around this monument are the smaller pyramids
of his wives.[8] King's daughters and king's sons, however, were not buried
as close to their father. King's sons often became high state officials and
were buried as such in the wider cemetery around the king's pyramid, but
also in other cemeteries. King's daughters were often married to high state
officials and were buried next to their husbands.

This practice of royal burials appears again in the Middle Kingdom.
In the mortuary temple of Mentuhotep II are incorporated five burials
of women with the titles "king's wife," "priestess of Hathor," and "king's
ornament."[9] A sixth woman had no title and evidently died very young,
given the small size of her coffins and from her skeleton (Mayet; see
Chapter 4). Their burials were placed in small chambers at the bottom
of a shaft. A seventh woman buried within the mortuary complex was the
king's wife and king's mother Tem, mother of Mentuhotep III, the son of
Mentuhotep II.[10] The same arrangement is visible for all Twelfth Dynasty
pyramid complexes. The pyramid of Senusret I is surrounded by several
smaller pyramids, all most likely belonging to the wives and daughters
of the king, although few names are preserved. Next to the pyramid of
Amenemhat II were found the three galleries discussed in Chapter 1, at
least two of them reserved for royal women. The only burial with a preserved name within the pyramid complex of Senusret II at Lahun is that
of a woman, in this case Sathathoriunet. All burials around the pyramid of
Senusret III at Dahshur were also of women.

HATHOR IN PRIVATE TOMB DECORATIONS

The type of arrangement just described is also known from private tombs of the period of about Senusret II to Senusret III. The tomb chapel of Ukh-hotep IV at Meir is in this respect especially remarkable. Ukh-hotep IV lived around the time of Senusret II and Senusret III and was governor at Qis in Middle Egypt, where Hathor was the main deity. His rock-cut tomb at Meir is in many ways exceptionally decorated. The tomb consists of three parts: a decorated chapel, a smaller inner chapel, also decorated, at the back, and the underground burial chambers, all undecorated. The decoration of the chapel and innermost chapel is remarkable, as they are filled to an extraordinary extent with royal symbols. Fertility figures are shown in the innermost chapel,[11] a motif that otherwise appears only on wall decorations of temples. In an inscription it is stated that Ukh-hotep IV "may appear as king of Upper and Lower Egypt."[12] The innermost chapel is decorated all around with a palace facade, and the sign "uniting the two lands" appears in the tomb,[13] again something normally connected only with kingship. In some scenes Ukh-hotep is shown holding an ankh sign,[14] also something so far found only in the royal sphere and in the realm of the temple. Ukh-hotep IV was married to at least eight women, all shown in the paintings of his tomb chapel in the innermost chamber: two of them are depicted in a prominent position sitting alone at the back of this chapel, not in the company of Ukh-hotep IV himself.[15] Also remarkable is the tomb chapel proper, where women appear in all scenes, with Ukh-hotep IV the only man. The activities in the marshes or religious festivals shown are all performed solely by women. Festivals in honor of Hathor are depicted in the tomb.[16] Although Ukh-hotep IV was not a king, he borrowed many elements that otherwise appear only in royal contexts. The special prominence of women in this tomb might relate to the local Hathor but also be connected to royalty and Hathor in general. Indeed, there is another tomb of about the same period in Qaw el-Kebir, belonging to the governor Wahka II.[17] The tomb decoration is very much destroyed, but the few surviving elements indicate that it was decorated in a similar way, giving women a prominent position in the tomb decoration. In Qaw el-Kebir, ancient Tjebu, Hathor was not the major deity. The local Hathor was evidently not the main motivation behind the scenes in Ukh-hotep IV's tomb, it was most likely Hathor in general.

HATHOR AND THE KING

Hathor was the main female deity in the Old and Middle Kingdoms and strongly connected to kingship.[18] Her name means "house of Horus" and implies that she was the mother of Horus, who was in turn also the king, as the king was the Horus on earth. In the early Middle Kingdom the king sometimes appears with the title "son of Hathor."[19] The king also had the royal title "Horus of Gold." This again seems to combine Horus with Hathor, as Hathor could also be called "Gold."[20] The strong connection between Hathor and the king is visible too in the late Eleventh Dynasty in the mortuary complex of King Mentuhotep II. Most wives of the king buried within his funerary complex had the title "priestess of Hathor."[21]

From this evidence it might be argued that the references to Hathor in the tomb of Ukh-hotep IV at Meir and in the tomb of Wahka II at Qaw el-Kebir were not simply indications of a strong local connection (Hathor was the main deity at Meir). It seems possible that these decorations emulated the connection of kingship to Hathor. This is supported by the presence of royal symbols in the decoration of both tombs.

The king's mother perhaps identified as Hathor was clearly the most important woman at the royal court.[22] The first lady was the king's mother, not the king's wife. This is clearly visible in the pyramid complex of Senusret III at Dahshur, where the king's mother had her dummy burial in the most important position, although it is most likely that she was buried somewhere else. For Senusret III it was important to have her present at the heart of his burial complex.

It seems that the royal women around the king were in some way connected to Hathor; either they were directly identified with Hathor or, in other periods, lesser queens were "priestesses of Hathor." With this strong connection to Hathor the king himself was placed among the gods.[23]

Hathor is also visible on several parts of the burial equipment in the court type burials. Her face appears on mirror handles and on boxes. Several of the women discussed have the goddess Hathor in their name, including Nubhetepti-khered, as "Nub," meaning "the Gold," is Hathor.[24] The crown of Sathathoriunet too seems to have a connection to Hathor.

THE KING'S CHILDREN

An important part of the royal court, especially in terms of its ritual functions, was the group labeled "king's children" ("mesu-nisut"). They appear in the king's festival, also known as the Sed festival. This festival
was the main celebration of kingship in ancient Egypt, celebrated in the
thirtieth year of a king's reign and after that every third year. There were,
however, many exceptions to this rule, when a king celebrated the festival
before his thirtieth year. There are about twelve ceremonies performed at
the festival, mainly known from the few depictions in temples. The king's
children appear at the beginning of the festival in a procession with the
king. They are shown sitting in a carrying chair, but from the preserved
depictions it is not possible to decide whether they are male or female, or
whether both sexes appear side by side. Perhaps the earliest representa-
tion of a "king's child" comes from a mace head of Narmer, where the
king is shown in front of a person sitting in a carrying chair.[25] Old Kingdom examples of representations of the king's children include the Sed-
festival reliefs of Niuserre from the Fifth Dynasty, where they are labeled
"king's children" and are shown individually, each in his or her own carrying chair. The king's children are also shown in the New Kingdom tomb
of Kheriuf, an official under King Amenhotep III. Here they are shaking
the Hathor sistrum, no longer shown in a carrying chair but depicted as
a row of young women. Dating from about the same time are the depictions from the temple at Soleb in Nubia, built under Amenhotep III. Here
they are again shown as young women with a sistrum.[26] Shortly afterward
they are represented on Sed-festival reliefs belonging to King Akhenaton
and are shown in a procession behind Queen Nefertiti. Once they are
depicted as several young women with hand-held fans, otherwise they appear in carrying chairs. The latter images are not clear enough to know
whether girls or boys are shown.[27] In the Sed-festival reliefs of Osorkon II
from Bubastis they appear behind the king and the king's wife. Here they
are again clearly shown as young women or girls.[28] The king's children
are also found on reliefs excavated at the palace of Apries at Memphis,
perhaps dating to the Twenty-sixth Dynasty. Here they again appear in a
carrying chair.[29] The reliefs perhaps copy older depictions, as the slightly
earlier reliefs of Osorkon II do not show the carrying chair for the king's
children.

The king's children appear in literary compositions as well. When the famous Sinuhe came back to Egypt after several adventures in Palestine, he was hailed with a song in praise of Hathor in front of the king's wife and the king's children.[30] Here, the king's wife and the king's children shake the sistrum of Hathor and rattle the menit (a kind of bead rattle) of Hathor.[31]

The depictions of the king's children as individuals sitting in a carrying chair or shrine connects them strongly with something known in ancient Egyptian as "reput." This is not easy to translate, as it could mean either "image of a woman" or "image of a goddess" and is most often written with the carrying chair.[32] It is also the name of a goddess, and it often seems impossible to decide whether, in a particular depiction or text reference, the meaning is reput the image or Reput the goddess. It might be even asked whether the Egyptians distinguished the two clearly. The important point is that Reput had a strong connection to rebirth and rituals around rebirth.[33] She was connected with Hathor from Denderah and with the male fertility god Min.[34]

Especially from the earlier depictions showing the king's children in a carrying chair, it almost seems that the king's children were identical with reputs. According to Werner Kaiser, the reputs could include the king's wife and even the king's mother.[35] He wonders whether a better translation of "king's children" would be "who has borne the king."[36] He argues that the reputs were important for rituals of rebirth relating to the king. There are, however, arguments against the identification with the king's wife and king's mother if the reputs are connected or even identical to the king's children. In the temple of Soleb, Queen Tiy appears next to the king's children.[37] In the representations of the Sed festival of King Osorkon II at Bubastis the king is always depicted with his wife Karoma.[38] Three daughters of the king are shown and even named,[39] but not labeled "king's children." The king's children also appear in other scenes and are evidently not identical, at least with the king's wife, as she appears in the same scene. The same setting is described in the story of Sinuhe, where the king's children even shake the sistrum and the king's wife appears too, not being one of them. From this evidence it might be argued that the king's children are indeed female children and do not include the king's wife. The translation "king's children" fits the available evidence better (Fig. 106).

Going back to the tomb of Ukh-hotep IV, one might wonder whether the high number of women in his tomb have—at least on one level—

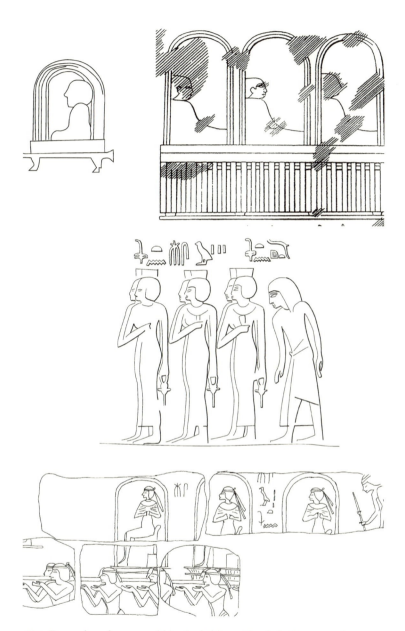

106. Examples of reput and king's children. Top left: figure on the mace
of Narmer; top right: reputs on a relief from the Sed-festival reliefs of
King Niuserre; middle: king's children on a relief in the Nubian temple
at Soleb, reign of Amenhotep III; bottom: reput shrines with the label
"king's children on block from Karnak, reign of Akhenaton." Redrawn
by the author from Quibell 1900, pl. XXVIb; von Bissing, Kees 1923,
Blatt 21, Schiff Giorgini, 1998, pl. 127; Gohary 1992, pl. I.

something to do with the king's children, in the way that this concept was copied by that powerful local governor. The many women shown and depicted in his tomb could have been considered his king's children, with the main function of guaranteeing the rebirth of Ukh-hotep IV.

Perhaps the same idea lies behind the pyramid complexes of the Middle Kingdom. The king was buried in the middle, and around him were positioned the tombs of the female members of his family. Indeed, one wonders whether they might be placed here as the king's children. Here, they might serve the same function, guaranteeing the rebirth of the king.[40] In this way the whole pyramid complex including the burials of the women was a "machine for surviving death," providing an endless eternal ritual for rebirth in which the king's children played an important part. A further point is the connection of the king's children with the reput. In several versions of the hour vigil of the Ptolemaic period, the reput played an important part. In the twelfth-day hour we read: "Oh living one, your reput is embracing you. In the first and sixth hour of the night it is said: oh my lord, come to (my) reput. In the ninth hour appears: Both reputs are joining with you."[41] As I have already noted several times in this book, the hour vigil was the most important aspect of the late Middle Kingdom burial equipment at the royal court and for people at the highest social level. Just as there were king's children around the actual burial of the king, there were reputs around the burial of the king in the context of the hour vigil.

*   *   *

In this interpretation, the royal women buried around the king were the king's children known mainly from Sed-festival depictions. The king's children were strongly connected to or even fully identified with reputs. The reputs were important in connection with rebirth. By placing the king's children around the king's tomb, the rebirth of the king was guaranteed. The king's children are furthermore strongly connected with Hathor, and the king's wife was identified with Hathor. By the placing of the king's wife next to the king, he was placed in the circle of deities. His divine status was confirmed. In their own burial equipment, however, the royal women were identified as the underworld god Osiris, something important for their transformation in the underworld. With the jewelry boxes placed in their burial chambers, their social identity as high-status women was confirmed.

Appendix

The Royal Women of the Twelfth Dynasty

The women are listed under the names of the relevant kings.

AMENEMHAT I

Mother

Nefret
Nefret bears the titles "member of the elite" and "king's mother." She is known from an offering table found next to the pyramid of the king at Lisht.[1] She was most likely the mother of Amenemhat I, as indicated by the find spot of the offering table.

Wife

Nefretatenenet
She is known only from a statue, now lost. The inscriptions call her "king's mother." It is stated that Senusret was born to Amenemhat and born of Nefretatenenet.[2]

Daughters

[Ita]kayt (?)
She appears on a relief fragment found in the mortuary temple of Amenemhat I at Lisht.[3] She is called "king's daughter of his body." The space

in front of her name is destroyed, and one wonders whether she was just called Kayt. There are several king's daughters with the name Itakayt. One of them was buried in a small pyramid next to that of Senusret I at Lisht.[4] Perhaps the two women are identical. Another attestation of a king's daughter with this name appears on a cylinder seal now in the Brooklyn Museum, next to the name of Amenemhat. It remains unclear which Amenemhat it refers to.[5]

Neferusheri
The name of this king's daughter appears on a weight found in a shaft next to the pyramid of Amenemhat I at Lisht. Nothing is known about her. The object is not yet published.[6]

SENUSRET I

Wife

Neferu
She was the daughter of Amenemhat I, the wife of Senusret I, and the mother of Amenemhat II.[7]

Daughters

[. . .]sobek
The inscription of "king's daughter" with the remains of this name was found on a fragment of a bowl at the pyramid complex of Senusret I at Lisht. The reconstruction of her name is uncertain and could be Neferu-sobek or Satsobek. A relation to Senusret I seems possible but is far from certain.[8]

Sebat
Sebat appears on a back slab of a statue found at Serabit el-Khadin on Sinai. She is mentioned next to the king's wife Neferu and Senusret I as "king's daughter of his body" and is therefore most likely the daughter of both.[9]

Itakayt: see [Ita]kayt (?) under Amenemhat I.

AMENEMHAT II

Senet

The king's mother Senet is a good candidate for the wife of Amenemhat II. She is known from two statues and bears several important titles, including "king's wife" and "king's mother."[10] There are two possibilities: that she was the wife of Amenemhat II and the mother of Senusret II, or that she was the wife of Amenemhat III and the mother of Sobekneferu. One important observation is the missing title "united with the white crown," common for royal women after Amenemhat II. Therefore, she might date under this king, when the title had not yet become fully standard.[11]

Ita; see the discussion on p. 54.

Khenmet; see the discussion on p. 60.

Itaweret; see the discussion on p. 61.

Khenmetneferhedjet

A king's daughter with this name is known from several objects, including cylinder seals and a statue. One cylinder seal bears the throne name of Amenemhat II. She may be identical with Khenmet.[12]

SENUSRET II

Wife

Khenmetneferhedjet Weret (I)

She was the wife of Senusret II and the mother of Senusret III. Next to the pyramid of the latter was found her dummy burial within a small pyramid. Her real burial was most likely at Lahun, next to the pyramid of her husband.[13] There is some disagreement in Egyptology whether Weret ("the elder") is her full name and Khenmetneferhedjet ("united with the white crown") just a title, or whether Khenmetneferhedjet is her name. Relief fragments found in her funerary temple belonging to her dummy pyramid at Dahshur indicate that Khenmetneferhedjet was her name, as this name appears sometimes without Weret.[14] There are several objects where a queen is just called Khenmetneferhedjet. It is not always certain whether these belong to this woman.[15]

Daughters

Nefret
Nefret is known from two statues found at Tanis.[16] A king's daughter with
the same name appears on a papyrus fragment found at Lahun.[17] It is possible that the two are identical. On one of the statues she bears several titles, one in connection with Senusret II ("the beloved one, the one united
with Khakheperre"). For that reason and because of her long title strings
it has been assumed that she was the wife of Senusret II. She does not,
however, bear the title "king's wife." Therefore it seems rather likely that
these references refer to a king's daughter.

Itakayt
A king's daughter Itakayt appears on a papyrus fragment found at Lahun,
next to Nefret mentioned above.[18] They are perhaps sisters.

SENUSRET III

Wives

Khenmetneferhedjet Weret (II)
Her name appears on a wooden board and on a canopic jar found in her
pyramid tomb next to the pyramid of Senusret III at Dahshur.[19] She must
be different from the queen Khenmetneferhedjet Weret (I) who had a
dummy pyramid nearby.

Khenmetneferhedjet Khered
This woman appears on a fragment of a papyrus found at Lahun.[20] Her
statue is listed in connection with the name of Senusret III. There are no
further secure attestations for her. There is, however, some chance that
she is identical with Khenmetneferhedjet Weret (II), having two different
epithets relating to two different stages in her life, being called Khered
("the child") when she was young and Weret ("the elder") later in her life.[21]

Nefret-henut
This king's wife is known only from her sarcophagus and fragments from
the chapel found in and next to her pyramid as part of the pyramid complex of Senusret III at Dahshur. Her other titles are "member of the elite,"
"united with the white crown," and "she who sees Horus and Seth."[22]
With some reservation it might be argued that she is identical with the

king's daughter Nefret who is attested under Senusret II. In the Middle Kingdom it was not uncommon to place a short and a long version of a name on different monuments, or even on the same one.

Daughters

Itakayt

Itakayt is known only from fragments found in the chapel of her pyramid next to that of Senusert III at Dahshur.[23] She bears the title "king's daughter of his body."[24] Perhaps she is identical to the king's daughter of the same name attested in a papyrus from Lahun (see above), which would make her the daughter of Senusret II and sister of Senusret III. A stone vessel found at Qatna in Syria bears the names and titles of a king's daughter Itakayt. It remains uncertain whether the vessel belongs to her or the women with the same name and titles dating under Senusret I.[25]

Senet-Senebtisi

Her sarcophagus was found in a gallery next to the pyramid of Senusret III. On her sarcophagus she is simply called "king's daughter."[26]

Menet

Her burial was found in a gallery next to the pyramid of Senusret III. On her sarcophagus and canopic jars she is simply called "king's daughter" and "united with the white crown."[27]

Sathathor; see the discussion on pp. 86–87.

Mereret/Meryt; see the discussion on pp. 92–93.

AMENEMHAT III

Wives

Aat

The king's wife Aat is known from an offering table and a fragment of a false door, both excavated at the pyramid of Amenemhat III at Dahshur. She was most likely his wife. Her burial was found in the pyramid. She died at the age of about twenty-five to thirty-five.[28]

Khenmetneferhedjet

Her burial was also found in the pyramid of Amenemhat III at Dahshur.

The name and the title "king's wife" appear on a cultic vessel. There is no further name after Khenmetneferhedjet, so it seems likely that this was indeed used as a name and not as a title. It appears unlikely that on such an important object just the titles without any names would be given. She was about twenty-three to twenty-seven years old when she died.[29]

Hetepti

She appears on a relief in the temple of Amenemhat III and Amenemhat IV in Medinet Maadi. There she is called "king's mother." She was therefore the mother of Amenemhat IV and most likely the wife of Amenemhat III.[30]

Daughters

Neferuptah

She was most likely a daughter of Amenemhat III. See the discussion on pp. 68–71.

Hathorhotep

She is known from the fragment of a canopic jar found in the pyramid of Amenemhat III at Dahshur.[31] The animal hieroglyphs on the fragment are incomplete, as is typical of the very end of Amenemhat's III reign and the following Second Intermediate Period. It remains unknown whether she was a daughter of Amenemhat III or of another king, perhaps of the Thirteenth Dynasty.

Sathathor

Her burial was located in the pyramid of Amenemhat III at Dahshur. Details of the burial have yet to be published.[32]

Chronology

Only kings mentioned in the text are listed here.

EARLY DYNASTIC PERIOD (C. 3000–2700 BCE)

First Dynasty
      Narmer
      Djer
      Semerkhet

OLD KINGDOM (C. 2700–2150 BCE)

Third Dynasty
      Djoser

Fourth Dynasty
      Khufu (Kheops)

Fifth Dynasty
      Sahure
      Niuserre
      Unas

Sixth Dynasty
      Teti
      Pepy I
      Pepy II

FIRST INTERMEDIATE PERIOD (C. 2150–2000 BCE)

Egypt was divided into two kingdoms

MIDDLE KINGDOM (C. 2000–1650 BCE)[1]

Eleventh Dynasty
>Mentuhotep II (c. 2008–1957)
>Mentuhotep III (c. 1957–1945)

Twelfth Dynasty
>Amenemhat I (c. 1939/8–1909)
>Senusret I (c. 1919–1875/4)
>Amenemhat II (c. 1877/6–1843/2)
>Senusret II (c. 1845/4–1837)
>Senusret III (c. 1837–1818)
>Amenemhat III (c. 1818/7–1773/2)
>Amenemhat IV (c. 1773–1764/3)
>Nefrusobek (c. 1763–1759)

Thirteenth Dynasty (c. 1759–1600 BCE
>Hetepibre Hornedjheriotef
>Awibre Hor
>Khendjer
>Neferhotep I

SECOND INTERMEDIATE PERIOD (C. 1650–1550 BCE)

Seventeenth Dynasty
>Nubkheperure Antef

NEW KINGDOM (C. 1550–1069 BCE)

Eighteenth Dynasty
>Ahmose (c. 1550–1525)
>Hatshepsut (1473–1458)
>Thutmose III (c. 1479–1425)

Amenhotep III (c. 1390–1352)
Akhenaton (c. 1352–1336)
Nefernefruaton (c. 1338–1336)
Tutankhamun (c. 1336–1327)

Nineteenth Dynasty
Ramses II (c. 1279–1213)
Sethy II (c. 1200–1194)
Tawesret (c. 1188–1186)

THIRD INTERMEDIATE PERIOD (C. 1069–664 BCE)

Twenty-first Dynasty
Psusennes (c. 1039–991)

Twenty-second Dynasty
Sheshonk II (c. 890)
Osorkon II (c. 874–850)

LATE PERIOD (664–332 BCE)

Twenty-sixth Dynasty
Apries (589–570)

PTOLEMAIC PERIOD (332–30 BCE)

ROMAN PERIOD (30 BCE–395 CE)

Notes

INTRODUCTION

1. Aldred 1971 is especially important in this respect.

2. Studies of Egyptian women include: Franke 1983, 326; Endesfelder 1989; Robins 1993; Graves-Brown 2008; Graves-Brown 2010.

3. The ruling queen Nitocris from the end of the Old Kingdom, known from later sources, may never have existed; see Ryholt 2000, 92–93.

4. Compare "king's mother" in Israel: Donner 1959, and in Ugarit: Ackerman 1998, 134.

5. Cooney 2008, 5.

6. "Royal women" in this book are kings' daughters, wives, and mothers. These are women directly related to the king by family ties expressed in the titles.

7. See, for example, the burial of Djehutynakht from Deir el-Bersheh (Doxey 2009).

8. Richards 2005, 176.

9. Junker 1919, 214–15.

10. http://www.begraebnis.at/begraebnis/seitelinks.php?nkat=Erdbestattung (retrieved 18 May 2011).

11. http://www.findadeath.com/Deceased/l/Bela%20Lugosi/bela_lugosi.htm (retrieved 25 December 2012).

12. Pearson 1999, 11.

13. Pearson 1999, 7.

14. Ucko 1969, 265.

15. Zillhardt 2009.

16. Zillhardt 2009, 12.

17. Summary of Egyptian coffins: Taylor 1989.

18. Erickson 2010, 14.

19. Kuhn 1992, 74, 78; Erickson 2010, 42–47.

20. Donnan 2007, 95–97.

21. Curtis 1995.

22. Obayashi 1992.

23. Obayashi 1992.

24. Dittrich 1981, 200–202.

25. Nashrabadi 1999, 64.

26. Salman, Andersen 2009, 173–74.

27. Philpott 1991, 192.

28. Miniaci, Quirke 2009.

29. Salman, Andersen 2009, 173–74 (the authors do not specify where they got this idea from; but banquets in the underworld are attested for the Etruscan and Greeks; Bonnefoy, Doniger 1992, 35).

30. Cavanagh 1996, 674.

31. Scharff 1947.

32. Haynes 2000, 148–49.

33. Müller-Karpe 1968, pl. 107c, 108.

34. Pearson 1999, 17–20, 166.

35. Emery 1954, 142.

36. Wilkinson 1999, 237; compare the discussion on human sacrifice in ancient Egypt and Nubia by van Dijk 2007.

37. Morkot 2000, 66.

38. Barrett 2007.

39. Thorp 2006, 190–91.

40. Woolley 1934, 35–38; Zettler 1998, 25–30.

41. Paludan 1994; Erickson 2010, 65–76.

42. Hill 1999.

43. Tooley 1995.

44. Compare n. 46 in Chapter 4.

45. Taylor 2001, 117–19.

46. Alexanian 1998, 19–22.

47. Seiler 2005, 162.

48. Steel 2004, 175.

49. Dittrich 1981, 77.

50. Dittrich 1981, 83–90.

51. Reeves 1990, 128–29; these figures are also known from other royal tombs of the New Kingdom: Reeves, Wilkinson 1996, 134–35.

52. Reeves 1990, 133.

53. Leitz 2002, 390–94 (with a list of the main functions of Anubis).

54. Altenmüller 1977, 842; Spencer 1982, 74–111; Snape 2011, 81–83.

55. Lüscher 1998, 54–57.

56. Ikram, Dodson 1998, 137–48; Taylor 2001, 200–208.

57. See, for example, Stierlin, Ziegler 1987, 130–34 and passim.

58. For a translation of the passage see Lichtheim 1975, 216–17.

59. Seidlmayer 2007.

60. Künzl 1989.

61. Haffner 1989, 108.

62. Schreiter 2001, 104.

63. Schuhmacher 1989.

64. Cavanagh 1996, 674.

65. Seidlmayer 2001, 241–45.

66. Gardiner, Sethe 1928.

67. Seidlmayer 2001.

68. Best described in Dubiel 2008.

69. Ikram, Dodson 1998, 137–46; Taylor 2001, 201–8.

70. Swain 1995.

71. Snodgrass 2010, 248.

72. Ionesov 2002, 102.

73. Robb 2000, 50.

CHAPTER 1

1. Mace, Winlock 1916; Podvin 1997, 99–101; Podvin 2000, 327.

2. Ranke 1935, 314, no. 25.

3. List of court type burials: Grajetzki 2010, 96–102.

4. Arnold 2008, 77–82.

5. Reeves 1990, 56.

6. Grajetzki 2010, 28–29.

7. Willems 1988, 159–60.

8. New York, MMA 08.200.45a, b.

9. Mace, Winlock 1916, 31–32.

10. Smith 1916.

11. On mummification in the Middle Kingdom in general: Ikram, Dodson 1998, 113–17; 156–57; David 2007, 85–97; Theis 2011b, 28–31.

12. New York, MMA 07.227.6; Mace, Winlock, 1916, 58–59.

13. New York, MMA 07.227.7; color image of circlet and rosettes: Aldred 1971, pl. 6.

14. New York, MMA 08.200.30; Aldred 1971, pl. 7; Seipel 2001, no. 29.

15. New York, MMA 08.200.43; Aldred 1971, pl. 8; Andrews 1990, fig. 12.

16. New York, MMA 08.200.41, Mace, Winlock, 1916, 66–67.

17. New York, MMA 07.227.8; Seipel 2001, fig. on p. 47 (in color), no. 30.

18. New York, MMA 07.227.11.

19. New York, MMA 07.227.9.

20. Other examples come from the tomb of Nakht at Abydos (Garstang 1902, pl. III; Bourriau 1988, 150, no. 163) and the tomb of Renseneb in Thebes (Carnarvon, Carter 1912, pl. LI); compare discussion in Lilyquist 2003, 296–98.

21. New York, MMA 07.227.12.

22. See, for example, the painted sweret beads on the coffins of the "two brothers" from Rifeh: David 2007, fig. 34 on p. 52.

23. Andrews 1994, 99.

24. Jéquier 1921, 49–51.

25. Willems 1997.

26. New York, MMA 08.200.29; Aldred 1971, pl. 9.

27. Jéquier 1921, 103–8.

28. Jéquier 1921, 110–11.

29. New York, MMA 08.200.42b; Patch 1995, 93–94, fig. 1.

30. Jéquier 1921, 91–93.

31. Patch 1995.

32. Patch 1995, 110–12.

33. New York, MMA 08.200.25, 08.200.26.

34. New York, MMA 08.200.27, 08.200.28.

35. Mace, Winlock 1916, 74.

36. Jéquier 1921, 165–68.

37. New York, MMA 07.227.15.

38. New York, MMA 07.227.16, 07.227.5.

39. New York, MMA 07.227.14; Petschel 2011, 241–42, 492 (no. 234).

40. Jéquier 1933b, pl. XII; compare for a recent translation: Allen 2005, 318.

41. Mace, Winlock 1916, 105, pl. XXVIII, H, I.

42. Abubakr 1937, 25–26; Wildung 1984b, 973.

43. Winlock 1941; Budka 2006 (for the Late Period); Eaton-Krauss 2008 (general discussion); Soliman 2009, 118–19 (Middle Kingdom example).

44. New York, MMA 07.227.1.–4a, b.

45. Arnold 1982, 53.

46. Schiestl 2009, 141–42.

47. Mace, Winlock 1916, 110, no. 14; Arnold 1988, 140.

48. Arnold 1982, 53 (Mace, Winlock 1916, 110, nos. 2–4).

49. Arnold 1982, 53.

50. Mace, Winlock 1916, 110, no. 17.

51. PT 510, 512, 515, 533, 536, 665, 666, 676; Assmann 2002, 370; Willems 1996, 175.

52. PT 536, translation follows Assmann 2002, 370.

53. Allen 2009, 331–32.

54. Mace, Winlock 1916, 110–11, nos. 15, 16.

55. Allen 2009, 332.

56. Willems 1996, 107, 119 (the vase more often appears alone).

57. Allen 1998, 48.

58. Hapy is one of the children of Horus (Ranke 1935, 291, 22). Hapy = Apis is another option (Ranke 1935, 291, 23). The writing of the name is not that clear in this respect. Although the writing supports the child of Horus, Apis is a more common name. For double names in the Middle Kingdom, see Vernus 1986; for the double names of Senebtisi, see Vernus 1986, 64, 101.

59. Ryholt 1997, 84.

60. Miniaci 2010, 117; Grajetzki 2010, 28–29.

61. Aston 2004, 93–94.

62. Brunton 1920 (excavation report); Petrie, Brunton, Murray 1923, 15–16 (additions to the excavation report); Dodson 2000a, 42–49 (summary of the discovery).

63. New York, MMA 16.1.45–48.

64. Petrie, Brunton, Murray 1923, 15–16.

65. MMA 16.1.2, Seipel 2001, no. 31.

66. CG 52641; JE 44919; Vilímková 1969, pl. 16; Aldred 1971, pl. 39.

67. Blackman 1953, pls. IX, XIX.

68. Allam 1963, 23–41.

69. Staehelin 1978, 79; however, Stavnik 1936 draws a connection to the "plant of Horbeit" and the god Nefertem.

70. Allam 1963, 29–31.

71. New York, MMA 16.1.3; Feucht 1967, 28, 161–62, no. 2; Vilímková, 1969, pl. 11; Desroches-Noblecourt 1979, fig. 231; Andrews 1990, fig. 15, 111; Aldred 1971, pl. 37.

72. Aldred 1971, 113–14; Wilde 2011, 36–39.

73. CG 52712, JE 44922; Feucht 1967, 28–31, 162, no. 3; Aldred 1971, pl. 38.

74. Aldred 1971, 192–93.

75. New York, MMA 16.1.20, 19.

76. New York, MMA 16.1.18; Seipel 2001, no. 35.

77. New York, MMA 16.1.16.

78. New York, MMA 16.1.24, Ben-Tor 2004, fig. 19, and Cairo CG 52689, JE 44921; Vilímková 1969, pl. 16; Seipel 2001, no. 36.

79. New York, MMA 16.1.22; Winlock 1934, pl. XII, D.

80. New York, MMA 16.1.8; Aldred 1971, pl. 40; Andrews 1990, fig. 16.

81. New York, MMA 16.1.15A; Seipel 2001, no. 33.

82. New York, MMA 16.1.7; Aldred 1971, pl. 36; Seipel 2001, no. 34.

83. Winlock 1934, 34–36.

84. Aldred 1971, 160.

85. New York, MMA 16.1.5; Aldred 1971, pl. 35.

86. New York, MMA 16.1.6; Aldred 1971, pl. 36; Seipel 2001, no. 32.

87. CG 52663, JE 44920; Desroches-Noblecourt 1979, fig. 245; Tiradritti 1998, fig. on p. 153.

88. New York, MMA 16.1.30a, b (razors); New York, MMA 16.1.27, 16.1.28 (whetstones); Brunton 1920, 37, pl. X; Winlock 1934, 62–66.

89. Brunton 1920, 37, pl. IX; Winlock 1934, 68–69, pl. XVI; Bevan 2007, 101.

90. New York, MMA 16.1.21; Winlock 1934, 66, fig. 5, no. 30; Brunton 1920, 37, pl. XI.

91. Brunton 1920, 37, pl. XI.

92. "Egyptian alabaster" or simply "alabaster" appearing in modern literature on ancient Egypt is in fact travertine (Aston, Harrell Shaw 2000, 59–60). However, the term "(Egyptian) alabaster" is widely used in Egyptology and will be used here too.

93. Brunton 1920, 37, pl. IX (top); Winlock 1934, 66–68, pl. XVI.

94. New York, MMA 21.2.62; Petrie, Brunton, Murray 1923, 42, pls. XXV.7, XXVI.

95. Pries 2011, 148; see Assmann 2002, 272–73; for the hour vigil in the funerary world of the Middle Kingdom see Willems 1997.

96. Theis 2011b, 50–51.

97. Translation according to Forman, Quirke 1996, 71; compare Grajetzki 2010, 93.

98. Allen 1998, 46–47.

99. Arnold 1982, 57–58; Allen 1998, 40.

100. Compare the chart in Tallet 2005, 21.

101. Brunton 1920, 27.

102. Roth 2001, 211–12.

103. Ben-Tor 2001.

104. Macadam 1951, pl. VI.

105. de Morgan 1903, 68–71; Grajetzki 1995; Grajetzki 2010, 26–28.

106. For the date of Keminub see Jánosi 1994.

107. Fay 1996, 47.

108. de Morgan 1903, 45–46, fig. 105 (the plan in the publication is assigned to Ita, but that seems to be a confusion; only Khenmet had a falcon collar as shown on the plan).

109. de Morgan 1903, 50–55; Podvin 1997, 155–58; Podvin 2000, 328–29; PM III (2), 886.

110. Russo 2012, 87.

111. Lapp 1993, 228–29; Russo 2012.

112. For this coffin see Mace, Winlock 1916, 47.

113. de Morgan 1903, 48.

114. Petschel 2011, 95.

115. Cairo CG 52982, JE 31069; Desroches-Noblecourt 1979, fig. 263; Müller, Thiem 1999, fig. 218; Petschel 2011, 93–97, 358, no. 13.

116. Philip 2006, 146.

117. Cairo CG 52994, 52995, 52063, 52892, 53011; JE 31077, 31079, 31083; Seipel 2001, no. 42, fig. on p. 54 (in color).

118. Jéquier 1921, 91–93.

119. de Morgan 1903, 48.

120. de Morgan 1903, 52, 54; compare the discussion in Mace, Winlock 1916, 71–72.

121. von Bissing 1907, 136–38; Cairo CG 18642–50.

122. Koura 1999, 217–19.

123. Koura 1999, 171–73.

124. Koura 1999, 173–76.

125. Koura 1999, 204–6.

126. Koura 1999, 193–95.

127. Koura 1999, 181–83.

128. Koura 1999, 177–80.

129. Koura 1999, 155–57.

130. Koura 1999, 175–76.

131. Koura 1999, 72–79.

132. Koura 1999, 79 (VII, 134).

133. Koura 1999, 58–63.

134. Interpretation as incense burner: Fischer 1980, 916 n. 10; Radwan 1983, 86–87, no. 217 (there are several other identical objects from Dahshur, without exact provenance, nos. 218–21; all most likely come from de Morgan's excavation); for the interpretation as lamp see: Müller 2006.

135. Junker 1929, 129–31.

136. Fay 1996, 30–32.

137. Sabbahy 2002.

138. Ranke 1935, 49, nos. 3, 5, 7.

139. de Morgan 1903, 55–68, 159–60; Podvin 1997; Podvin 2000, 329; PM III (2), 886.

140. Ranke 1935, 276, 17.

141. de Morgan 1903, 55.

142. Picture of the collar: Aldred 1971, pl. 11 (in color).

143. de Morgan 1903, 64, nos. 36–48; Vilímková 1969, pl. 18; Aldred 1971, pl. 30.

144. de Morgan 1903, 55; CG 52044–45, JE 31091; Aldred 1971, pl. 12; Tiradritti 1998, fig. on p. 144.

145. de Morgan 1903, 60.

146. CG 52859, JE 31104; Vilímková 1969, pl. 13; Aldred 1971, pl. 28 (in color); Andrews 1990, fig. 82; Ikram, Dodson 1998, pl. XII.

147. CG 52860, JE 31105; Vilímková 1969, pl. 12; Tiradritti 1998, fig. on p. 145; Ikram, Dodson 1998, pl. XIII.

148. Lilyquist 1993, 36–37; Markowitz, Lacovara 2009, 60, proposes a Minoan craftsman working in Egypt.

149. Wolters 1983, 69–71; Lilyquist 1993, 31–51; Wilde 40–41 (for the Middle Kingdom).

150. CG 52975, JE 31126.

151. CG 52978, JE 31125.

152. CG 52976, JE 31124.

153. CG 52979, JE 31121.

154. Vilímková 1969, pl. 17 a–e; Aldred 1971, pl. 29, fuller description on pp. 186–88.

155. Fitton 2009, 65.

156. Fitton, Meeks, Joyner 2009, 23–24, figs. 101, 102.

157. Cairo CG 52914, 52955–56, 52958; Aldred 1971, pl. 31.

158. Cairo CG 18651; von Bissing 1907, 138–39.

159. Cairo CG 18652–59, 18661; von Bissing 1907, 139–40.

160. Arnold 2006, 48 n. 3.

161. Allen 1998, 42.

162. On swans in ancient Egypt see Houlihan 1988, 50–52.

163. Engelbach 1915, pl. XXIII; in general: Jéquier 1921, 330–31.

164. Davies, Gardiner, Davies 1920, pls. XVII, XVIII.

165. Reeves 1990, 130.

166. Faulkner, Andrews 1985, 95.

167. PT utterance 267, 366a/b; utterance 509, 1122 a/b.

168. de Morgan 1903, 57; compare for the spells on Middle Kingdom coffin lids: Willems 1988, 171–74.

169. de Morgan 1903, 68.

170. Stünkel 2006, 155–56.

171. Fay 1996, 46.

172. Aldred 1971, 186.

173. Roth 2001, 279–83.

174. de Morgan 1903, 71–77.

175. PM III (2), 886.

176. Picture of the collar and of one bracelet: Aldred 1971, pl. 10.

177. A photographic image: Houlihan 1988, 50–51, figs. 66a, b.

178. de Morgan 1903, 74.

179. Farag, Iskander 1971, ix.

180. Farag, Iskander 1971 (the excavation report); Podvin 1997, 173–74; Dodson 2000b (summary of the burial), Theis 2011a, 110 (no. 121, on the pyramid).

181. Arnold 1987, 35.

182. Farag, Iskander 1971, 17–24.

183. Grajetzki 2005a.

184. Willems 1988, 174.

185. Farag, Iskander 1971, 92–95.

186. Willems 1988, 211.

187. Gautier, Jéquier 1902, pls. XXXII–XXV.

188. Farag, Iskander 1971, 31.

189. Farag, Iskander 1971, 45; Tiradritti 1998, fig. on p. 140 (the flail: JE 90200).

190. For glass before the New Kingdom: Nicholson, Henderson 2000, 195, compare Lilyquist 1993, 53–55.

191. JE 90199; Tiradritti 1998, fig. on pp. 152–53; Andrews 1990, fig. 26.

192. Lilyquist 2003, 127–28.

193. Petrie 1890, 15, pl. V.

194. Schiestl 2009, 149, 152; Kopetzky 2010, 134–35.

195. Schiestl 2009, 142; Kopetzky 2010, 127.

196. Petrie 1890, 15, pl. V; compare the discussion: Arnold 1982, 58.

197. Allen 1998, 47.

198. Cairo CG 9438. It is far from certain that the magical wand belongs to Neferuptah, daughter of Amenemhat III. The wand was found at Lisht. This Neferuptah is therefore sometimes treated as daughter of Senusret I (Schmitz 1976, 191). This too is far from certain; compare also Grdseloff 1951.

199. The list of sources: Farag, Iskander 1971, 101–5.

200. Allen 1998, 47.

201. Schiestl 2009, 149 n. 1442.

202. Petrie 1890, 17, discussed in full in Miniaci 2010, 116.

203. Aldred 1971, pl. 50.

204. Petrie 1890, 17.

205. de Morgan 1895, 107–15; Podvin 1997, 169–72; Podvin 2000, 333–34; PM III (2), 889.

206. Allen 1998, 47.

207. Lilyquist 1979a, fig. 73.

208. The only other example appears in the tomb of King Awibre Hor: de Morgan 1895, fig. 222.

209. Jéquier 1921, 173–76.

210. de Morgan 1895, 110, fig. 260.

211. Donadoni Roveri 1969, 71, fig. 15b.

212. Soliman 2009, 116–18.

213. Soliman 2009, 105–7.

214. de Morgan 1903, 34, figs. 81, 83.

215. Jéquier 1933a, 36–37, figs. 6–28, pl. VIII.

216. Miniaci, Quirke 2008, 20–21.

217. Grajetzki 2007, 49–50.

218. Mace, Winlock 1916, 48.

219. Mace, Winlock 1916, 66 n. 2.

220. de Morgan 1895, 112, pl. XXXVIII; compare Wilkinson 1971, 73.

221. Montet 1928, 172, pl. XCVIII.

222. Aldred 1971, pls. 82–83; compare also Jéquier 1921, 43–45.

223. Reeves 1996.

224. Aldred 1971, pl. 32.

225. Petschel 2011, 246, 500 (no. 246).

226. de Morgan 1895, 111, fig. 264.

227. Lüscher 1990, 27, 69.

228. de Morgan 1895, 115, fig. 269; Cairo CG 4007–10.

229. de Morgan 1895, 104, fig. 24.

230. Ranke 1935, 192, 2.

231. Hodjash, Berlev 1982, 93 (s).

232. D. Fouqet, in de Morgan 1895, 150.

233. Stirland 1999, 30–33.

234. de Morgan 1895, 128.

235. von Beckerath 44–45 (full discussion); Ryholt 1997, 216, 339–40.

236. Ben-Tor 2001.

237. Ryholt 1997, 38–39.

238. Ryholt 1997, 218.

239. Ryholt 1997, 35, fig. 1; 38–40.

240. Arnold 2002, 27 (the measurements are not certain).

241. Arnold 2002, 58.

242. Arnold 2002, 59.

243. Stünkel 2006.

244. Arnold 2002, 64; Tallet 2005, 15–16.

245. de Morgan 1895, 60–44.

246. Arnold 2002, 70.

247. CG 52001, JE 30857; Feucht 1967, 27, 161, no. 1 (with full bibliography); Aldred 1971, pl. 33; Desroches-Noblecourt 1979, fig. 323; Müller, Thiem 1999, 219, fig. 201 (in color); Tiradritti 1998, figs. on pp. 136, 148; PM III (2), 883.

248. CG 52041, JE 38435; Aldred 1971, pl. 34.

249. Oppenheim 1995, 11.

250. Andrews 1981, 95 (list of similar amulets from the Middle Kingdom).

251. CG 53137, JE 30865; Andrews 1981, 91 (list of similar lion amulets from the Middle Kingdom); compare also the gold lions found in the burial of Queen Khenmet-nefer-hedjet-weret, Oppenheim 1995, 10.

252. CG 53136, JE 30858; Seipel 2001, 57, no. 46, color picture on p. 58; Tiradritti 1998, fig. on 149; Andrews 1981, 94 (list of similar objects from the Middle Kingdom); compare also the seven golden cowrie shells found in the burial of Queen Khenmet-nefer-hedjet-weret, Oppenheim 1995, 11.

253. Seipel 2001, 57, no. 47, color picture on p. 59.

254. Allen 1998, 40; Kopetzky 2010, 123 n. 723, 135.

255. de Morgan 1895, 62, fig. 133.

256. Arnold 2002, 74, mentions a further king's daughter Sat . . . (rest of name not preserved). However, this is a "ghost princess," by error discussed twice in the publication. Once, in discussing tomb 11, he refers to the remains of a canopic chest, where only the title "king's daughter" is preserved. He sees the remains of the name Sat, but these remains of the name are not visible on the published fragments. There is only the title "king's daughter." In the discussion of tomb 5 (Arnold 2002, 71) he refers again to the same canopic chest, this time noting that there are no remains of the name. The text of the canopic box is depicted in de Morgan 1895, 57, fig. 125.

257. Ryholt 1997, 39–40 n. 104 (known from a scarab; Petrie Museum UC 11595).

258. Bietak, Forstner-Müller 2009, 111–12.

259. de Morgan 1895, 64–72; Arnold 2002, 70.

260. Aldred 1971, 194–95.

261. CG 52002, JE 30875; Feucht 1967, 31–33, 163, no. 4; Vilímková 1969, pl. 9; Aldred 1971, pl. 41; Desroches-Noblecourt 1979, fig. 234; Tiradritti 1998, figs. on pp. 136–37, 139 (top), 150–51; Andrews 1990, fig. 112; PM III (2), 884.

262. CG 52003, JE 30875; Feucht 1967, 31–33, 163–64, no. 5; Vilímková 1969, pl. 10; Aldred 1971, pl. 42; PM III (2), 884.

263. Aldred 1971, 194.

264. Farag, Iskander 1971, pls. vi–viii.

265. CG 53070; Tiradritti 1998, fig. on pp. 140–41; Desroches-Noblecourt 1979, fig. 233.

266. CG 53168; JE 30888.

267. CG 53078, JE 30893.

268. CG 53074; Vilímková 1969, pl. 20.

269. CG 53075; Desroches-Noblecourt 1979, fig. 240; Seipel 2001, no. 53.

270. CG 52026, JE 30886; CG 52027, JE 30886; Seipel 2001, no. 52.

271. CG 52056, JE 30883.

272. CG 53096–53099, JE 30906; Seipel 2001, no. 51 (two lions and beads reconstructed as an armlet).

273. The mirrors are reconstructed in Lilyquist 1979a, 31–32 n. 358.

274. CG 53079–81; JE 30897, 30897.

275. Cairo CG 52238 (no. 33); CG 52239 (no. 34), Wilkinson 1971, 77, pl. XI, B, C; Lilyquist 1993, figs 8e, 8f on p. 78.

276. Cairo CG 53071; Seipel 2001, no. 50.

277. Aston, Harrell, Shaw 2000, 40, CG 18778.

278. Möller, Schubart 1910, 44 (calling them un-Egyptian); Lilyquist 1993, 37; Wilkinson 1971, 77.

279. de Morgan 1895, 69, figs. 147, 150, 153.

280. de Morgan 1895, 69, fig. 152.

281. de Morgan 1895, 69, fig. 146.

282. de Morgan 1895, 69, fig. 151.

283. Aldred 1971, 194.

CHAPTER 2

1. See n. 46 in Chapter 4.

2. Compare the short summary of such burials in Engelbach 1923, 2–3 (Wady I and Wady II).

3. Late Middle Kingdom tomb chapels have been excavated in recent years at Thebes: Nelson, Kalos 2000.

4. Seidlmayer 1987, 184–85.

5. Lilyquist 1979a, 83; Pearson 1999, 95–123; Díaz-Andreu 2005, 38–39.

6. Firth, Gunn 1926, 59–60.

7. Cairo CG 52752, JdE 47847; the personal adornments are depicted in color in Vilímková 1969, pl. 21a.

8. Cairo CG 52753, JdE 47848.

9. Cairo CG 52755, JdE 47845.

10. Cairo CG 52756, JdE 47844.

11. Cairo CG 52754, JdE 47846.

12. Firth, Gunn 1926, 60–61.

13. Ranke 1935, 285, 20; the name means "daughter of Ip."

14. Allen 1950, 72–73; Lapp 1993, 281; Gestermann 2010; Grajetzki 2010, 24.

15. de Morgan 1895, 35–37, figs. 73–76.

16. Excavation report: Engelbach 1923; a recent summary on the burials: Grajetzki 2004b; an evaluation of the social stratification of the late Middle Kingdom burials: Richards 2005, 90–98, 112–18; on the chronology see Kemp, Merrillees 1980, 23–57.

17. Tombs 17, 49, 105, 108, 110, 121, 162, 171, 280, 608.

18. Tombs 3, 4, 5, 8, 11, 22, 30, 35, 43, 57, 58, 64, 67, 70, 81, 92, 93, 96, 104, 106, 109, 118, 119, 122, 128, 129, 132, 133, 134, 138, 141, 143, 159, 161, 190,

246, 250, 256, 262, 264, 271, 284, 285, 293, 302, 320, 336, 337, 341, 347, 348, 353, 357, 365, 377, 381, 383, 385, 386, 390, 394, 397, 398, 399, 501, 605, 606, 611, 614, 620.

19. Some were found basically intact; of others only the inlaid eyes were preserved. The eyes might also belong to anthropoid coffins or mummy masks: tombs 128, 246, 250, 285 (information from tomb card), 320, 341, 347, 394, 397, 501, 605.

20. Tombs 5, 35, 67, 70, 96, 109, 122, 132, 293, 608.

21. Tombs 8, 11, 30, 43, 92, 93, 129, 134, 271, 284, 336, 353, 377, 381, 386, 390, 399, 611.

22. Tombs 3, 70, 96, 104, 109, 118, 143, 159, 190, 284, 285, 320, 341, 348, 357, 377, 605, 614.

23. Bourriau 2003, 57.

24. Grajetzki 2004b, 53–56.

25. Hayes 1953, 312, fig. 203.

26. Miniaci 2011.

27 On the problems of "eyes" in (Old Kingdom) burials, compare de Meyer 2011.

28. Engelbach 1923, 14–15.

29. Aldred 1971, pl. 78.

30. Aldred 1971, 141.

31. Staehelin 1978, 82.

32. Engelbach 1923, 15–16; Grajetzki 2004b, 31–33; Bagh 2011, 141–43.

33. Reconstruction: Feucht 1967, 44–45, 166, no. 9.

34. The stela is now in the Ny Carlsberg Glyptotek ÆIN 1664 (Copenhagen), Jørgensen 1996, 182–83, no. 65; Bagh 2011, 141.

35. Engelbach 1915 (the excavation report); an evaluation for the social stratification of the burials in the cemetery is published in Richards 2005, 121–24.

36. Engelbach 1915, 11–13.

37. Manchester Museum, inv. no. 5966; Feucht 1957, 39–41, 165–66, no. 8.

38. Manchester Museum, inv. no. 5968.

39. Manchester Museum, inv. no. 5967.

40. Dubiel 2008, 155.

41. For these people, their burials, and their titles, see Seidlmayer 1990, 216–33; Seidlmayer 2007.

42. For the importance of H. Jones see: Pinch-Brock 2007, 31–39.

43. Garstang 1907.

44. Garstang 1907, 113–14, figs. 102–7.

45. The list of names found in the tombs at Beni Hassan indeed state "son" (Garstang 1907, pl. VIII).

46. Garstang 1907, 146, fig. 144.

47. Brunton 1948, 55, pl. XLIII.

48. Petrie 1907, 13.

49. Garstang 1902, 2 (description of tombs and finds).

50. Doxey 1997.

51. Petrie 1901b, 43; Podvin 1997, 121–22; Podvin 2000, 330.

52. Color picture of the golden fish: Pouls 1997.

53. The evidence was reevaluated in Bourriau 2009, which presents a tomb register. I take only the tombs dated MK/SIP or SIP (Middle Kingdom, Second Intermediate Period) into account.

54. Tomb nos. Y5, Y81, Y432, Y511, Y512, Y480.

55. Tomb nos. Y480, Y413, Y453, Y224, Y411, Y422, Y423, Y428, Y435, Y437, Y505, Y510, Y514.

56. Junker 1920, 147; Lilyquist 1979a 35, 397.

57. Lilyquist 1979a, 35 n. 397 (list of examples found in burials). About eight examples were excavated in burials of the Middle Kingdom. A further torque was found by John Garstang in tomb 345 A'07 in Abydos. The tomb group included a bronze mirror, stone vessels, scarabs, a green glaze crocodile, shells, silver ornaments for a necklace, and tweezers; Snape 1986, 216, 437.

58. Montet 1928, 123, pls. LXVII, LXX (more than forty examples found in the "Montet jar" at Byblos).

59. Junker 1920, 153.

60. Junker 1920, 159 (description of the burial).

61. Randall-MacIver, Woolley 1911, 200–201

CHAPTER 3

1. Blackman 1953, pl. XI (choker with shell pendants?).

2. Keimer 1948, 23.

3. Compare the discussion with full bibliography in Pinch 1993, 211–14.

4. Pinch 1993, 215–17.

5. Waraksa 2009, 16.

6. Budin 2011, 117–35, especially 126–35.

7. Helck 1975.

8. Pinch 1993, 225.

9. Type I of Pinch 1993, 198–99 (she includes figures of different materials).

10. Wildung 1985a, 139, no. 65.

11. Hayes 1953, 219; Bourriau 1988, 126–27, no. 121.

12. Wilkinson 1971, 20; Andrews 1990, 43.

13. Wilkinson 1971, 37–43.

14. Grajetzki 2004a, fig. on p. 23.

15. Leiden A0.11a; Raven 1989.

16. Cairo JE 39390; Wildung 1984a, fig. 74 on p. 85; compare Arnold 2008, 82 n. 165 (with further literature).

17. Blackman 1953, pl. XIV; Forman, Quirke 1996, figs. on pp. 104–5.

18. Curto 1988, fig. 48; Zanelli 1989, figs. 7–8.

19. Aldred 1971, pl. 18, p. 183.

20. Newberry 1893b, pl. XIII.

21. Garstang 1907.

22. Jéquier 1921, 62–71.

23. Mace, Winlock 1916, 65.

24. New York, MMA 12.183.16 (the object is not yet published, but a picture is accessible via the database of the museum).

25. de Morgan 1895, 99–100, fig. 231.

26. Wildung 1985a, 54–55, no. 21.

27. Pozzi Battaglia 2009.

28. Wildung 1985a, 139, no. 65.

29. Andrews 1990, 117.

30. Bothmer 1960, 76–77.

31. Junker 1943, 223, fig. 89.

32. In general: Dubiel 2008, 154–57; further example of a shell found on a breast: Cecil 1903, 68.

33. Jéquier 1921, 58–60.

34. Wildung 1985a, 139, cat. no. 65; Caubet, Pierrat-Bonnefois 2005, 37, fig. 64.

35. Engelbach 1923, 15.

36. Aldred 1971, pl. 32.

37. Aldred 1971, pl. 24.

38. See the back of pectorals in Aldred 1971, pls. 73–74, 76, 81.

39. Feucht 1967, 164–65, no. 6 (perhaps orginally found at Byblos?); 166, no. 10 (originally from Dahshur?).

40. Andrews 1990, 117.

41. Aldred 1971, 146, pl. 15.

42. Blackman 1953, pls. XI, XV.

43. Dunn Friedman 1998, 212, no. 80; Markowitz, Haynes, Freed 2002, 70, 18.

44. Aldred 1971, pl. 30.

45. Newberry 1893a, pl. XXIX; for a color photo: Aldred 1971, pl. 32.

46. Aldred 1971, 160.

47. Petrie 1930, pl. XXIV.

48. Aldred 1971, 160–61.

49. Middle Kingdom body chains have so far not been discussed. However,

Fletcher 2008, 251, 395, discusses them for Ptolemaic Period Egypt in connection with Aphrodite.

50. Examples include Kaiser 1967, 45, no. 458; Wildung 1985a, no. 65; Wildung 1985b, 41–42, cat. no. 29; Caubet, Pierrat-Bonnefois 2005, 37, fig. 64.

51. Pavlov, Hodjash 1985, pl. 45; Keimer 1948, pl. XIII, 5.

52. Boardman 1996, 4.

53. Rummel 2007a, 35, no. 19; another example: Pinch 2006, 127, fig. 67.

54. Petrie 1930, pl. XXIV.

55. Serpico 2008, 131–32, fig. 57.

56. Engelbach 1923, 14.

57. Vandier d'Abbadie 1946, 189–90, pls. CXXII, CXXIII, 2868; Peck 1978, 138–39, no. 68.

58. Montet 1951, 83–84, no. 775, fig. 31, pl. LV.

59. Boardman 1996, 4.

60. Pinch 2006, 126.

61. Fay 1990, 58.

62. Pinch 2006, 107, fig. 55.

63. Dubiel 2008, 149.

64. Keimer 1948, 20–21.

65. Brunton, Caton-Thompson 1928, 15, pl. VIII (Badari tomb 5735); Brunton 1937, 37 (Mostagedda tomb 592); Andrews 1990, 57.

66. Patch 2002.

67. Baba, Yoshimura 2010, fig. on p. 11 (middle).

68. CG 28084; for the dating see Willems 1988, 76–77.

69. Aston, Harrell, Shaw 2000, 45–46.

70. Aston, Harrell, Shaw 2000, 50–52.

71. Aston, Harrell, Shaw 2000, 62–63.

72. Aston, Harrell, Shaw 2000, 39–40.

73. Hölzl 2001, 43, nos. 27–28.

74. Seidlmayer 2001, 235.

75. Quirke 2007a, 249–50.

76. Bourriau 1988, 126–27.

77. Ikram, Dodson 1998, 147.

78. Information kindly supplied by Janet Johnson (UCL).

79. Garstang 1907, 110.

80. Hayes 1953, 306–9; compare also the comments in Winlock 1942, 225, on the jewelry of Wah.

81. Aldred 1971, 178 (referring to the broad collar of Senebtisi).

82. Aldred 1971, 179.

83. Guilhou 2003.

84. Translation according to Faulkner 1969, 316.

85. Haslauer, in Seipel 2001, 33–34, no. 18.

86. Aldred 1971, 179 (on the jewelry of real life in the jewelry boxes).

87. Bianchi 1986.

88. Kitchen 1963 (with further literature).

89. Schmitz 1976, 202.

90. Roth 2001, 279–83.

91. Blackman 1953, pl. XIX.

92. Winlock 1932; Bourriau 1988, 153–54, no. 172.

93. A similar situation still exists today in the Western world. While women can wear almost all types of clothing and jewelry, including all those regarded as typical of men (e.g., suits and ties), there are still many types of women's clothing (e.g., skirts) not widely accepted for men.

94. Seidlmayer 1990, 310.

95. Greer 1971, 58–59.

96. For a translation: Lichtheim 1975, 216.

CHAPTER 4.

1. Gramsci 2007, 2311–13; English translation and further discussion of Gramsci's idea: Crehan 2002, 106–7.

2. Crehan 2002, 137–45.

3. Seidelmayer 2001, 235.

4. Myśliwiec 2008, 13.

5. For an overview of these buildings see the collection of papers in *Archéo-Nil* 18 (December 2008) (*La Naissance de l'architecture funéraire*).

6. Stevenson 2009, 159–215.

7. Grajetzki 2003, 7–14.

8. Frankfort 1930, 214, pl. XXX; Andrews 1990, 43.

9. Reisner 1908, 29–33, pls. 4–8; Andrews 1990, 20, fig. 11.

10. Petrie 1901a, 16–19, frontispiece.

11. Petrie 1901a, 16 (assigns them to Djer's queen); Aldred 1971, 173, color images: pl. 1.

12. Ikram, Dodson 1998, 320; Owens, Tucker, Hassan 2009, 248.

13. Junker 1929, 120–31.

14. See, for example, the jewelry found at Gizeh, shaft 316: Seipel 2001, 33–37.

15. Compare the remarks of Mackay 1915, 8.

16. Grajetzki 2003, 15–26.

17. Grajetzki 2003, 27–39.

18. Allen 2006.

19. Baines, Yoffee 1998.

20. O'Connor 2000, 21–24.

21. Seidlmayer 2001, 240–45.

22. Dunn Friedman 1998, 212 n. 80.

23. Hassan 1932, 44.

24. Kaiser 1969, 56–68.

25. Andrews 1990, 175.

26. Hassan 1936, 139–50; color photographs of the diadem and the "insect" necklace: Aldred 1971, pls. 4–5; reconstructed bead-net dresses: Jick 1988; Rigault 1999; Gomez-Deluchi 2005.

27. See, e.g., Markowitz, Haynes, Freed 2002, 118, no. 51.

28. A large number of copper offering tables and copper vessels were found in the undisturbed (still unpublished) tomb of Ptahshepses Impy at Gizeh: Radwan 1983, 61–62, nos. 154 A–K, pls. 28–31; Markowitz, Haynes, Freed 2002, 102–3, no. 39.

29. Seidlmayer 1990; Seidlmayer 2001.

30. Brunton 1948, 36–37, pl. XL.

31. For the sequence of Middle Kingdom governors see Grajetzki 1997 and Melandri 2011; for the burials of the First Intermediate Period at Qaw see Seidl-mayer 1990, 123–210.

32. Brunton 1927, 40; Brunton 1928, pl. LXVI.

33. Garstang 1907.

34. Grajetzki 2003, 39–51.

35. Hayes 1953, 303–5.

36. Grajetzki 2003, 51–53; the jewelry equipment in provincial cemeteries is described by Dubiel 2008.

37. Winlock 1921, 51–53; Winlock 1942, 44–46.

38. James 1974, 37–38, no. 85, pl. XXXII; for a discussion of these spells compare Willems 1988, 122–27.

39. Winlock 1942, 44, pl. 10; she was perhaps a woman from Nubia. Compare Zibelius-Chen 2007, 396.

40. Grajetzki 2005b, 24–25.

41. Arnold 1992, 54–55.

42. Arnold 1992, 54–58.

43. Seidlmayer 1990, 310.

44. Frankfort 1930, 219, pl. XXXVII.

45. Important exceptions are the coffin of the "chief lector priest" Sesenebnef found at Lisht (Thirteenth Dynasty; Grajetzki 2010, 30–31; L1–2Li) and the coffin of the Second Intermediate Period queen Mentuhotep from Thebes (Geisen 2004), both with inside decoration.

46. In general see: Bourriau 1991. "Shabtis" of the early Middle Kingdom are not shown as mummies, and I would not like to call them "shabtis" (Hayes 1953, 327); on the first heart scarabs see Quirke 2003, Lorand 2008.

47. Bourriau 1991.

48. Grajetzki 2004a, 46–49.

49. Kemp, Merrillees 1980, 167–68.

50. de Morgan 1895, 87–106; Aufrère 2001.

51. His human remains are now a skeleton and are stored today in the Egyptian Museum, Cairo. The skeleton was well preserved, with remains of flesh still on the head (Owens, Tucker, Hassan 2009, 249).

52. Patch 1995, 104.

53. Engelbach 1915, 13, 19, 23–25.

54. Gautier, Jéquier 1902, 74–79.

55. The myth is described as a whole by Plutarch: Gwyn Griffiths 1970.

56. Willems 1997.

57. Gardiner 1917; Grajetzki 2010, 89–94.

58. Montet 1951, pl. LXXVI.

59. Grajetzki 2010, 67.

60. de Morgan 1895, 95, de Morgan 1903, 60; Gauthier, Jéquier 1902, 79.

61. Theis 2011b.

62. In this way indicated by Gnirs 2009, 105.

63. This is also visible in tomb decorations of New Kingdom queens, such as in the tomb of Nefertari, wife of Ramses II; compare: McCarthy 2002.

64. Examples: Nubhetepti-khered (see Chapter 1); Hayes 1953, fig. 201 on p. 310 ("steward" Khnumhotep from Meir); de Morgan 1895, fig. 27 on p. 21 (from the mastaba of the vizier Khnumhotep at Dahshur); compare discussion in Rogge 1986, 57 n. 146.

65. Rummel 2007a, fig. 114 on p. 81 (tomb of Geheset at Thebes).

66. Renfrew 1986, 146–50.

67. Enmarch 2008, 85 (Leiden I 344 recto, 3.8); amethyst is mentioned in the text. This may be another indicator that the text was composed in the late Middle Kingdom, as this semiprecious stone was especially popular in this period (Aston, Harrell, Shaw 2000, 51).

68. Engelbach 1915, pl. XXIII; compare Jéquier 1921, 329–30.

69. Other late Middle Kingdom burials of this type not described in this book: Ankhet and unknown woman at Rifeh (set of well-decorated coffins, mummy masks, little jewelry: Petrie 1907, 12–13).

70. There are well-recorded burials without canopic equipment but with signs of mummification, e.g., the burials of Geheset at Thebes (Lösch et al. 2007, 100–101) and Ankhet at Lisht (Arnold 1992, 54–55).

71. A similar necklace (obsidian beads with silver caps) was found in the burial of Hapy Ankhtifi at Meir: New York, MMA 12.183.13a, b; mentioned in Hayes 1953, 236. A picture is available in the museum's database.

72. Carnarvon, Carter 1912, 54–55.

73. Carnarvon, Carter 1912, 60.

74. Seidlmayer 1990, 428.

75. Garstang 1902, pl. III (E. 105), pl. XV (E.105); compare Bourriau 1988, 150, no. 163.

76. Burials with decorated coffins belong to type 2.

77. Bourriau 1991.

78. Grajetzki 2004b.

79. Willems 2006, 149–50.

80. Seidlmayer 2001, 231–40; compare the discussion of Wilfong 2010, 169–73.

81. Brunton 1930, pls. V–VIII (tomb register), tombs 1001 (mask), 7045 (anthropoid coffin?), 7125, 7171 (stuccoed coffins); for the dating of the cemetery see Bourriau 2010, 23–29.

82. See n. 95 (Chapter 1) for literature on the hour vigil.

83. Kamal 1901; Leclant 1979, fig. 334; Grajetzki 2010, 96.

84. Grajetzki 2010, 90.

85. Assmann 2002, 215.

86. Willems 1988, 206.

87. Jéquier 1933b, pl. XII; compare for a recent translation: Allen 2005, 318.

88. Reeves 1990, 112–13.

89. Montet 1951, 41–42, 50, pls. XXXI–XXXII; compare Aston 2009, 52.

90. Peebles 1971, 69.

91. Compare the discussion in Stevenson 2009, 160–61.

92. Assmann 1997, 131–32.

93. Kemp, Merrillees 1980, 167–68.

94. Miniaci, Quirke 2009.

95. Seidlmayer 1987, 193.

96. Renfrew 1986, 146–50.

97. Szpakowska 2008, 196, comes to a similar conclusion

98. Compare a case in the New Kingdom where the magical bricks are restricted to a limited number of burials of the highest ruling class. The bricks were evidently affordable by almost everyone, but it seems that not everyone had access to the rituals connected to the bricks; see Franzmeier 2010.

99. For the late Middle Kingdom in general: Quirke 1990, 1–8.

100. Franke 1991.

101. Newberry 1893a, pls. XI, XXIX.

102. Gestermann 1995, 49.

103. Grajetzki 2010, 103–4.

104. For example, several coffin fragments found at Hu, which are close in style to coffins from Thebes and may have been produced there (Grajetzki 2010, 15–22).

105. See a shabti found at Esna: Downes 1974, 5, fig. 4.

106. Vila 1976 (Vila argues for a local production of mummy masks).

107. Franke 1994, 105–17 (discussion for Elephantine).

108. Grajetzki 2003, 54–61.

109. Whelan 2007.

110. Grajetzki 2010, 39–43.

111. Grajetzki 2010, 57–58.

112. Forstner-Müller 2008, 48–49; Schiestl 2009, 118–19.

113. Forstner-Müller 2008, 56–57; Schiestl 2009, 92–93.

114. Forstner-Müller 2008, 169–74.

115. Petrie 1909, 6–10, pls. XXII–XXIX; Miniaci 2011, 65–66.

116. Data on Queen Ahhotep: Ryholt 1997, 275–77. There are perhaps two queens with the same name.

117. von Bissing 1900; Miniaci 2011, 55–56; for Dra Abu el-Naga in general see Miniaci 2009.

118. Miniaci 2011.

119. Gnirs 2009, 105–6; Graves-Brown 2010, 39.

120. Aldred 1971, 19.

121. Smith 1992; Grajetzki 2003, 66–83.

122. First full publication: Winlock 1948; the whole tomb group is republished in Lilyquist 2003. Lilyquist also reexcavated the tomb.

123. Steindorff 1937, 199–200.

124. Smith 1992, 220.

125. Grajetzki 2003, 84–93.

126. Budka 2010.

127. Taylor 1999.

128. Davis et al. 1908, 31–32.

129. Aldred 1971, 233–35.

130. Davis et al. 1908, 38–39.

131. Davis et al. 1908, 43–44.

132. Gauthier 1921, 21–27; on the burial in general: Aston 2009, 64–65; the pectoral is also depicted in Stierlin, Ziegler 1987, figs. 116–17.

133. Compare the discussions of undisturbed Twenty-sixth Dynasty burials: Bareš 1999, 26–27.

134. Dunham 1963, 366–73.

135. Lohwasser 2001, 167.

136. Hodder 2006, 212.

137. Bacus 2007.

138. For example, in Middle Bronze Age Greece: Kilian-Dirlmeier 1997, 103; Iron Age Italy: Robb 2000, 51; Megiddo: Guy 1938, 170–71.

139. Robb 2000, 51.

140. Glob 1970, 17–98; Müller-Karpe 1985, 126–35; compare more recently on gender: Harding 2000, 406.

141. Guliaev 2003.

142. Müller-Karpe 1979; Müller-Karpe 1985, 155–94.

143. Taylor 1996, 68; compare Harrington 2007.

144. Kenyon 1965, 577.

145. Martin 1971, nos. 354, 475, 1107.

146. Ben-Tor 2007, 121.

147. Kenyon 1965, 315.

148. Guy 1938, pls. 108–9, 118.

149. Guy 1938, 57–58, pls. 26, 115.

150. The burial is not yet fully published; compare for a summary: Matthiae 1981, 206–14, pls. 46–49; Matthiae 1984, 24–25.

151. Matthiae 2008a.

152. Matthiae 2008b.

153. The dating of the tombs is not certain; compare Lilyquist 1993, 41–44; Schiestl 2007, 265 n. 5.

154. Schiestl 2007 (the remains of the Egyptian-style coffin were found in tomb I).

155. Montet 1928, 143–48, 155–202.

156. Woolley 1934, 73–91; a more recent view on the jewelry of the tomb is presented in Pittman 1998.

157. Seager 1912 (the excavation report).

158. Seager 1912, 30.

159. Seager 1912, 31.

160. Seager 1912, 32.

161. Haller 1954, 123–48; Müller-Karpe 1985, 71–88.

162. Benzel 2008.

163. Reuther 1968, 172–73.

CHAPTER 5

1. See in general, for the tombs of queens in the Old and Middle Kingdoms, Jánosi 1996.

2. Davis 1904, 6–7 (canopic jars of the king's son Amenemhat in the tomb of Thutmosis IV).

3. Hornung 1995, 125; compare Gabolde 1998, 118–24.

4. Kozloff, Bryan 1992, 43–44 (on the daughters and family of Amenhotep III).

5. Ziegler 1999a.

6. Curto 1988, fig. 48; Ziegler 1999b, no. 7b.

7. El Awady 2006.

8. Stadelmann 1991, 195, 201.

9. Sabbahy 1997.

10. Compare in general Graves-Brown 2010, 135–36.

11. Blackman 1953, pl. XV.

12. Blackman 1953, pl. XV.

13. Blackman 1953, pl. XIII.

14. Blackman 1953, pls. XI, XVIII.

15. Blackman 1953, pl. XVI.

16. Staehelin 1978, 78 (Hathor is not named in the tomb, but there are many references to her).

17. Petrie 1930, pls. 23–27 (all men shown are priests, sons of Wahka or fertility figures).

18. Gillam 1995; Graves-Brown 2010, 132–33.

19. Fischer 1968, 52 n. 209.

20. Troy 1986, 55.

21. Troy 1986, 157; Gillam 1995, 231–32.

22. Roth 2001, 304.

23. Roth 2001, 339; Altenmüller 1997, 15–19.

24. Staehelin 1978, 81–82; Gillam 1995, 234.

25. Kaiser 1983.

26. Schiff Giorgini 1998, pls. 94–95, 127, 130, 131.

27. Gohary 1992, pl. I.

28. Naville 1892, pl. XVI.

29. Kaiser 1987, fig. 4.

30. Troy 1986, 59.

31. Troy 1986, 89; king's children appear also outside a ritual context, and here they could include boys; see also Roth 2001, 62 n. 339. "King's children" in a ritual context and in administrative and biographical inscriptions seems to have different meanings.

32. Troy 1986, 79–83.

33. Kaiser 1983, 295.

34. Kaiser 1983, 284.

35. Troy 1985, 89–91; Kaiser 1983, 295.

36. Kaiser 1983, 290.

37. Schiff Giorgini 1998, pls. 94–95.

38. Naville 1892, pls. II 10, III 13, IV bis, XVI.

39. Naville 1892, pl. IV 1.

40. Ben-Tor 2004, 23.

41. Kaiser 1983, 284–85.

APPENDIX

1. Roth 2001, 217–20, 432–33; Jánosi 2010.

2. Champollion 1824, 196–97, pl. X, 2; Roth 2001, 220–24.

3. Simpson 1954, 267, pl. XX, fig. 2; Schmitz 1976, 191.

4. Arnold 1992, 24–25, pls. 17c, 19b, 20a–c; Theis 2011a, 100–101 (no. 109).

5. James 1974, 44 (104a), pl. XXXV.

6. Hayes 1953, 176–77.

7. Schmitz 1976, 190; Roth 2001, 433–34.

8. Schmitz 1976, 192; Arnold 1992, 58, no. 23, pls. 70.23, 71a (23).

9. Gardiner, Peet 1952, pl. XXI (71); Fay 1996, 47 (Amenemhat II is also mentioned in the inscription, so it remains an option that she was his daughter).

10. Roth 2001, 242–45, 582, figs. 112, 113.

11. Callender 2005, 212.

12. Perdu 1977, 69–70.

13. Stünkel 2006, 153–55.

14. Stünkel 2006, 155–56.

15. Perdu 1977 (list of sources). A further parallel for such an ambiguity is the name or title Semathor, three times attested in the late Middle Kingdom. Once it appears on coffin fragments found at Abydos (Grajetzki 2010, 6–7, the reference to Ranke 1935, 313, 24, there should be deleted—it is a misreading of a name and title by Ranke); once on a stela from Abydos in connection with the name Nebetiunet (Peet 1914, 113, pl. 24.3); and once on a stela from Thebes and connected with the name Sobekhotep (Bazin, el-Enany 2010, 10). The examples on these stelae might give the impression that Semathor was a title in the late Middle Kingdom, as Semathor is attested in the New Kingdom for royal women. However, the title indicates a close relationship to the king, not visible for these women. Furthermore, Horus/Hor appears rarely in titles of private individuals in the Middle Kingdom (see the list of titles in Ward 1986, 156–64, and Stefanović 2009, passim; compare also the list in Troy 1986, 183–84, where the titles combined with Horus are royal). Therefore, I prefer to regard Semathor as a woman's name. The two examples cited in connection with a second name might just refer to double names

16. Cairo CG 382; CG 381 is an almost identical statue, but the original inscriptions are not preserved; Schmitz 1976, 192.

17. Borchardt 1899, 91.

18. Borchardt 1899, 91.

19. Stünkel 2006, 149.

20. Berlin 10.003: Borchardt 1899, 71.

21. Arnold 2002, 118.

22. Arnold 2002, 61–63, pl. 119.

23. Theis 2011a, 82 (no. 88).

24. Arnold 2002, 63–66.

25. Ahrens 2010.

26. Arnold 2002, 72.

27. Arnold 2002, 72 (sarcophagus); de Morgan, 1895, 59, fig. 126 (canopic jars).

28. Strouhal, Klír 2006, 142.

29. Strouhal, Klír 2006, 141.

30. Roth 2001, 440–41.

31. de Morgan 1903, 105, fig. 154.

32. Arnold 1987, 94.

CHRONOLOGY

1. The kings' reigns of the Middle Kingdom are according to Detlef Franke in Hayes 1953 (reprint 1990), 401.

Egyptian Tombs and Excavation Reports

The following are the tombs discussed in this book and their associated excavation reports.

Queen Ahhotep
von Bissing 1900.

Ankhet, Lisht
Arnold 1992, 54–58.

King Awibre Hor
de Morgan 1895, 87–106.

Henutmehyt
Taylor 1999.

Hetepet, Saqqara
Firth, Gunn 1926, 59–60.

Ita, Dahshur
de Morgan 1903, 50–55.

Itaweret, Dahshur
De Morgan 1903, 72–77.

Kama, Tell Moqdam
Gauthier 1921, 21–27.

Khenmet, Dahshur
de Morgan 1903, 55–68.

Mayet
Winlock 1921, 51–53; Winlock
1942, 44–46.

Menhata, Menuwai, Meruta
Winlock 1948, Lilyquist 2003.

Mereret, Dahshur
de Morgan 1895, 64–72.

Mernua
Dunham 1963, 366–73.

Neferuptah, Hawara
Farag, Iskander 1971.

Nubhetepti-khered
de Morgan 1895, 107–15.

Renseneb (Thebes)
Carnarvon, Carter 1912, 54–55.

Sathathor, Dahshur
de Morgan 1895, 60–44.

Sathathoriunet, Lahun
Brunton 1920; Petrie, Brunton,
Murray 1923, 15–16.

Sathathormeryt, Dahshur
de Morgan 1903, 74–77.

Satip, Dahshur
de Morgan 1895, 35–37.

Sawadjet was found at Riqqeh
Engelbach 1915, 13, 19, 23–25.

Seneb, Tomb 487 Beni Hassan
Garstang 1907, 113–14, figs.
102–7.

Senebtisi, Lisht
Mace, Winlock 1916.

Weser and Tanefert, Aniba
Steindorff 1937, 199–200.

ABYDOS

Naqada tomb
Frankfort 1930, 214, pl. XXX.

Tomb 108
Garstang 1902, 2.

Tomb 1008
Frankfort 1930, 219, pl. XXXVII.

BUHEN

Tomb K8
MacIver, Woolley 1911, 200–201.

GIZA

Shaft 133
Hassan 1932, 44.

Tomb 294
Hassan 1936, 139–50.

HARAGEH

Tomb 72
Engelbach 1923, 14–15.

Tomb 124
Engelbach 1923, 15–16.

Tomb 154
Engelbach 1923, pl. LIX (tomb
register).

Tomb 357
Engelbach 1923, pl. LXI (tomb
register).

HU

Tomb W 32
Petrie 1901b, 43.

KUBANIEH NORTH

Tomb 15.l.1
Junker 1920, 147.

Naga ed-Deir, Tomb 1532
Reisner 1908, 29–33, pls. 4–8.

MATMAR

Tomb 521
Brunton 1948, 55, pl. XLIII.

Tomb 1316
Brunton 1948, 36–37, pl. XL.

QAU

Tomb 1735
Brunton 1927, 40; Brunton 1928,
pl. LXVI.

RIFEH

Girl's Tomb
Petrie 1907, 13.

RIQQEH

Tomb 124
Engelbach 1915, 11–13.

SAQQARA, TETI PYRAMID CEMETERY

Tomb 129
Firth, Gunn 1926, 60–61.

Tomb 206
Firth, Gunn 1926, 61.

TELL EL-DAB'A

A/II-m/16
Forstner-Müller 2008, 169–74.

THEBES

Qurna princess
Petrie 1909, 6–10, pls. XXII–
XXIX.

KV 56
Davis et al. 1908, 31–32.

Bibliography

Abbreviations

ASAE	Annales du Service des Antiquités de l'Egypte (Cairo)
BIFAO	Bulletin de l'Institut Français d'Archéologie Orientale (Cairo)
BMMA	Bulletin of the Metropolitan Museum of Art (New York)
BSAE	British School of Archaeology in Egypt (New York)
CdE	Chronique d'Égypte (Brussels)
EES	Egypt Exploration Society (London)
EVO	Egitto e Vicino Oriente (Pisa)
GHP	Golden House Publications (London)
GOF	Göttinger Orientforschungen (Wiesbaden)
JARCE	Journal of the American Research Center in Egypt (Boston)
JEA	Journal of Egyptian Archaeology (London)
JEOL	Jaarbericht van het Vooraziatisch-egyptisch Genootschap Ex Oriente Lux (Leiden)
JNES	Journal of Near Eastern Studies (Chicago)
MDAIK	Mitteilungen des Deutschen Archäologischen Instituts, Abteilung Kairo (DAIK) (Mainz/Cairo/Berlin/Wiesbaden)
OLA	Orientalia Lovaniensia Analecta (Louvain)
OMRO	Oudheidkundige Mededelingen uit het Rijksmuseum van Oudheden (Leiden)
RdE	Revue d'Égyptologie (Paris)
SAK	Studien zur Altägyptischen Kultur (Hamburg)
ZÄS	Zeitschrift für ägyptische Sprache und Altertumskunde (Berlin/Leipzig)

Abubakr, A. M. 1937. *Untersuchungen über die altägyptischen Kronen.* Glückstadt.

Ackerman, S. 1989. *Warrior, Dancer, Seductress, Queen: Women in Judges and Biblical Israel.* New York.

Ahrens, A. 2010. "A Stone Vessel of Princess Itakayet of the 12th Dynasty from Tomb VII at Tell Mišrife/Qatna (Syria)." *Ägypten und Levante* 20: 15–29.

Aldred, C. 1971. *Jewels of the Pharaohs: Egyptian Jewellery of the Dynastic Period.* London.

Alexanian, N. 1998. "Ritualrelikte an Mastabagräber des Alten Reiches." In *Stationen, Beiträge zur Kulturgeschichte Ägyptens*, ed. H. Guksch, D. Polz, 3–22. Mainz am Rhein.

Allam, S. 1963. *Beiträge zum Hathorkult bis zum Ende des Mittleren Reiches.* Münchner Ägyptologische Studien 4. Berlin.

Allen, J. P. 2005. *The Ancient Egyptian Pyramid Texts.* Atlanta.

———. 2006. "Some Aspects of the Non-royal Afterlife in the Old Kingdom." In *The Old Kingdom Art and Archaeology: Proceedings of the Conference Held in Prague, May 31–June 4, 2004*, ed. M. Bárta, 9–17. Prague.

Allen, S. J. 1998. "Queens' Ware: Royal Funerary Pottery in the Middle Kingdom." In *Proceedings of the Seventh Interntional Congress of Egyptologists, Cambridge, 3–9 September 1995* (OLA 82), ed. C. J. Eyre, 39–48. Louvain.

———. 2009. "Funerary Pottery in the Middle Kingdom: Archaism or Revival?" In *Archaism and Innovation: Studies in the Culture of Middle Kingdom Egypt*, ed. D. P. Silverman, W. K. Simpson, J. Wegner, 319–39. Yale Egyptological Seminar. New Haven.

Allen, T. G. 1950. *Occurences of Pyramid Texts with Cross Indexes of These and Other Egyptian Mortuary Texts.* Chicago.

Altenmüller, H. 1977. "Grabausstattung und -beigaben." In *Lexikon der Ägyptologie*, ed. W. Helck, E. Otte, vol. 2, 838–46. Wiesbaden.

———. 1997. "Auferstehungsritual und Geburtsmythos." *SAK* 24: 1–21.

Andrews, C. A. R. 1981. *Catalogue of Egyptian Antiquities in the British Museum VI: Jewellery I: From the Earliest Times to the Seventeenth Dynasty.* London.

———. 1990. *Ancient Egyptian Jewellery.* London.

———. 1994. *Amulets of Ancient Egypt.* London.

Arnold, D. 1987. *Der Pyramidenbezirk des Königs Amenemhet III. in Dahschur.* Mainz am Rhein.

———. 1992. *The Pyramid Complex of Senwosret I: The South Cemeteries of Lisht, III.* New York.

———. 2002. *The Pyramid Complex of Senwosret III at Dahshur: Architectural Studies.* New York.

———. 2008. *Middle Kingdom Tomb Architecture at Lisht.* New York.

Arnold, Do. 1982. "Keramikbearbeitung in Dahschur 1976–1981." *MDAIK* 38: 25–65.

———. 1988. "Pottery." In D. Arnold, *The Pyramid of Senwosret I: The South Cemeteries of Lisht, I*, 106–46. New York.

———. 2006. "The Fragmented Head of a Queen Wearing the Vulture Headdress." In *Timelines: Studies in Honour of Manfred Bietak*, OLA 149, ed. E. Czerny, I. Hein, H. Hunger, D. Melman, A. Schwab, 47–54. Louvain.

Assmann, J. 1997. *Das kulturelle Gedächtnis: Schrift, Erinnerung und politische Identität in frühen Hochkulturen*. Munich.

———. 2002. *Altägyptische Totenligurgien, 1: Totenliturgie in den Sargtexten des Mittleren Reiches*. Heidelberg.

Aston, B., J. Harrell, I. Shaw. 2000. "Stone." In *Ancient Egyptian Materials and Technology*, ed. P. T. Nicholson, I. Shaw, 5–77. Cambridge.

Aston, D. A. 2004. *Tell el-Dab'a XII: A Corpus of Late Middle Kingdom and Second Intermediate Period Pottery*. Vienna.

———. 2009. *Burial Assemblages of Dynasty 21–25, Chronology—Typology—Developments*. Contributions to the Chronology of the Eastern Mediterranean 21. Vienna.

Aufrère, S. H. 2001. "Le roi Aouibrê Hor: Essai d'interprétation du matériel découvert par Jacques de Morgan à Dahchour (1894)." *BIFAO* 101: 1–41.

El Awady, T. 2006. "The Royal Family of Sahure, New Evidence." In *Abusir and Saqqara in the Year 2005*, ed. M. Barta, F. Coppens, J. Krejčí, 191–218. Prague.

Baba, M., S. Yoshimura. 2010. "Dahshur North: Intact Middle and New Kingdom Coffins." *Egyptian Archaeology* 37 (Autumn): 9–12.

Bacus, E. A. 2007. "Expressing Gender in Bronze Age North East Thailand: The Case of Non Nol Tha." In *Archaeology and Women, Ancient and Modern Issues*, ed. S. Hamilton, R. D. Whitehouse, K. I. Wright, 312–34. Walnut Creek, CA.

Bagh, T. 2011. *Finds from W. M. F. Petrie's Excavations in Egypt in the Ny Carlsberh Glyptotek*. Copenhagen.

Baines J., N. Yoffee. 1998. "Order, Legimitacy, and Wealth in Ancient Egypt and Mesopotamia." In *The Archaic State: A Comparative Perspective*, ed. G. Feinman and J. Marcus, 199–260. Santa Fe, NM.

Bareš, L. 1999. *Abusir IV, The Shaft Tomb of Udjahirresnet at Abusir*. Prague.

Barrett, T. H. 2007. "Human Sacrifice and Self-Sacrifice in China: A Century of Revelations." In *The Strange World of Human Sacrifice*, ed. J. N. Bremmer. Studies in the History and Anthroplogy of Religion 1, 237–58. Louvain.

Bazin, L., K. el-Enany. 2010. "La stèle d'un 'chancelier du roi et prophète d'Amon' de la fin du moyen empire à Karnak (Caire JE 37507)." *Karnak* 13: 1–23.

von Beckerath, J. 1964. *Untersuchungen zur politischen Geschichte der Zweiten Zwischenzeit in Ägypten*. Glückstadt.

Ben-Tor, D. 2001. "Beauty and the Beetle: A Princess on a Scarab of the Late Middle Kingdom—13th Dynasty (ca. 1775–1700 BCE)." *The Israel Museum Journal* 19: 22–23.

————. 2004. "Two Royal-Name Scarabs of Amenemhat II from Dahshur." *Metropolitan Museum Journal* 39: 17–33.

————. 2007. *Scarabs, Chronology, and Interconnections: Egypt and Palestine in the Second Intermediate Period*. Orbis Biblicus et Orientalis. Series Archaeologica. Fribourg

Benzel, K. 2008. "Beads." In J. Akruz, K. Benzel, J. M. Evans, *Beyond Babylon, Art, Trade, and Diplomacy in the Second Millennium B.C.*, 213. New York.

Bevan, A. 2007. *Stone Vessels and Values in the Bronze Age Mediterranean*. Cambridge.

Bianchi, R. S. 1986. "Tätowierung." In *Lexikon der Ägyptologie VI*, ed. W. Helck, E. Otto, 145–46. Wiesbaden.

Bietak, M., I. Forstner-Müller. 2009. "Der Hyksos-Palast bei Tell el-Dab'a: Zweite und dritte Grabungskampagne (Frühling 2008 und Frühling 2009)." *Ägypten und Levante* 19: 91–125.

von Bissing, F. W. 1900. *Ein thebanischer Grabfund aus dem Anfang des Neuen Reiches*. Berlin.

————. 1907. *Steingefässe* (Catalogue Général des Antiquités Égyptiennes du Musée du Caire, nos. 18065–18793). Vienna.

von Bissing, F. W., H. Kees. 1923. *Das Re-Heiligtum des Königs Ne-woser-Re (Rathures)*. Leipzig.

Blackman, A. M. 1953. *The Rock Tombs of Meir VI*. London.

Boardman, J. 1996. "The Archaeology of Jewelry." In *Ancient Jewelry and Archaeology*, ed. A. Calinescu, 3–13. Bloomington, IN.

Bonnefoy, Y., W. Doniger. 1992. *Roman and European Mythologies*. Chicago.

Borchardt, L. 1899. "Der zweite Papyrusfund von Kahun und die zeitliche Festlegung des mittleren Reiches der ägyptischen Geschichte." *ZÄS* 37: 89–103.

Bothmer, B. V., in collaboration with H. de Meulenaere, H. W. Müller. 1960. *Egyptian Sculpture of the Late Period, 700 B.C. to A.D. 100*. Ed. E. Riefstahl. New York.

Bourriau, J. 1988. *Pharaohs and Mortals*. Cambridge.

————. 1991. "Patterns of Change in Burial Customs During the Middle Kingdom." In *Middle Kingdom Studies*, ed. S. Quirke, 3–20. New Malden, U.K.

————. 2003. "The Contribution of the Excavation of Lisht North Cemetery to Middle Kingdom Studies." In *Discovering Egypt from the Neva: The Egyptological Legacy of Oleg D. Berlev*, ed. S. Quirke, 51–9. Berlin.

————. 2009 "Mace's Cemetery Y at Diospolis Parva." In *Sitting Beside Lepsius: Studies in Honour of Jaromir Malek at the Griffith Institute*, OLA 185, ed. D. Magee, J. Bourriau, S. Quirke, 39–98. Louvain.

————. 2010. "The Relative Chronology of the Second Intermediate Period: Problems in Linking Regional Archaeological Sequences." In *The Second Intermediate Period (Thirteenth–Seventeenth Dynasties)*, OLA 192, ed. M. Marée, 11–37. Louvain.

Brunton, G. 1920. *Lahun I: The Treasure*. London.

———. 1927. *Qau and Badari I*. London.

———. 1928. *Qau and Badari II*. London.

———. 1930. *Qau and Badari III*. London.

———. 1937. *Mostagedda and the Tasian Culture*. London.

———. 1948. *Matmar*. London.

Brunton G., G. Caton-Thompson. 1928. *The Badarian Civilisation and Predynastic Remains near Badari*. BSAE 46. London.

Budin, S. L. 2011. *Images of Woman and Child from the Bronze Age*. Cambridge.

Budka, J. 2006. "Deponierungen von Balsamierungsmaterial und Topfnester im spätzeitlichen Theben (Ägypten): Befund, Kontext und Versuch einer Deutung." In *Archäologie und Ritual: Auf der Suche nach der rituellen Handlung in den antiken Kulturen Ägyptens und Griechenlands*, ed. J. Mylonopoulos, H. Roeder, 85–103. Vienna.

———. 2010. *Bestattungsbrauchtum und Friedhofsstruktur im Asasif: Eine Untersuchung der spätzeitlichen Befunde anhand der Ergebnisse der österreichischen Ausgrabungen in den Jahren 1969–1977*. Vienna.

Callender, V. G. 2005. Review of Roth 2001. *JEA* 91: 207–15.

Carnarvon, H., Earl of, H. Carter. 1912. *Five Years' Explorations at Thebes: A Record of Work Done 1907–1911*. London.

Caubet, A., G. Pierrat-Bonnefois. 2005. *Faïences de l'antiquité, de l'Égypte à l'Iran*. Paris.

Cavanagh, W. G. 1996. "The Burial Customs." In *Knossos North Cemetery, Early Greek Tombs II*, ed. J. N. Goldstream, H. W. Catling, 651–75. London.

Cecil, Lady W. 1903. "Report on the Work Done at Aswân." *ASAE* 4: 51–73.

Champollion, J.-F. 1824. *Précis du système hiéroglyphique des anciens Égyptiens*. Paris.

Cooney, K. M. 2009. "The Problem of Female Rebirth in New Kingdom Egypt: The Fragmentation of the Female Individual in Her Funerary Equipment." In *Sex and Gender in Ancient Egypt*, ed. C. Graves-Brown, 1–25. Swansea.

Crehan, K. 2002. *Gramsci, Culture and Anthropology*. London.

Curtis, J. 1995. "Gold Face-Masks in the Ancient Near East." In *The Archaeology of Death in the Ancient Near East*, ed. S. Campbell, A. Green, 226–31. Oxford.

Curto, S. 1988. "Antico Regno." In *Civiltà degli Egizi: Le credenze religiose*, ed. A. M. Donadoni Roveri, 44–61. Milan.

van Dijk, J. 2007. "Retainer Sacrifice in Egypt and Nubia." In *The Strange World of Human Sacrifice*, ed. J. N. Bremmer. Studies in the History and Anthroplogy of Religion 1, 135–55. Louvain.

David, R. 2007. *The Two Brothers: Death and Afterlife in Middle Kingdom Egypt*. Bolton.

Davies, N. de G., A. H. Gardiner, N. de G. Davies. 1920. *The Tomb of Antefoker,*

Vizier of Sésostris I and of His Wife Senet. The Theban Tombs series, second memoir. EES. London.

Davis, T. M. 1904. *The Tomb of Thoutmôsis IV*. London.

Davis, T. M., G. Maspero, E. Ayrton, G. Daressy, E. H. Jones. 1908. *The Tomb of Siphtah*. London.

Desroches-Noblecourt, C. 1979. "Die Umgestaltung des Stoffs oder die angewandte Kunst." In Leclant 1979: 227–75.

Díaz-Andreu, M. 2005. "Gender Indentity." In M. Díaz-Andreu, S. Lucy, S. Babi, D. N. Edwards, *The Archaeology of Identity*, 13–42. London.

Dittrich, E. 1981. *Grabkult im Alten China*. Cologne.

Dodson, A. 2000a. "Lahun and Its Treasure." *KMT* 11.1 (Spring): 38–49.

———. 2000b. "The Intact Pyramid Burial of the 12th Dynasty Princess Neferuptah." *KMT* 11.4 (Winter): 41–47.

Donadoni Roveri, A. M. 1969. *I sarcofagi egizi dalle origini alla fine dell'antico regno*. Rome.

Donnan, C. B. 2007. *Moche Tombs at Dos Cabezas*. Los Angeles.

Donner, H. 1959. "Art und Herkunft des Amtes der Königinmutter im Alten Testament." In *Festschrift Johannes Friedrich zum 65. Geburtstag am 27. August 1958 gewidmet*, ed. R. von Kienle et al., 105–45. Heidelberg.

Downes, D. 1974. *The Excavations at Esna, 1905–1906*. Warminster.

Doxey M. D. 1997. "Pectoral in the Shape of a Shell, Cowrie Shell Beads." In *Searching for Ancient Egypt*, ed. D. Silverman, 196–97. Dallas.

———. 2009. "The Djehutynakht's Burial Goods." In *The Secrets of Tomb 10A, Egypt 2000 BC*, ed. R. E. Freed, L. M. Berman, D. M. Doxey, N. S. Picardo, 137–49. Boston.

Dubiel, U. 2008. *Amulette, Siegel und Perlen: Studien zu Typologie und Tragesitte im Alten und Mittle ren Reich*. Fribourg.

Dunham, D. 1963. *The Royal Cemeteries of Kush V: The West and South Cemeteries at Meroë*. Boston.

Dunn Friedman, F. 1998. *Gifts of the Nile: Ancient Egyptian Faience*. New York.

Eaton-Krauss, M. 2008. "Embalming Caches." *JEA* 94: 288–93.

Emery, A. B. 1954. *Great Tombs of the First Dynasty II*. London.

Endesfelder, E. 1989. "Die Stellung der Frauen in der Gesellschaft des Alten Ägypten." In *Waren sie nur schön? Frauen im Spiegel der Jahrtausende*, ed. B. Schmitz, U. Steffgen. Kulturgeschichte der antiken Welt 42, 23–68.

Engelbach, R. 1915. *Riqqeh and Memphis VI*. London.

———. 1923. *Harageh*. London.

Enmarch, R. 2008. *A World Upturned: Commentary on and Analysis of* The Dialogue of Ipuwer and the Lord of All. Oxford.

Erickson, S. N. 2010. "Han Dynasty Tomb Structures and Contents." In *China's Early Empires: A Re-appraisal*, ed. M. Nylan, M. Loewe, 13–82. Cambridge.

Farag, N., Z. Iskander. 1971. *The Discovery of Neferwptah*. Cairo.

Faulkner, R.O. 1969. *The Ancient Egyptian Pyramid Texts*. Oxford.

Faulkner, R. O., C. Andrews. 1985. *Book of the Dead*. London.

Fay, B. 1990. *Ancient Egyptian Jewelry in the Collection of the Verein zur Förderung des Ägyptischen Museums in Berlin-Charlottenburg e.V.* Mainz am Rhein.

———. 1996. *The Louvre Sphinx and Royal Sculpture from the Reign of Amenemhat II*. Mainz am Rhein.

Feucht, E. 1967. *Die königlichen Pektorale, Motive, Sinngehalt und Zweck*. Bamberg.

Firth, C. M., B. Gunn. 1926. *Teti Pyramid Cemeteries*. Cairo.

Fischer, H. G. 1968. *Dendera in the Third Millennium B.C.* New York.

———. 1980. "Lampe." In *Lexikon der Ägyptologie* III, ed. W. Helck, W. Westendorf, 913–17. Wiesbaden.

Fitton, J. L. 2009. "Links in a Chain, Aigina, Dahshur and Tod." In *The Aigina Treasure*, ed. L. Fitton, 61–65. London.

Fitton, J. L., N. Meeks, J. Joyner. 2009. "The Aigina Treasure: Catalogue and Technical Report." In *The Aigina Treasure*, ed. J. L.Fitton, 17–24. London.

Fletcher, J. 2008. *Cleopatra the Great*. London.

Forman, W., S. Quirke. 1996. *Hieroglyphs and the Afterlife in Ancient Egypt*. London.

Forstner-Müller, I. 2008. *Tell el-Dab'a XVI: Die Gräber des Arials A/II von Tell el-Dab'a*. Vienna.

Franke, D. 1983. *Altägyptische Verwandtschaftsbezeichnungen im Mittleren Reich*. Hamburger Ägyptologische Studien, H 3. Hamburg.

———. 1991. "The Career of Khnumhotep III of Beni Hasan and the So-called Decline of the Normarchs." In *Middle Kingdom Studies*, ed. S. Quirke, 51–67. New Malden, U.K.

———. 1994. *Das Heiligtum des Heqaib auf Elephantine*. Studien zur Archäologie und Geschichte Altägyptens 9. Heidelberg

Frankfort, H. 1930. "The Cemeteries of Abydos: Work of the Season 1925–26." *Journal of Egyptian Archaeology* 16: 213–19.

Franzmeier, H. 2010. "Die magischen Ziegel des Neuen Reiches—Material und immaterieller Wert einer Objektgruppe." *MDAIK* 66: 93–105.

Gabolde, M. 1998. *D'Akhenaton à Toutânkhamon*. Paris.

Gardiner, A. H. 1917. Review of Mace, Winlock 1916. *JEA* 4: 203–6.

Gardiner, A. H., K. Sethe. 1928. *Egyptian Letters to the Dead, Mainly from the Old and Middle Kingdom*. London.

Gardiner, A. H., T. E. Peet. 1952. *The Inscriptions of Sinai, Part I*. 2nd ed., rev. and augmented by J.Černý. London.

Garstang, J. 1902. *El-Arabah, a Cemetery of the Middle Kingdom: Survey of the Old Kingdom Temenos: Graffiti from the Temple of Sety*. London.

———. 1907. *The Burial Customs of Ancient Egypt: As Illustrated by Tombs of the*

Middle Kingdom: Being a Report of Excavations Made in the Necropolis of Beni Hassan During 1902–3–4. London.

Gauthier, M. H. 1921. "À travers la Basse-Égypte." *ASAE* 1921: 17–39.

Gautier, J.-E., G. Jéquier. 1902. *Mémoire sur les fouilles de Licht.* Cairo.

Geisen, C. 2004. *Die Totentexte des verschollenen Sarges der Königin Mentuhotep aus der 13. Dynastie.* Studien zum Altägyptischen Totenbuch 8. Wiesbaden.

Gestermann, L. 1995. "Der politische und kulturelle Wandel under Sesostris III.— Ein Entwurf." In *Per aspera ad astra: Wolfgang Schenkel zum neunundfünfzigsten Geburtstag*, ed. L. Gestermann, H. Sternberg-El Hotabi, 31–50. Kassel.

———. 2010. "Ein verlorener Sarg des Mittleren Reiches aus Dahsur." In *Honi soit qui mal y pense: Studien zum pharaonischen, griechisch-römischen und spätantiken Ägypten zu Ehren von Heinz-Josef Thissen*, ed. H. Knuf, C. Leitz, D. von Recklinghausen, 49–56. Louvain.

Gibson, P. C. 2000. "Redressing the Balance: Patriarchy, Postmodernism and Feminism." In *Fashion Cultures: Theories, Explorations and Analysis*, ed. S. Bruzzi, P. C. Gibson, 349–61. London.

Gillam, R. A. 1995. "Priestesses of Hathor: Their Function, Decline and Disappearance." *JARCE* 32: 211–37.

Glob, P. V. 1970. *The Mound People: Danish Bronze-Age Man Preserved.* London.

Gnirs, A. M. 2009. "Ägyptische Militärgeschichte als Kultur- und Sozialgeschichte." In *Militärgeschichte des pharaonischen Ägypten*, ed. R. Gundlach, C. Vogel, 65–141. Paderborn, Munich.

Gohary, J. 1992. *Akhenaten's Sed-festival at Karnak.* London, New York.

Gomez-Deluchi, S. 2005. "Bead-net Dress." In *Excavating Egypt: Great Discoveries from the Petrie Museum of Egyptian Archaeology, University College London*, ed. B. Teasley Trope, S. Quirke, P. Lacovara, 192. Atlanta.

Grajetzki, W. 1995. "Der Schatzmeister Amenhotep und eine weitere Datierungshilfe für Denkmäler des Mittleren Reiches." *Bulletin de la Société d'Égyptologie de Genève* 19: 5–11.

———. 1997. "Bemerkungen zu den Bürgermeistern (ḥзtj-ᶜ) von Qaw el-Kebir im Mittleren Reich." *Göttinger Miszellen* 156: 55–62.

———. 2003. *Burial Customs in Ancient Egypt: Life and Death for Rich and Poor.* London.

———. 2004a. *Tarkhan: A Cemetery at the Time of Egyptian State Formation.* London.

———. 2004b. *Harageh: An Egyptian Burial Ground for the Rich Around 1800 BC.* London.

———. 2005a. "The Coffin of the 'King's Daughter' Neferuptah and the Sarcophagus of the 'Great King's Wife' Hatshepsut." *Göttinger Miszellen* 205: 55–66.

———. 2005b. *Sedment: Burials of Egyptian Farmers and Noblemen over Centuries.* London.

———. 2007. "Box Coffins in the Late Middle Kingdom and Second Intermediate Period." *EVO* 30: 41–54.

———. 2010. *The Coffin of Zemathor and Other Rectangular Coffins of the Late Middle Kingdom and Second Intermediate Period.* GHP 15. London.

Gramsci, A. 2007. *Quaderni del Carcere (Volumen terzo), Quaderni 12–29.* Turin.

Graves-Brown, C. 2008. *Sex and Gender in Ancient Egypt: Don Your Wig for a Joyful Hour.* Swansea.

———. 2010. *Dancing for Hathor: Women in Ancient Egypt.* London, New York.

Grdseloff, B. 1951. "La princesse Neferouptah de Lisht." *ASAE* 51: 147–51.

Greer, G. 1971. *The Female Eunuch.* London.

Guilhou, N. 2003. "La parure du mort d'après le cercueils du moyen empire." *Egypte, Afrique & Orient* 30 (August): 65–72.

Guliaev, V. I. 2003. "Amazons in the Scythia: New Finds at the Middle Don, Southern Russia." *World Archaeology* 35.1: 112–25.

Gwyn Griffiths, J. 1970. *Plutarch's de Iside et Osiride.* Cardiff.

Guy, P. L. O. 1938. *Megiddo Tombs.* Oriental Institute Publications 33. Chicago.

Haffner, A. 1989. "Das Gräberfeld von Wederath-Belginium vom 4. Jahrhundert vor bis zum 4. Jahrhundert nach Christi Geburt." In *Gräber—Spiegel des Lebens, zum Totenbrauchtum der Kelten und Römer am Beispiel des Trevere-Gräberfeldes Wederath-Belginum,* ed. A. Haffner, 37–130. Mainz am Rhein.

Haller, A. 1954. *Die Gräber und Grüfte von Assur.* Berlin.

Harding, A. F. 2000. *European Societies in the Bronze Age.* Cambridge.

Harrington, S. 2007. "Stirring Women, Weapons, and Weaving: Aspects of Gender Identity and Symbols of Power in Early Anglo-Saxon England." In *Archaeology and Women: Ancient and Modern Issues,* ed. S. Hamilton, R. D. Whitehouse, K. I. Wright, 335–52. Walnut Creek, CA.

Hassan, S. 1932. *Excavations at Giza 1929–1930.* Cairo.

———. 1936. *Excavations at Giza 1930–1931, II.* Cairo.

Hayes, W. C. 1953. *The Scepter of Egypt I: From the Earliest Times to the End of the Middle Kingdom.* New York (reprint 1990).

Haynes, S. 2000. *Etruscan Civilization: A Cultural History.* Los Angeles.

Helck, W. 1975. "Beischläferin." In *Lexikon der Ägyptologie* I, ed. W. Helck, E. Otto, 684–86. Wiesbaden.

Hill, M. 1999. "Note on the Dating of Certain Serving Statuettes." In *Egyptian Art in the Age of the Pyramids,* 386–87. New York.

Hodder, I. 2006. *Catalhöyük: The Leopard's Tale.* London.

Hodjash, S., O. Berlev. 1982. *The Egyptian Reliefs and Stelae in the Pushkin Museum of Fine Arts, Moscow.* Leningrad.

Hölzl, C. 2001. "Katalogummern 26–30: Schmuck aus der Nekropole von el-Lischt." In Seipel 2001: 41–43.

Hornung, E. 1995. *Echnaton: Die Religion des Lichtes.* Zürich.

Houlihan, P. F. 1988. *The Birds of Ancient Egypt.* Cairo.

Ikram, S., A. Dodson. 1998. *The Mummy in Ancient Egypt: Equipping the Dead for Eternity.* London.

Ionesov, V. I. 2002. *The Struggle Between Life and Death in Proto-Bactrian Culture.* New York.

James, T. G. H. 1974. *Corpus of Hieroglyphic Inscriptions in the Brooklyn Museum, I.* Brooklyn, NY.

Jánosi, P. 1994. "Keminub—Eine Gemahlin Amenemhets II.?" In *Zwischen den beiden Ewigkeiten: Festschrift Gertrud Thausing,* ed. M. Bietak, 94–101. Vienna.

———. 1996. *Die Pyramidanlagen der Königinnen: Untersuchungen zu einem Grabtyp des Alten und Mittleren Reiches.* Vienna.

———. 2010. "'He is the son of a woman of Ta-Sety . . .'—The Offering Table of the King's Mother Nefret (MMA 22.1.21)." In *Offerings to the Discerning Eye: An Egyptological Medley in Honor of Jack A. Josephson,* ed. S. D'Auria, 201–8. Culture and History of the Ancient Near East. Leiden.

Jéquier, G. 1921. *Les frises d'objets des sarcophages du Moyen-Empire.* Mémoires publiés par l'Institut français d'archéologie orientale du Caire, 47. Cairo.

———. 1933a. *Fouilles à Saqqarah: Deux pyramides du moyen empire.* Cairo.

———. 1933b. *Pyramides des reines Neit et Apouit.* Cairo.

Jick, M. 1988. "Bead Net-dress." In *Mummies and Magic: The Funerary Arts of Ancient Egypt,* ed. S. D'Auria, P. Lacovara, C. H. Roehring, 78–79. Boston.

Jørgensen, M. 1996. *Catalogue Egypt I (3000–1550 B.C.), Ny Carlsberg Glyptotek.* Copenhagen.

Junker, H. 1919. *Bericht über die Grabungen des Akademie der Wissenschaften in Wien auf den Friedhöfen von El-Kubanieh-Süd, Winter 1910–1911.* Vienna.

———. 1920. *Bericht über die Grabungen des Akademie der Wissenschaften in Wien auf den Friedhöfen von El-Kubanieh-Nord, Winter 1910–1911.* Vienna.

———. 1929. *Gîza I: Die Mastabas der IV. Dynastie auf dem Westfriedhof.* Vienna.

———. 1943. *Gîza V I: Die Mastabas des Nfr (Nefer), Kdfjj (Kedfi), K3hjf (Kahjef) und die westlich anschließenden Grabanlagen.* Vienna.

Kaiser, W. 1967. *Ägyptisches Museum Berlin.* Berlin.

———. 1969. "Die Tongefässe." In *Das Sonnenheiligtum des Königs Userkaf, II,* ed. H. Ricke. Beiträge zur ägyptischen Bauforschung und Altertumskunde 8, 49–82. Wiesbaden.

———. 1983. "Zu den [mwt-njswt] der älteren Bilddarstellungen und der Bedeutung von rpw.t." In *MDAIK* 39: 261–96.

———. 1987. "Die dekorierte Torfassade des spätzeitlichen Palastbezirkes von Memphis." *MDAIK* 43: 123–54.

Kamal, A. B. 1901. "Rapport sur les fouilles executées à Deîr-el-Bershé." *ASAE* 2: 206–22.

Keimer, L. 1948. *Remarques sur le tatouage dans l'Égypte ancienne.* Cairo.

Kemp, B., R. S. Merrillees. 1980. *Minoan Pottery in Second Millennium Egypt*. Mainz am Rhein.

Kenyon, K. M. 1965. *Excavations at Jericho II: Tombs Excavated in 1955–58*. London.

Kilian-Dirlmeier, I. 1997. *Das Mittelbronzezeitliche Schachtgrab von Ägina*. Mainz.

Kitchen, K. A. 1963. "A Long-lost Portrait of Princess Neferure from Deir el-Bahri." *JEA* 49: 38–40.

Kopetzky, K. 2010. *Tell el-Dab'a XX, Die Chronologie der Siedlungskeramik der Zweiten Zwischenzeit in Tell el-Dab'a, Teil I: Text*. Vienna.

Koura, B. 1999. *Die "7–Heiligen Öle" und andere Öl- und Fettnamen: Eine lexikographische Untersuchung zu den Bezeichnungen von Ölen, Fetten und Salben bei den Alten Ägyptern von der Frühzeit bis zum Anfang der Ptolemäerzeit (von 3000 v. Chr.–ca. 305 v. Chr.)*. Aegyptiaca Monasteriensia, 2. Aachen.

Kozloff, A. P., B. M. Bryan. 1992. *Egypt's Dazzling Sun: Amenhotep III and His World* (with L. M. Berman and an essay by E. Delange). Cleveland.

Kuhn, D. 1992. "Zwischen dem Sarg in der Erdgrube und dem Kammergrab aus Ziegelstein, Gräber aus der Zeit der Streitenden Reiche und der Han-Zeit in chinesischen Ausgrabungsberichten (1988–1991)." In D. Kuhn, *Arbeitsmaterialien aus chinesischen Ausgrabungsberichten (1988–1991) zu Gräbern aus der Han- bis Tang-Zeit*, 23–137. Würzburg.

Künzl, E. 1989. "Die Zahnarztgräber 1600 und 1539." In *Gräber—Spiegel des Lebens, zum Totenbrauchtum der Kelten und Römer am Beispiel des Trevere-Gräberfeldes Wederath-Belginum*, ed. A. Haffner, 289–98. Mainz am Rhein.

Lapp, G. 1993. *Typologie der Särge und Sargkammern von der 6. bis 13. Dynastie*. Studien zur Archäologie und Geschichte Altägyptens 7. Heidelberg.

Leclant, J. 1979. *Ägypten I: Das Alte und das Mittlere Reich*. Munich.

Leitz, C. 2002. *Lexikon der ägyptischen Götter und Götterbezeichnungen*, vol. 1: *A–i*. OLA 110. Louvain.

Leospo, E. 1989. "Propitiary Rites, Aspects of Daily Life, Work and Free Time Activities as Depicted on Painted Linen and Wall Decorations." In *Egyptian Civilization: Monumental Art*, ed. A. M. Donadoni Roveri, 186–247. Turin.

Lichtheim, M. 1975. *Ancient Egyptian Literature*, vol. 1: *The Old and the Middle Kingdom*. Berkeley.

Lilyquist, C. 1979a. *Ancient Egyptian Mirrors: From the Earliest Times Through the Middle Kingdom*. Munich.

———. 1979b. "A Note on the Date of Senebtisi and Other Middle Kingdom Groups." *Serapis* 5: S. 27–28.

———. 1993. "Granulation and Glass: Chronological and Stylistic Investigations at Selected Sites, ca. 2500–1400 B.C.E." *Bulletin of the American Schools of Oriental Research*, nos. 290–91: 29–94.

———. 2003. *The Tomb of Three Foreign Wives of Thutmosis III*. New York.

Lohwasser, A. 2001. *Die königlichen Frauen im antiken Reich von Kusch, 25. Dynastie bis zur Zeit des Nastasen.* Wiesbaden.

Lopatta, M. 2006. "Das Festbankett des Gaufürsten und sein Ritualgeschirr." In *Timelines: Studies in Honour of Manfred Bietak*, ed. E. Czerny, I. Hein, H. Hunger, D. Melman, A. Schwab, 197–205. OLA 149. Louvain.

Lorand, D. 2008. "Quatre scarabées de coeur inscrits à tête humaine." *CdE* 83: 20–24.

Lösch, S., A. R. Zink, S. Panzer, E. Hower-Tilmann, A. G. Nerlich. 2007. "Eine Nubierin in Ägypten? Anthropologisch-paläopathologische Untersuchungen an den menschlischen Überresten der Geheset." In *Für die Ewigkeit geschaffen: Die Särge des Imeni und der Geheset*, ed. D. Polz, 100–106. Mainz am Rhein.

Lüscher, B. 1990. *Untersuchungen zu ägyptischen Kanopenkästen.* Hildesheim.

———. 1998. *Untersuchungen zu Totenbuch Spruch 151.* Studien zum Altägyptischen Totenbuch 2. Wiesbaden

Macadam, M. F. L. 1951. "A Royal Family of the Thirteenth Dynasty." *JEA* 37: 20–28.

Mace, A. C., H. E. Winlock. 1916. *The Tomb of Senebtisi at Lisht.* New York.

Mackay, E. 1915. "Kafr Ammar, IIIrd to VIth Dynasty Burials." In W. M. Flinders Petrie, E. Mackay, *Heliopolis, Kafr Ammar and Shurafa*, 8–10. London.

Markowitz, Y. J., J. L. Haynes, R. E. Freed. 2002. *Egypt in the Age of the Pyramids.* Boston.

Markowitz, Y. J., P. Lacovara. 2009. "Egypt and the Aigina Treasure." In *The Aigina Treasure*, ed. L. Fitton, 59–60. London.

Martin , G. T., 1971. *Egyptian Administrative and Private-Name Seals.* Oxford.

Matthiae, P. 1981. "Osservazione sui gioielli delle tombe principesche di Mardikh IIIB." *Studi Eblaiti* 4: 205–25.

———. 1984. "New Discoveries at Ebla; The Excavations of the Western Palace and the Royal Necropolis of the Amorite Period." *Biblical Archaeology* 47.1: 18–32.

———. 2008a. "Beaded Band." In *Beyond Babyon, Art Trade and Diplomacy in the Second Millennium B.C.*, ed. J. Aruz, K. Benzel, J. M. Evans, 37–38. New York.

———. 2008b. "Earring or Nose Ring." In *Beyond Babyon, Art Trade and Diplomacy in the Second Millennium B.C.*, ed. J. Aruz, K. Benzel, J. M. Evans, 38. New York.

McCarthy, H. L. 2002. "The Osiris Nefertari: A Case Study of Gender, Decorum and Regeneration." *JARCE* 39: 173–95.

Melandri, I. 2011. "Nuove considerazioni su una statua da Qaw El-Kebir al Museo delle Antichità Egizie di Torino." *Vicino & Medio Oriente* 15: 249–70.

Meskell, L. 1999. *Archaeologies of Social Life: Age, Sex, Class Etcetera in Ancient Egypt.* Oxford.

————. 2004. *Object Worlds in Ancient Egypt*. Oxford.

de Meyer, M. 2011. "Inlaid Eyes on Old Kingdom Coffins: A History of Misidentification." *JEA* 97: 201–3.

Miniaci, G. 2009. "The Necropolis of Dra Abu el-Naga." In *Seven Seasons at Dra Abu el-Naga, The Tomb of Huy (TT 14): Preliminary Results*, ed. M. Betrò, P. De Vesco, G. Miniaci. Pisa.

————. 2010. "The Incomplete Hieroglyphs System at the End of the Middle Kingdom." *RdE* 61: 113–34.

————. 2011. *Rishi Coffins and the Funerary Culture of Second Intermediate Period Egypt*. GHP Egyptology 17. London.

Miniaci, G., S. Quirke. 2008. "Mariette at Dra Abu el-Naga and the Tomb of Neferhotep: A Mid-13th Dynasty Rishi Coffin (?)." *EVO* 31: 5–25.

————. 2009. "Reconceiving the Tomb in the Late Middle Kingdom: The Burial of the Accountant of the Main Enclosure Neferhotep at Dra Abu al-Naga." *Bulletin de l'Institut Français d'Archaeologie Orientale* 109: 339–83.

Möller, G., W. Schubart. 1910. *Ägyptische Goldschmiedearbeiten: Mitteilungen aus der Ägyptischen Sammlung*. Königliche Museen zu Berlin 1. Berlin.

Montet, P. 1928. *Byblos et l'Égypte, quatre campagnes de fouilles 1921–1924*. Paris.

————. 1951. *Les constructions et le tombeau de Psousennès a Tanis*. La nécropole royale de Tanis, 2. Paris.

de Morgan, J. 1895. *Fouilles a Dahchour, Mars–Juin 1894*. Vienna.

————. 1903. *Fouilles a Dahchour 1895*. Vienna.

Morkot, R. 2000. *The Black Pharaohs: Egypt's Nubian Rulers*. London.

Müller, H. W., E. Thiem. 1999. *The Royal Gold of Ancient Egypt*. London.

Müller, V. 2006. "Die Entwicklung der Gefäßformen "Cup-and-Saucer" in Ägypten und Palästina." In *Timelines: Studies in Honour of Manfred Bietak*, vol. 2, ed. E. Czerny, I. Hein, H. Hunger, D. Melman, A. Schwab, 259–77. OLA 149. Louvain.

Müller-Karpe, H. 1968. *Handbuch der Vorgeschichte II: Jungsteinzeit*. Munich.

————. 1979. "Fu Hao von Anyang." *Beiträge zur Allgemeinen und Vergleichenden Archäologie*, 1: 1–68.

————. 1985. *Frauen des 13. Jahrhunderts v. Chr.* Mainz am Rhein.

Myśliwiec, K. 2008. *Saqqara II: The Upper Necropolis, Part I: The Catalogue with Drawings*. Warsaw.

Nashrabadi B. M. 1999. *Untersuchungen zu den Bestattungssitten in Mesopotamien in der ersten Hälfte des ersten Jahrtausend v. Chr.* Mainz am Rhein.

Naville, E. 1892. *The Festival-Hall of Osorkon II in the Great Temple of Bubastis (1887–1889)*. London.

Nelson, M., M. Kalos. 2000. "Concessions funéraires du Moyen Empire découvertes au nord-ouest du Ramesseum." *Memmonia* 11: 131–51.

Newberry. P. E. 1893a. *El Bersheh I*. London.

———. 1893b. *Beni Hassan I*. London.

Nicholson P. T., J. Henderson. 2000. "Glass." In *Ancient Egyptian Materials and Technology*, ed. P. T. Nicholson, I. Shaw, 195–224. Cambridge.

Obayashi, H., ed. 1992. *Death and Afterlife: Perspectives of World Religions*. London.

O'Connor, D. 2000. "Society and Individual in Early Egypt." In *Order, Legitimacy and Wealth in Ancient States*, ed. J. Richards, M. van Burden, 21–34. Cambridge.

Oppenheim, A. 1995. "A First Look at Recently Discovered 12th Dynasty Royal Jewelry from Dahsur." *KMT* 6.1 (Spring): 10–11.

———. 2002. "Appendix." In Arnold 2002: 123–46.

Owens, L. S., T. L. Tucker, F. A. Hassan. 2009. "The Potential and Future of Egyptian Bioarchaeology: Management Strategies for Ancient Human Remains." In *Managing Egypt's Cultural Heritage*, ed. F. A. Hassan, G. J. Tassie, A. de Trafford, L. Owens, J. van Wetering, 206–57. London.

Paludan, A. 1994. *Chinese Tomb Figurines*. Oxford.

Patch, D. C. 1995. "A 'Lower Egyptian' Costume: Its Origin, Development, and Meaning." *JARCE* 32: 93–116.

———. 2002. "The Beaded Garment of Sit-werut." In *Egyptian Museum Collections Around the World*, vol. 2, ed. M. Eldamaty, M. Trad, 905–16. Cairo.

Pavlov, V. V., S. I. Hodjash. 1985. Египетская пластика малых форм. Moscow.

Pearson, M. P. 1999. *The Archaeology of Death and Burial*. Stroud, United Kingdom.

Peck, W. H. 1978. *Egyptian Drawings*. Photographs by J. G. Ross. London.

Peebles, C. 1971. "Moundville and Surrounding Sites: Some Structural Considerations of Mortuary Practices." In *Approaches to the Social Dimensions of Mortuary Practices*, ed. J. A. Brown, 68–91. Memoirs of the Society for American Archaeology no. 25. Washington

Peet, T. E. 1914. *Cemeteries of Abydos II*. London.

Perdu, O. 1977. "Khenemet-Nefer-Hedjet: Une princesse et deux reines du Moyen Empire." *RdE* 29: 68–85.

Petrie, F., G. Brunton, M. A. Murray. 1923. *Lahun II*. London.

Petrie, W. M. F. 1890. *Kahun, Gurob and Hawara*. London.

———. 1901a. *The Royal Tombs of the Earliest Dynasties*. Part II. London.

———. 1901b. *Diospolis Parva: The Cemeteries of Abadiyeh and Hu, 1898–9*. London.

———. 1907. *Gizeh and Rifeh*. London.

———. 1909. *Qurneh*. London.

———. 1930. *Antaeopolis: The Tombs of Qau*. British School of Archaeology in Egypt, 51. London.

Petschel, S. 2011. *Den Dolch betreffend: Typologie der Stichwaffen von der prädynastischen Zeit bis zur 3. Zwischenzeit*. Philippika 36. Wiesbaden.

Philip, G. 2006. *Metalwork and Metalwork Evidence of the Late Middle Kingdom and the Second Intermediate Period (Tell el-Dab'a XV)*. Vienna.

Philpott, R. 1991. *Burial Practices in Roman Britain: A Survey of Grave Treatment and Furnishing, A.D. 43–410*. Oxford.

Pinch, G. 1993. *Votive Offerings to Hathor*. Oxford.

———. 2006. *Magic in Ancient Egypt*. 2nd ed. London.

Pinch-Brock, L. 2007. "The Short, Happy Life of Harold Jones, Artist and Archaeologist." In *Who Travels Sees More: Artists, Architects and Archaeologists Discover Egypt and the Near East*, ed. Diane Fortenberry, 31–39. Oxford.

Pittman, H. P. 1998. "The Jewelry." In Zettler 1998: 87–122.

Podvin, J.-L. 1997. *Composition, position et orientation du mobilier funéraire dans les tombes Égyptiennes privées du moyen empire à la basse époque*. Lille.

———. 2000. "Position du mobilier funéraire dans les tombes égyptiennes privées du moyen empire." *MDAIK* 56: 277–334.

Porter, B., R. L. B. Moss. 1927–1952. *Topographical Bibliography of Ancient Egyptian Hieroglyphic Texts, Reliefs and Paintings*. 7 vols. Oxford. 2nd ed. 1960–.

Pouls, M. A. 1997. "Amulet in the Shape of a Fish." In *Searching for Ancient Egypt*, ed. D. Silverman, 236, no. 78. Dallas.

Pozzi Battaglia, M. 2009. "Statuetta femminile." In E. D'Amicone, M. Pozzi Battaglia, *Egitto Maivisto: Le dimore eterne di Assiut e Gebelein*, 208–9. Turin.

Pries, A. H. 2011. *Die Stundenwachen im Osiriskult: Eine Studie zur Tradition und späten Rezeption von Ritualen im Alten Ägypten*. Wiesbaden

Quibell, J. E. 1900. *Hierakonpolis*. Part I. London.

Quirke, S. 1990. *The Administration of Egypt in the Late Middle Kingdom*. New Malden, U.K.

———. 2003. "Two Thirteenth Dynasty Heart Scarabs." *JEOL* 37: 31–40.

———. 2007a. "Women of Lahun (Egypt 1800 BC)." In *Archaeology and Women: Ancient and Modern Issues*, ed. S. Hamilton, R. D. Whitehouse, K. I. Wright, 246–62. Walnut Creek, CA.

———. 2007b. "Book of the Dead Chapter 178: A Late Middle Kingdom Compilation or Excerpts." In *Life and Afterlife in the Middle Kingdom and Second Intermediate Period*, ed. S. Grallert, W. Grajetzki, 105–27. London.

Radwan, A. 1983. *Die Kupfer- und Steingefäße Ägyptens (von den Anfängen bis zum Beginn der Spätzeit)*. Munich.

Randall-MacIver, D., C. L. Woolley. 1911. *Buhen*. Philadelphia.

Ranke, H. 1935. *Die ägyptischen Personennamen*. Glückstadt.

Raven, M. 1989. "The Antef Diadem Reconsidered." *OMRO* 68: 77–90.

Reeves, N. 1990. *The Complete Tutankhamun: The King, the Tomb, the Royal Treasure*. London.

———. 1996. "A Newly-discovered Royal Diadem of the Second Intermediate Period." *Minerva* 7, no. 2 (March/April): 47–48.

Reeves, N., R. H. Wilkinson. 1996. *The Complete Valley of the Kings*. London.

Reisner, G. A. 1908. *The Early Dynastic Cemeteries of Naga-ed-Dêr*. Leipzig.

Renfrew, C. 1986. "Varna and the Emergence of Wealth in Prehistoric Europe." In *The Social Life of Things: Commodities in Cultural Perspective*, ed. A. Appadurai, 141–68. Cambridge.

Reuther, O. 1968. *Die Innenstadt von Babylon (Merkes)*. Osnabrück.

Richards, J. 2005. *Society and Death in Ancient Egypt: Mortuary Landscapes of the Middle Kingdom*. Cambridge.

Rigault, P. 1999. "Dress in Beaded Netting." In *Egyptian Art in the Age of the Pyramids*, 306, no. 94. New York.

Robb, J. 2000. "Female Beauty and Male Violence in Early Italian Society." In *Naked Truths: Women, Sexuality, and Gender in Classical Art and Archaeology*, ed. A. O. Koloski-Ostrow, C. L. Lyons, 43–65. London.

Robins, G. 1993. *Women in Ancient Egypt*. London.

Rogge, E. 1986. "Totenmasken und mumienförmige Särge." Unpublished Ph.D. thesis. Vienna.

Roth, S. 2001. *Die Königsmütter des Alten Ägypten*. Mainz.

Rummel, U., ed. 2007a. *Begegnungen mit der Vergangenheit: 100 Jahre in Ägypten*. Cairo.

Rummel, U. 2007b. "Auferstehung und Versorgung im Jenseits: Die bildlichen Darstellungen im Sarg des Imeni." In *Für die Ewigkeit geschaffen: Die Särge des Imeni und der Geheset*, ed. D. Polz, 81–99. Mainz am Rhein.

Russo, B. 2012. "Funerary Spells at Saqqara South: Some Considerations About the Inscriptions of Anu's Coffin (Sq20X) and Their Date." *ZÄS* 139: 80–92.

Ryholt, K. S. B. 1997. *The Political Situation in Egypt During the Second Intermediate Period, c. 1800–1550 B.C.* Copenhagen.

———. 2000. "The Late Old Kingdom in the Turin King-List and the Identity of Nitocris." *ZÄS* 127: 87–100.

Sabbahy, L. K. 1997. "The Titulary of the Harem of Nebhepetre Mentuhotep, Once Again." *JARCE* 34: 163–66.

———. 2002. "The Female Family of Amenemhat II: A Review of the Evidence." In *Hommages à Fayza Haikal*, ed. N. Grimal, 239–44. Bibliothèque d'étude 138, Le Caire.

Salman, M. I., S. F. Andersen. 2009. *The Tylos Period Burials in Bahrain*, vol. 2: *The Hamad Town DS3 and Shakhoura Cemeteries*. Aarhus.

Scharff, A. 1947. *Das Grab als Wohnhaus in der ägyptischen Frühzeit*. Vol. 6. Sitzungsberichte der Bayerischen Akademie der Wissenschaften. Philosophisch-historische Klasse, Jahrg. 1944–46. Munich.

Schiestl, R. 2007. "The Coffin from Tomb I at Byblos." *Ägypten und Levante* 17: 265–71.

————. 2009. *Tell el-Dab'a XVIII: Die Palastnekropole von Tell el-Dab'a, die Gräber des Areals F/I der Straten d/2 und d/1*. Vienna.

Schiff Giorgini, M. 1998. *Soleb V: Le temple, bas-reliefs et inscriptions*. Cairo.

Schmitz, B. 1976. *Untersuchungen zum Titel s3–njswt "Königssohn."* Bonn.

Schreiter, C. 2001. "Nachtrag: Die Xantener Malerbefunde." In B. Jansen, C. Schreiter, M. Zelle, *Die römischen Wandmalereien aus dem Stadtgebiet der Colonia Ulpia Traiana, I: Die Funde aus den Privatbauten*, 101–6. Mainz.

Schuhmacher, F.-J. 1989. "Das frührömische Grab 978 mit Beil und Axt Waffen oder Werkzeuge?" In *Gräber—Spiegel des Lebens, zum Totenbrauchtum der Kelten und Römer am Beispiel des Trevere-Gräberfeldes Wederath-Belginum*, ed. A. Haffner, 247–54. Mainz am Rhein.

Seager, R. B. 1912. *Explorations in the Island of Mochlos*. Boston.

Seidlmayer, S. J. 1987. "Wirtschaftliche und Gesellschaftliche Entwicklung im Übergang vom Alten zum Mittleren Reich, ein Betrag zur Archäologie der Gräberfelder der Region Qau-Matmar in der Ersten Zwischenzeit." In *Problems and Priorities in Egyptian Archaeology*, ed. J. Assmann, G. Burkard, V. Davies, 175–217. London.

————. 1990. *Gräberfelder aus dem Übergang vom Alten zum Mittleren Reich*. Studien zur Archäologie und Geschichte Altägyptens 1. Heidelberg.

————. 2001. "Die Ikonographie des Todes." In *Social Aspects of Funerary Culture in the Egyptian Old and Middle Kingdoms: Proceedings of the International Symposium Held at Leiden University, 6–7 June, 1996*, ed. H. Willems, 205–52. Louvain.

————. 2007. "People at Beni Hassan: Contributions to a Model of Ancient Egyptian Rural Society." In *The Archaeology and Art of Ancient Egypt: Essays in Honor of David B. O'Connor* 2, ed. Z. A. Hawass, 351–68. Annales du Service des Antiquités de l'Égypte, Cahiers; 36. Cairo.

Seiler, A. 2005. *Tradition & Wandel: Die Keramik als Spiegel der Kulturentwicklung, Theben in der Zweiten Zwischenzeit*. Mainz am Rhein.

Seipel, W. 2001. *Gold der Pharaonen*. Vienna.

Serpico, M. 2008. "Sediment." In *Unseen Images: Archive Photographs in the Petrie Museum*, vol. 1: *Gurob, Sedment and Tarkhan*, ed. J. Picton, I. Pridden, 99–184. London.

Simpson W. K. 1954. "Two Middle Kingdom Personifications of Seasons." *JNES* 13: 265–68.

Smith, G. E. 1916. "Notes on the Mummy." In A. C. Mace, H. E. Winlock, *The Tomb of Senebtisi at Lisht*, 119–20. New York.

Smith, S. T. 1992. "Intact Tombs of the Seventeenth and Eighteenth Dynasties from Thebes and the New Kingdom Burial System." *Mitteilungen des Deutschen Archäologischen Instituts, Abt. Kairo* 48: 193–231.

Soliman, R. 2009. *Old and Middle Kingdom Theban Tombs*. London.

Snape, S. 1986. "Mortuary Assemblages from Abydos." Unpublished Ph.D. thesis. Liverpool.

———. 2011. *Ancient Egyptian Tombs: The Culture of Life and Death*. Malden, MA.

Snodgrass, A. 2010. "Archaeology in China." In *China's Early Empires: A Reappraisal*, ed. M. Nylan, M. Loewe, 232–50. Cambridge.

Spencer, A. J. 1982. *Death in Ancient Egypt*. London.

Stadelmann, R. 1991. *Die ägyptischen Pyramiden: Vom Ziegelbau zum Weltwunder*. 2nd ed. Mainz am Rhein.

Staehelin, E. 1978. "Zur Hathorsymbolik in der ägyptischen Kleinkunst." *ZÄS* 105: 76–84.

Stavnik, E. 1936. "Une suggestion au sujet de la couronne de la princesse Sat-Hathor-Yount." *RdE* 2: 165–71.

Steel, L. 2004. *Cyprus Before History: From the Earliest Settlers to the End of the Bronze Age*. London.

Stefanović, D. 2009. *The Non-Royal Regular Feminine Titles of the Middle Kingdom and Second Intermediate Period*. GHP Egyptology 11. London.

Steindorff, G. 1937. *Aniba II*. Glückstadt.

Stevenson, A. 2009. *The Predynastic Egyptian Cemetery of El-Gerzeh: Social Identities and Mortuary Practices*. Orientalia Lovaniensia Analecta 186. Louvain.

Stierlin, H., C. Ziegler. 1987. *Tanis, vergessene Schätze der Pharaonen*. Munich.

Stirland, A. 1999. *Human Bones in Archaeology*. 2nd ed. Shire Egyptology. Risborough, United Kingdom.

Strouhal, E., P. Klír. 2006. "The Anthropological Examination of Two Queens from the Pyramid of Amenemhat III at Dahshur." In *Abusir and Saqqara in the Year 2005: Proceedings of the Conference Held in Prague (June 27–July 5, 2005)*, ed. M. Bárta, F. Coppens, J. Krejčí, 133–46. Prague.

Stünkel, I. 2006. "The Relief Decoration of the Cult Chapels of Royal Women in the Pyramid Complex of Senusret III at Dahshur." In *Abusir and Saqqara in the Year 2005: Proceedings of the Conference Held in Prague (June 27–July 5, 2005)*, ed. M. Bárta, F. Coppens, J. Krejčí, 147–66. Prague.

Swain, S. 1995. "The Use of Model Objects as Predynastic Egyptian Grave Goods: An Ancient Origin for a Dynastic Tradition." In *The Archaeology of Death in the Ancient Near East*, ed. S. Campbell, A. Green, 35–37. Oxford.

Szpakowska, K. 2008. *Daily Life in Ancient Egypt: Recreating Lahun*. Malden, MA.

Tallet, P. 2005. *Sésostris III et la fin de la XIIe dynastie*. Paris.

Taylor, J. 1989. *Egyptian Coffins*. Shire Egyptology. Risborough, United Kingdom

———. 1999. "The Burial Assemblage of Henutmehyt: Inventory, Date and Provenance." In *Studies in Egyptian Antiquities: A Tribute to T. G. H. James* (Occasional Paper 123), ed. W. V. Davies, 59–72. London.

———. 2001. *Death and the Afterlife in Ancient Egypt*. London.

Taylor, T. 1996. *The Prehistory of Sex: Four Million Years of Human Sexual Culture.* London.

Theis, C. 2011a. *Corpus Pyramidum Aegyptiacarum.* Göttinger Miszelle, 9. Göttingen.

———. 2011b. *Deine Seele zum Himmel, dein Leichnam zur Erde, zur idealtypischen Rekonstruktion eines altägyptischen Bestattungsrituals.* Studien zur Altägyptischen Kultur, 12. Hamburg.

Thorp, R. L. 2006. *China in the Early Bronze Age.* Philadelphia.

Tiraditti, F., ed. 1998. *Egyptian Treasures from the Egyptian Museum in Cairo.* Vercelli.

Tooley, M. J. 1995. *Egyptian Models and Scenes.* Princes. Risborough, United Kingdom.

Troy, L. 1986. *Patterns of Queenship.* Stockholm.

Ucko, P. J. 1969. "Ethnography and Archaeological Interpretation of Funerary Remains." *World Archaeology* 1, no. 2 (October): 262–80.

Vandier d'Abbadie, J. 1946. *Catalogue des Ostraca Figurés de Deir el-Medineh III.* Cairo.

Vernier, E. S. 1909. *Bijoux et orfèvreries.* Fascicule 2. Cairo.

———. 1925. *Bijoux et orfèvreries.* Fascicule 4. Cairo.

Vernus, P. 1986. *Le surnom au moyen empire.* Studia Pohl 13. Rome.

Vila, A. 1976. "Les masques funéraires." In *Mirigissa III—Les necropolis,* ed. J. Vercoutter, 151–263. Paris.

Vilímková, M. 1969. *Egyptian Jewellery.* London.

Virolleaud, C. 1922. "Decouverte a Byblos d'un hypogee de la douzième dynastie Égyptienne." *Syria* 3, no. 4: 273–90.

Waraksa, E. A. 2009. *Formal Figurines from the Mut Precinct: Context and Ritual Function.* Göttingen.

Ward, A.W. 1986. *Essays on Feminine Titles of the Middle Kingdom and Related Subjects.* Beirut.

Whelan, P. 2007. *Mere Scraps of Rough Wood? 17th–18th Dynasty Stick Shabtis in the Petrie Museum and Other Collections.* GHP Egyptology 6. London.

Wilde, H. 2011. *Innovation und Tradition: zur Herstellung und Verwendung von Prestigegütern im pharaonischen Ägypten.* GOF Aegypten 49. Wiesbaden.

Wildung, D. 1984a. *Sesostris und Amenemhet: Ägypten im Mittleren Reich.* Munich.

———. 1984b. "Zur Formgeschichte der Landeskronen." In *Studien zu Sprache und Religion Ägyptens* (FS W. Westendorf), vol. 2: *Religion,* 967–80. Göttingen.

———. 1985. *La femme au temps des pharaons.* Mainz am Rhein.

———. 1985b. *Entdeckungen: Ägyptische Kunst in Süddeutschland.* Mainz am Rhein.

Wilfong, T. G. 2010. "Gender in Ancient Egypt." In *Egyptian Archaeology,* ed. W. Wendrich, 164–79. Malden, MA.

Wilkinson, A. 1971. *Ancient Egyptian Jewellery*. London.

Wilkinson, T. A. 1999. *Early Dynastic Egypt*. London.

Willems, H. 1988. *Chests of Life*. Leiden.

———. 1996. *The Coffin of Heqata (Cairo JdE 36418)*. OLA 70. Louvain.

———. 1997. "The Embalmer Embalmed: Remarks on the Meaning of the Decoration of Some Middle Kingdom Coffins." In *Essays on Ancient Egypt in Honour of Herman te Velde*, ed. J. van Dijk, 343–72. Groningen.

———. 2006. *Les textes des sarcophages et la démocratie*. Paris.

Williams, B. 1976. "The Date of Senebtisi at Lisht and the Chronology of Major Groups and Deposits of the Middle Kingdom." *Serapis* 3: 41–55.

Winlock, H. E. 1921. "Excavations at Thebes: The Egyptian Expedition 1920–21." *BMMA* 16, no. 2: 29–53.

———. 1923. "Museum Excavations in Thebes." *BMMA* 18: 11–39.

———. 1932. "Pearl Shells of Sen'n-Wosret I." In *Studies Presented to F. L. L. Griffith*, 388–92. London.

———. 1934. *The Treasure of El Lahun*. New York.

———. 1941. *Materials Used at the Embalming of King Tut-'ankh-Amun*. New York.

———. 1942. *Excavations at Deir el Bahri: 1911–1931*. New York.

———. 1948. *The Treasure of Three Egyptian Princesses*. New York.

Wolters, J. 1983. *Die Granulation, Geschichte und Technik einer alten Goldschmiedekunst*. Munich.

Woolley, C. L. 1934. *The Royal Cemetery: Ur Excavations II*. New York.

Zanelli, F. 1989. "Frammenti di decorazione parietale." In *Passato e Futuro del Museo Egizio Torino*, ed. A. M. Donadoni Roveri, 19–20. Turin.

Zettler, R. L. 1998. "The Royal Cemetery of Ur." In *Treasures from the Royal Tombs of Ur*, ed. R. L. Zettler, L. Horne, 21–32. Philadelphia.

Zibelius-Chen, K. 2007. "Die Medja in altägyptischen Quellen." *SAK* 36: 391–405.

Ziegler, C. 1999a. "Boundary Stela of King Djoser." In The Metropolitan Museum of Art New York, *Egyptian Art in the Age of the Pyramids*, 172. New York.

———. 1999b. "Decorated Fragments from the Chapel of King Djoser at Heliopolis." In The Metropolitan Museum of Art New York, *Egyptian Art in the Age of the Pyramids*, 175–76. New York.

Zillhardt, R. 2009. *Kinderbestattungen und die soziale Stellung des Kindes im Alten Ägypten—Unter besonderer Berücksichtigung des Ostfriedhofes von Deir el-Medine*. Göttinger Miszellen 6. Göttingen.

Web Resource

Database of the Metropolitan Museum of Art: http://www.metmuseum.org/collections/search-the-collections

Index

Acknowledgments

This book has been made possible only with the help of many people. Foremost, I wish to thank Stephen Quirke and Paul Whelan for reading my English, and Deborah Blake for reading my English and accepting the manuscript for the University of Pennsylvania Press. Paul Whelan also supplied several high-quality drawings and reconstructions. For other images I would like to thank Juan R. Lázaro, Gianluca Miniaci, and Daniela Rosenow. My thanks to Robert Bianchi for information on Harageh tomb 124. Further help came from Ulrike Dubiel in the shape of several stimulating discussions and a Topoi grant that allowed me a solid period of access to the Egyptological library of the Free University in Berlin, providing this book with its finishing touches. Kerstin Hoffmann from Topoi provided me with the insightful articles on identity. Last but not least, I am grateful to the anonymous reviewers for their valuable comments.